THE
HEALTHFUL
CHEF ™

by

E.N. HETHERINGTON, M.D.

A Cookbook for
people who wish to lower
their cholesterol
and for
people with diabetes

ACKNOWLEDGEMENTS

We are grateful to our many friends who were "guinea pigs" for the taste testing of these recipes. They helped with suggestions and shared their secrets with us.

I am especially grateful to my wife who suffered through the throes of creativity and tasting, and whose most terrible condemnation of a new dish was that it was "interesting." She did the typing, the collation, contacted people and created her own dishes also. Without her tacit agreement and interest in my health, this would not have happened. Lest I seem an ogre, in my defense, I was practicing medicine all this time.

Special thanks go to Mary Ann Mulcahey, our dietitian consultant, who assisted us in ways that we didn't know we needed assistance.

And thanks to Charlie, whose childhood has been interrupted by his parents in the sometimes grim, but mostly pleasant, pursuit of creating this book.

Publisher: The Healthful Chef, Inc.

Editor: E.N. Hetherington, M.D.

Associate Editor: Janet Hetherington

Published by The Healthful Chef, Inc.
P.O. Box 2085
Danville, IL 61834-2085
(217) 442-8782

© 1989 The Healthful Chef, Inc.   ISBN-0-9622454-2-9   **Printed in USA**

FROM THE AUTHOR

This edition of THE HEALTHFUL CHEF™ has been analyzed with the assistance of a dietitian to list the caloric and nutrient content per serving of each recipe.

Specifically these recipes inform you on a per serving basis of the amount of calories, fiber, protein, total fat, saturated fat, monounsaturated fat, polyunsaturated fat, cholesterol, Vitamin C, calcium and sodium.

Many other nutrients were obtained in the analysis, but not all are listed. My specific aim, to increase monounsaturated fats in the diet, is the reason for the extra attention paid to fats.

For people with special dietary needs, consult your physician before acting on nutritional information in this book. Every effort has been made to ensure that this information is as accurate as possible; however, the accuracy or suitability for any specific medically imposed diet is not guaranteed.

For those on salt restricted diets an (*) asterisk has been placed after those ingredients which are high in sodium. If these are eliminated, there will be a change in taste which may or may not be acceptable.

This is the first in a series of books having to do with health problems. The second book will address the problem of many people; lack of time to cook. We plan a book on microwave cooking of recipes similar to those in this edition. Also in the works is a cookbook with many of our favorite ethnic recipes modified for fat controlled, high taste results.

E.N. Hetherington, M.D.

The nutritional analyses in this book are based on USDA standards.

Specific brand names of ingredients which have been named include:

Sprinkle Sweet® is a trademark of the Pillsbury Company.

Egg Beaters® is a trademark of the Nabisco Company.

Butter Buds® is a trademark of the Cumberland Packing Company.

TABLE OF CONTENTS

INTRODUCTION

It is estimated that at least one third of American adults, younger as well as older, have an elevated cholesterol reading. It is becoming more evident that cholesterol levels in younger people are supposed to be lower than those of older people. What is acceptable in an older person is cause for alarm in a younger person. Autopsies done on young American soldiers killed in the Korean and Vietnamese wars showed a very high incidence of early atherosclerosis and, in many instances, far advanced coronary artery disease. These young Americans were in the 19-21 year of age group.

It is obvious that cholesterol deposits don't occur overnight, but are a lifelong process. The American Medical Association recommends that physicians start checking cholesterol levels at much earlier ages, and, depending upon the family history, even in preschoolers. The sooner a prudent diet is started, the longer and more useful life will be. It is my belief that this book will contribute to that goal: a prudent diet and a better life.

Rx – Taste

This book was conceived because most cholesterol lowering diets are devoid of flavor. When people go on diets that do not include the taste of their culture, they will revert back to that taste. To supply the taste of our culture without the original fat is the purpose of this book.

After a lacunar infarct (stroke, to non-medical people) and a cholesterol of over 300, it became necessary for me to change my lifestyle. A hectic, busy medical practice and typical American diet had gotten me in trouble. I had to switch to a more controlled way of life which included a different diet.

At first it would appear that creating a low fat diet is easy—you simply quit using fat or oils or butter or margarine or lard—anything that tastes good! It quickly became obvious that I had learned to eat my former diet because it was tasty! It soon became apparent that eating a low fat diet was a terrible way to live! As a physician, I knew that the fats I must avoid were hidden in what I and most Americans consider to be the essentials of our way of life: red meat, dairy products and fried foods. However, it was necessary to deny myself these goodies if I were to fully regain the use of my right arm and to stop more damage from occurring. So the matter of taste, along with texture and aroma, became the goal, keeping in mind that the content must always be devoid of the original problem-causing fats.

This was quite a challenge. I had to eliminate fat-laden ingredients and find substitutes that would meet our exacting taste requirements. As a result of this quandary, my wife, Jan, and I spent two years perfecting these recipes. We had marathon cooking sessions, sometimes taking fifteen tries to get the right combination of ingredients. If the recipe was greeted with comments like "Interesting," we knew it needed more work. Only when a recipe passed our taste tests did we try it on others. These efforts reproduced many of our favorite recipes and incorporated some of the latest medical thinking into almost identically flavored dishes such as braised sirloin tips, fettuccine alfredo, beef stroganoff and ice cream, to name a few. Not every food can be copied because of texture (i.e. steaks), but the recipes almost duplicate both taste and texture. You think not? Read on.

Fortunately, we live in a time when there is an abundance of choices, such as evaporated skim milk, low salt boullion, low fat yogurt, herbs and spices—all easily available. Once the innovative use of these ingredients becomes understandable, most cooks find a whole new world of food in their own kitchens.

Forget Cholesterol!

One of the great farces foisted upon the American public is the inordinate attention given to cholesterol in our food. Forget the word "cholesterol." This is not the problem—FAT is the problem. Only animal sources contain cholesterol. No plant sources contain cholesterol, and advertising otherwise is misleading. Advertisements that claim vegetable oils contain "no cholesterol" are not false advertising, but since cholesterol content of food is usually not relevant to the problem, the attention given this facet of our nutrition by the advertisers is not pertinent.

My first recipes did not incorporate fats or oils of any kind in their composition. Later, as more research material became available, it was evident that the omega 9 oil, olive oil, did things that an absence of fat in the diet simply would not do. Olive oil raises the high density lipoproteins (HDL) and lowers the low density lipoproteins (LDL), which is the name of the game.

Saturated Fats
the bad guys

There are many kinds of fat. The one most used in the American diet is animal fat or saturated fat: lard, bacon grease, and butter, to name a few. These fats have one thing in common—they are solid at room temperature. A fat that becomes solid at room temperature is a saturated fat. The only exceptions to this are coconut oil and palm or palm kernel oil which are of vegetable origin. They are, however, as saturated as the animal fats. At the present time we do not recommend the use of coconut, palm or palm kernel oil in the preparation of foods because of the saturation factor. Watch out, though. These oils are used extensively in commercially prepared foods! Fortunately, the ingredients are listed and it is astounding to find the number of food items in which the manufacturers use these saturated oils. Another one of our commonly used cooking fats is a commercial preparation of coconut oil and hydrogenated fat which is highly touted by the manufacturer because it does not have a "fat" taste. Read those labels and avoid coconut, palm and palm kernel oils! A diet high in saturated fat has been linked to breast cancer.

Red meat is 50% saturated fat and there is no way that it can be prepared so that the fat is removed from the meat. People tell me that they know how to cook it so that the fat is removed. My answer to them is to cool the meat and wipe it on their best blouse or shirt and see what sort of streak they get. Some of the widely used prepared imitation meat protein products such as textured "bacon", "sausage" and "hamburger patties" also have saturated fat. You can see this by allowing the fat that oozes from the product to congeal and become solid at room temperature.

Chicken and fish have about the same amount of cholesterol as beef, pork or lamb. The difference is in the type of fat. There is more saturated fat in the red meats.

Some of our favorite foods, such as hot dogs, have a legal maximum of 40% fat. However, when I calculate the amount of fat in some of these weiners, I can get readings as high as 70% from the package labels. To their credit, some of the manufacturers are now creating extremely low fat meats, particularly luncheon meats which have less than a gram of fat in each slice. Select those products with the fewest grams of fat.

Most of our cheeses have high saturated fat levels and are to be avoided. Some cheeses, such as Parmesan, are highly flavored and small amounts can be grated on food for a maximum of flavor and a small amount of fat. In those cases when the cheese is in slices or slabs, the intake of saturated fat goes up.

2% milk is also touted as low fat. Considering that whole milk is 3.3% saturated fat, it is difficult for me to see that this can be labeled as low fat. It might be labeled as lower fat, but the fat is not a minimal amount until 1% or skimmed is reached. Cottage cheese, if you read the label, is labeled "creamed" cottage cheese and has a high saturated fat content. However, now you can buy much lower fat cottage cheeses, 1%, and even dry cottage cheese.

Butter, of course, is one of the epitomes of the saturated fat class. I have advised my patients for years that I see no advantage to using margarine. Margarine fails the room temperature solidity test because it has hydrogen attached to the unsaturated fat. Hydrogenation raises the saturation 5–10% over the unhydrogenated state. In addition, margarine contains polyunsaturates, and I recommend eating foods with a higher level of monounsaturates rather than polyunsaturates. When butter and margarine are both eliminated from the diet, people ask what substitute can be used. I recommend olive oil and various flavorings (see recipes for suggestions).

Omega 3 Fats
the better guys

Most fish are low in fat, and even the oily ocean fish contain the right kind of fat, eicosapentaenoic acid (EPA) and docosahexaenoic acid (DHA). Sardines, herring, mackerel, salmon, cod, haddock, bluefish and tuna are examples of fish that have more than average amounts of EPA.

Eskimoes have less cholesterol effects in their arteries, but have an increased incidence of colon cancer. Their healthier arteries do not appear to be related to lower blood cholesterol, as it would seem from their diet. The mechanism is not clear, but the lower cholesterol levels appear to be related to a decreased clotting process. Several medical conditions, diabetes being the most common, have an increased clotting condition. Eicosapentaenoic acid (EPA) and docosahexaenoic acid (DHA) are the major active ingredients of fish oil. However, EPA blocks insulin and can make diabetes more difficult to control. This, among several other reasons, is why doctors do not recommend fish oil capsules.

At one time it was thought that shrimp, lobster and oysters were too high in cholesterol to be considered in a cholesterol lowering regime. However, they are quite low in total fat which makes them acceptable. Instead of an "all you can eat" approach to these foods, they should be cooked in a sauce or as part of a recipe. Squid and octopus are foods that have been used in other cultures but seem to cause revulsion to the American palate. I personally find them enjoyable. It is recommended that seafood be included at least three times a week. This is a minimum requirement and more is better.

Omega 6 Oils
the good/bad guys

Omega 6 oils are the most commonly used oils in this country and constitute the major oils about which we are inundated with advertising. These are safflower, corn, cottonseed, soybean and sunflower oils. These do lower cholesterol; however, these cause some increase in platelet aggregation (clotting) against the walls of the arteries. This appears to have some part in the atherosclerotic process.

In addition, these are oils that are hydrogenated and made into margarine. When you read labels, and you should make this a habit, you will see that many commercial preparations have "hydrogenated" vegetable oil. Hydrogen is added to relatively harmless oils, which increases the saturation, making them less desirable than the original oil. You can find hydrogenated oil listed in such things as soda crackers, candy, cake mixes, several of the dry soup mixes, popcorn oils, creamy peanut butter and coffee whiteners, to name a few. Fortunately, the manufacturers are required to list the ingredients so they can be identified. Omega 6 oils, even when not hydrogenated, are usually highly polyunsaturated. Here I depart from the herd. I don't believe a preponderance of polyunsaturated fats is as beneficial as monounsaturated. While polyunsaturated oils do lower LDL, which is good, they also lower HDL, which is not so good. This apparently increases the atherosclerotic process.

Most people are aware that saturated fats are not good for you, but we have been misinformed on the relative value of the polyunsaturated vegetable oils which claim to have no cholesterol. Recent research indicates that a diet high in either polyunsaturated or saturated fats has a relationship to carcinoma of the colon.

Usually I discuss palm oil, palm kernel oil and coconut oil along with the Omega 6 oils since they are so ubiquitous. There is some evidence that a mixture of Omega 6 margarine or salad dressing with coconut oil is probably more detrimental than eating pure coconut oil. As an example, if, during a meal, you eat margarine and have a cookie or piece of cake made with coconut oil, which most store bought cookies and cakes contain, cholesterol deposits are greatly accelerated.

Omega 9 Oils
the best guys

This brings us to the Omega 9 oils. There are three major oils in this category. One is peanut oil, which has about 46% monounsaturated oil. The second one is canola oil which is 55% monounsaturated oil. I prefer olive oil with 72% monounsaturated oil, and in addition, the least amount of polyunsaturated oil in this group. The variations between olive oil, peanut oil, and coconut oil are very small chemically, but there is a vast difference in the effect that each has on the metabolism in the body. I believe the most healthful diet for our arteries is based on using olive oil. Because of this belief, my wife and I have spent over two years creating the recipes you find in **The Healthful Chef**™. Studies indicate that frequent small amounts of olive oil are most beneficial in lowering cholesterol.

About Our Diet

There are some general remarks at this point that should be made. After World War II the American diet underwent a radical departure from what it had been. Before then we didn't know what a pizza was, nor did we have "hamburger joints" with french fries and those high fat "breakfast sandwiches." Convenience foods were unknown and the reason they sell so well now is because they taste "good"–good being fat and salty.

In addition the American diet has become too high in protein. The recommendation today for lowering blood cholesterol is to have two 3 ounce servings of a non-meat protein and not over 6 teaspoons of any sort of fat in a day, and also not over 100 milligrams of cholesterol per day. The low cholesterol recommendation is associated with the fact that there is cholesterol only in animal products. It is necessary to have protein in a diet. Protein is found in some plant sources. Animal protein contains certain vitamins and minerals that plant sources don't have. These vitamins and minerals are necessary to your health. For this reason, some animal protein should be included in your diet. Strictly vegetarian diets may cause dietary deficiencies.

Many of the recipes I have included in this book have no animal protein in them simply because I feel that most Americans will search out animal proteins anyway and will get as much or more protein as recommended on a daily basis. The American Diabetic Association's routine 1500 calorie diet has a total of only 6 ounces of protein daily, and includes eggs, cheese and meats. The diet has been recommended for many years even though the importance of the cholesterol and fat content of food was not realized when the diet was first developed. There have been studies, particularly by nephrologists, which show that high protein diets can destroy the diabetic kidney. From that standpoint alone it would behoove us all to cut down on the tremendous amount of protein that we eat whether or not it carries with it a heavy fat load. Turkey breast, chicken breast, pork tenderloin and fish are used in these recipes because of their low fat content. Until research clarifies the metabolic processes involved, I avoid using egg yolks because their fat profile resembles bacon fat.

As I mentioned earlier, some things cannot be duplicated; i.e., steaks and chops because of their consistency. However, the sauces that we are familiar with can be duplicated without the use of meat. There are foods available in standard grocery stores which can be adapted for use in these recipes and most were developed with this in mind. Exotic flavorings are avoided when possible and some things, such as conversion of artificial sweeteners and sugar, are made easy by using equivalent measures. People who wish to avoid salt can do so by eliminating some of the heavily salted foods such as bouillon cubes and canned vegetables. Fresh or frozen vegetables should be used instead of canned. The amount of salt in canned vegetables is considerable.

People who are interested in lowering their cholesterol find they automatically increase the amount of fruit, vegetables and whole grains they eat. Using these recipes is a way of ensuring a balanced, tasty and healthful diet while keeping cholesterol levels down. This diet has been consumed by me almost exclusively for the past two years with a significant improvement in my general well being and stamina. My cholesterol has gone from 330 to 150, albeit with help from medications. I am one of the many people who cannot lower their cholesterol to an acceptable level in spite of a stringent diet. These people need cholesterol lowering medication as determined by their physician. The diet, however, remains the cornerstone of cholesterol control. The combination of a healthful diet and medication has allowed me to maintain my medical practice and to serve as medical director of a Health Maintenance Organization.

Grubs & Berries

Contemplation of the original human diet at the time we emerged as a distinct species is revealing in that the only food available was what nature provided. Other animals were competing for survival and each sought its own niche and its own food. Man's niche did not supply much environmental fat or protein, so it would seem that sophisticated chemical and metabolic adaptations for these foodstuffs would not have been developed.

Man was a grazer on what we consider to be a vegetarian diet. Archeologists find no evidence that man ate fish before 40,000 years ago. There was no dairy industry, so milk and cheese were not available. Man's search for protein drove him to eat things we consider unsavory: bugs and grubs. At any rate, there wasn't a lot of protein. This suggests that our protein needs are less than we think necessary today. The digestive effort made by us to assimilate the protein load we eat today is considerable, making it reasonable to conclude that this is an unusual food for us. Later, man discovered that fire made other animals tasty and allowed him to live in more hostile climes. There was little fat or oil in man's original diet since nature provided none. There was no sugar except honey, and as painful as it was to eat, it did not add much to survival.

Modern man has taught himself that meat, dairy products and sugar are necessities, not luxuries. The feeling I get is that we do not need these products very much for our metabolism and particularly not for our health.

Originally, I was interested in this line of reasoning as a means to help people lose weight, having seen so many people uselessly throw their money away on fad diets. I recommended then that the total daily protein load should equal in bulk the palm of the hand. I have not, however, recommended a vegetarian diet, since dietary deficiencies could result. Vitamin and mineral supplements miss the point; a diet should be complete through a variety of foods eaten. Some of the benefits of a more natural diet are missed by supplementation.

Hints & Helps

Read the labels! You'll be appalled at what you are eating!

Olive oil is used exclusively in these recipes because it is the only oil that has been universally found in all tests to be beneficial. Other oils have been excluded and olive oil has been substituted in all the recipes where any kind of fat, butter or other oil is recommended in standard recipes. Margarines specifically are ignored because they have increased saturation plus increased polyunsaturates. Any fat which is solid at room temperature should be avoided. Coconut, palm and palm kernel oils are the exceptions to this statement. They are liquid at room temperature and as saturated as animal fat, and are highly atherogenic. They are found in commercial cooking in such diverse things as cereal, cookies, candy, cake mixes, potato chips—to name a few.

There are about 300 different kinds of olives, and olive oil is a blend of these. Each brand has a different taste, and you may need to try two or three different brands to find the taste you prefer. The more flavorful olive oils are preferred by some, but Americans seem to prefer the more bland taste.

Oat bran has been incorporated into as many recipes as possible because of the cholesterol lowering effect of oat bran. Barley and many fruits do the same thing. Wheat bran, corn bran and other brans do increase intestinal bulk but they do not absorb the bile as does oat bran. Fats, except those contained in certain protein compounds such as fish, certain types of meat and fowl, have been avoided. No attempt to label this cooking as no cholesterol has been made because if a no cholesterol diet is attempted, it eliminates all animal products automatically.

Milk is always skim milk and cottage cheese is never more than 1%. Most cheeses are eliminated because of the high fat content. However, I use two cheeses. One is farmers cheese (check the label for fat content; they vary from brand to brand). It will give flavor and consistency to things if it is a part of the recipe. The other is freshly grated Parmesan. Commercially grated Parmesan is not used because the taste of freshly grated Parmesan allows a small amount to be used to obtain the flavor.

In many recipes, sweetness is obtained by the use of artificial sweetener. The type used is that which is equivalant to sugar, measure for measure. Diabetics can use these recipes and nondiabetics merely have to substitute sugar for the sweetener. A tablespoon of sugar is added for every ½ cup sweetener in cooked recipes, and is included in the nutritional analysis for each recipe. This keeps down the bitter taste which sometimes comes with the use of artificial sweeteners.

Freshly ground pepper is used exclusively at our house since commercially ground pepper usually has a stronger taste.

Beef and chicken flavor can be obtained by using bouillon cubes or instant bouillon. There is a low sodium bouillon available for both beef and chicken. However, potassium chloride is substituted for sodium chloride and too much of it becomes rather bitter.

Since commercially canned broths, stocks and vegetables are very high in sodium, we have reduced the sodium in our diet by using our own homemade broths, stocks and home canned vegetables, all of which are salt-free. The nutritional analysis of the recipes in this book is based upon commercially canned products (broth, tomatoes, etc.). You can decrease your sodium intake from the amounts listed for each recipe by using home prepared, salt-free products or purchased frozen vegetables.

Cocoa is used instead of chocolate squares, usually 3 tablespoons of cocoa and 1 tablespoon olive oil for each ounce of chocolate square. Cocoa is used because it has the cocoa fat removed: by analysis cocoa fat is almost identical to butter.

There are many herbs and spices used in these recipes. "Hand rubbed" means between the palms, for such things as basil, oregano and thyme. Others are crushed in a pestle or blender. All are prepared "at the pot." It is my hope that this book will foster experimentation with a variety of herbs and spices.

Most people are unfamiliar with herbs and spices and want to be led to exact amounts. It has been difficult for me to list these amounts because when I cook I usually throw "some" of these into the pot. When you become used to the flavors, you will be able to predict what the outcome will be, and you'll be more comfortable in trying them.

When I make bread, I use no oils, eggs, butter or milk, and find that my bread works as well as all the complicated recipes you can find. The lack of sugar in my bread recipes does not compromise the rising of the bread. Although I quantitate measurements for this book, bread making is not an exact science.

In recipes calling for eggs, I use 2 egg whites for each egg. If an emulsifing factor is needed, I use liquid egg substitute.

If you have a dehydrator, you may be able to preserve such things as mushrooms and onions plus fruits and vegetables. I have found this to be the best way to preserve mushrooms and onions, and it has the added advantage of making preparation easy. You just pick up a handful of dehydrated onions, crush them, and throw them in the pot. Mushrooms are more delicate and should be treated better than this.

Textured protein should be bought without fats. Most health food stores have textured protein, both chicken and beef. Some of the frozen textured protein products, "bacon," "sausage," "hamburger patties," which are sold to people because of religious beliefs have saturated fat in them. The labels should be examined and these products avoided.

Most of these recipes are the result of experimentation and failures and I urge people starting this sort of cookery to be willing to accept failures, determine what caused the failure, and change it. Some of the recipes are better if allowed to blend overnight than when they are freshly cooked, and others, particularily those with textured protein, get worse overnight and should be eaten immediately. Every recipe has been prepared many times by us and all have been taste-tested by our family and friends.

By the time people reach "Medicare" age they are paying for their lifestyles. By decreasing harmful fats and increasing fiber from vegetables and fruits in the diet, a reduction in vascular disease and some forms of cancer can be accomplished. This could create a great savings in our total national medical bills as well as an improved quality of life.

I do not intend this as a book on nutrition for the human being, but rather as an attempt to approximate the taste of our culture without the types of fat that we are used to. My real interest is in trying to make a controlled fat diet more tasty and interesting and something that you can look forward to at the next meal!

BIBLIOGRAPHY

1. "American Health Association 1988 Heart Facts." Dallas, American Heart Association 1988; 11.

2. "Report of the National Cholesterol Education Program Expert Panel on Detection, Evaluation and Treatment of High Blood Cholesterol in Adults." **Archives Internal Medicine** 1988 Jan; 148(1): 36–69.

3. McManus, B. M. "Coronary Risk Assessment (Part 1)." **Lipid Letter** 1987 March; (4)2.

4. Kreisberg, R. A. "Hypercholesterolemia Dietary and Pharmacotherapy." **Hospital Practice** 1987; 22(4): 197–232.

5. Dunn, F. L. "Lipids and Diabetes: Guidelines for Treatment." **Clinical Diabetes** 1986 March; 4(2): 34–40.

6. Manninen, V. "Cholesterol Transport by High Density Lipoprotein." **Cardiovascular Reviews & Reports** 1989 August; 10(8): 40–43.

7. Wilson, P. W. F., et al. "High Density Lipoproteins and Mortality: The Framingham Heart Study." **Arteriosclerosis** 1988 Nov/Dec; 8(6): 737–741.

8. Jones, P. H., Gotto, A. M. "Gauging Patient's Risks and Instituting Dietary Control." **Consultant** 1989 March; 29(8): 130–162.

9. Chisolm III, G. W. "The Oxidative Modification of LDL: Implications in Diabetes Mellitus." **Lipid Letter** 1988 Nov; 5(5).

10. Kwiterovich, P., Beneson, G. S. "Pediatrics and Cholesterol Related Issues." **Lipid Letter** 1989 April; 6(2).

11. Steiner, G. (Editorial). "From an Excess of Fat, Diabetics Die." **JAMA** 1989 July 21; 262(3): 398–399.

Nutritional
and Fat Content
Comparison

Based on USDA
Standards

♥ Your doctor tells you to eat more fiber, but where do you find it? You'll probably be surprised at where to find some of the nutrients you need for good health. Read on!

Fiber: pears, elderberry, blackberries, avacodo*, kale, figs, grapefruit, lime, lemon, kiwi*, oranges, melons, peaches, pineapple, plantain*, plums, peas and beans.

Calcium: beet greens, beans, canned salmon and canned mackerel, mushrooms, poppy seeds, milk products and ocean perch.

Folacin: found in most foods, including fish and meat, but especially high concentrations are found in peas, celery, tomatoes, spinach, beans, lentils, rye, buckwheat, and soy flour.

Vitamin C: green peppers, kiwi*, oranges, papaya*, and strawberries, plus most fruits and vegetables.

B12: oysters*, Atlantic herring, Atlantic mackerel, clams and rabbit*.

Iron: apricots, blackberries, gooseberries, prunes, most greens, beans, most meat and fish, tomatoes, soybeans*, lentils*, clams* and oysters*.

*Indicates foods highest in nutrient listed

FAT SATURATION COMPARISON
COOKING OILS

	% Saturated	% Mono	% Poly
Canola	7	55	33
Corn	13	24	59
Coconut	86	6	2
Cottonseed	26	19	51
Olive	14	72*	9
Palm	49	37	9
Palm Kernel	81	11	2
Peanut	19	46	30
Safflower	9	12	74
Sesame	15	40	40
Soybean	15	23	58
Sunflower	10	20	66
Walnut	9	23	63

FAT SATURATION COMPARISON
NUTS AND SEEDS

	% Saturated	% Mono	% Poly
Almonds	9	65*	21
Brazil	24	35	36
Cashews	20	59	17
Coconut	89	4	1
Filberts	7	79*	10
Macadamia	15	80*	2
Peanuts	14	50	32
Pecans	8	63*	25
Pine nuts	15	38	42
Pistachios	12	68*	15
Pumpkin Seeds	20	31	48
Sesame Seeds	14	38	44
Sunflower Seeds	11	19	66
Walnuts (Eng.)	9	23	63

* We recommend those foods with higher monounsaturated fats.

FAT CONTENT OF SOLID FATS

	% Saturated	% Mono	% Poly
Bacon	35	48	12
Beef	50	42	4
Butter	63	29	4
Chicken	30	45	21
Cocoa Butter	60	33	3
Egg Yolk	33	40	15
Lard	39	45	11
Margarine, hard 60%	23	43	30
Margarine, hard 80%	20	45	32
Margarine, soft 40%	20	41	36
Mayonnaise, soybean	15	29	49
Vegetable Shortening	25	44	26

NUTRIENT COMPARISON OF CHEESE

1 oz. each	Calories	Gm Protein	Gm Fat	Gm Saturated
American-slice	106.0	6.28	8.84	5.57
American-jar	92.8	5.55	6.98	4.37
Blue Cheese	99.8	6.09	8.14	5.29
Brie Cheese	94.8	5.87	7.84	4.94
Cheddar	114.0	7.05	9.38	5.97
Colby	112.0	6.73	9.08	5.72
Cottage 4%	29.0	3.54	1.21	.81
Cottage 1%	20.6	3.51	.29	.18
Cream	98.8	2.10	9.87	6.22
Feta	74.9	4.49	6.19	4.23
Gouda	101.0	7.06	7.72	4.98
Gruyere	117.0	8.44	9.05	5.35
Monterey Jack	106.0	6.93	8.56	5.42
Mozzarella(skim)	79.9	7.61	4.67	3.07
Parmesan	129.0	11.80	8.50	5.40
Provolone	99.8	7.13	7.54	4.83
Ricotta(part skim)	39.2	3.23	2.25	1.39
Romano	110.0	9.00	7.63	4.84
Roquefort	105.0	6.10	8.93	5.45
Swiss	107.0	8.03	7.79	5.03

NUTRIENT COMPARISON OF MEATS

3 oz.cooked	Calories	Gm Protein	Gm Total Fat	Gm Saturated	Gm Mono	Gm Poly	mg Cholesterol	mcg B_{12}
Beef								
Chuck Roast (lean)	230	26.4	13.0	5.3	5.8	.5	90	2.1
Ground	231	21.0	15.7	6.2	6.9	.6	74	2.0
Rib Roast	204	22.1	11.7	4.9	5.1	.4	68	2.5
Round Roast (lean)	189	26.9	8.2	2.9	3.8	.3	81	2.1
Rump Roast (lean)	153	25.2	5.7	2.2	2.4	.2	60	2.8
Chicken								
Breast (no skin)	140	26.4	3.0	.9	1.1	.7	72	.3
Dark Roast	174	23.3	8.3	2.3	3.0	1.9	79	.3
Light Roast	147	26.3	3.8	1.1	1.3	.8	72	.3
Thigh (no skin)	178	22.1	9.3	2.6	3.5	2.1	80	.3
Duck								
Roast	171	20.0	9.5	3.6	3.2	1.2	76	.3
Lamb								
Chop (broiled)	186	25.2	8.0	3.5	3.2	.5	80	2.1
Leg Roast	163	23.3	7.0	2.8	2.6	.5	76	1.6
Rib Roast	194	22.4	10.4	4.8	4.5	.5	75	1.7
Pork								
Ham (canned)	142	17.8	7.2	2.4	3.5	.8	35	.7
Ham Roast	207	18.3	14.3	5.1	6.7	1.5	52	.5
Loin Chop (broiled)	269	23.4	18.8	6.8	8.6	2.2	82	.6
Rib Roast (lean)	210	24.0	11.7	4.1	5.3	1.4	67	.5
Sausage Patty	300	15.9	25.2	8.8	11.3	3.1	66	1.4
Spareribs	338	24.7	25.8	10.0	12.1	3.0	103	.9
Tenderloin	141	24.0	4.1	1.4	1.8	.5	79	.5
Rabbit	168	24.1	6.1	2.6	1.3	2.1	77	10.2
Turkey								
Dark, Roast	159	24.3	6.1	2.1	1.4	1.8	72	.3
Ground	191	22.1	11.1	3.8	4.6	2.7	71	1.9
Light, Roast	133	25.5	2.7	.9	.5	.7	60	.3
Veal								
Cutlet (lean)	154	28.1	3.8	1.3	1.6	.6	117	1.6
Rib Roast (lean)	136	21.7	4.8	1.7	2.3	.5	115	1.6

NUTRIENT COMPARISON OF FISH

3 oz. raw	Calories	Gm Protein	Gm Total Fat	Gm Saturated	Gm Mono	Gm Poly	mg Cholesterol	mg Calcium
Bass	121	16.8	5.4	.8	1.8	2.2	47	10
Bluefish	105	17.0	3.6	.8	1.5	.9	50	6
Catfish	99	15.5	3.6	.8	1.4	.9	49	34
Clams	63	10.9	.8	.1	0	.2	29	39
Cod	70	15.1	.6	.1	0	.2	37	14
Flounder	77	16.0	1.0	.2	.2	.3	41	15
Haddock	67	16.1	.6	.1	.1	.2	49	28
Halibut	94	17.7	2.0	.3	.6	.7	27	40
Herring (Atlantic)	134	15.3	7.7	1.7	3.2	1.8	51	49
Herring (Pacific)	168	13.9	11.8	2.8	5.8	2.1	66	49
Lobster	77	16.0	.8	.1	.2	.3	81	25
Mackerel (Atlantic)	174	15.8	11.8	2.8	3.5	4.1	60	10
Mackerel (Pacific)	135	18.4	8.5	3.1	2.6	2.5	68	68
Northern Pike	75	16.4	.6	.1	.1	.2	33	49
Octopus	70	12.7	.9	.2	.1	.2	41	45
Oysters	69	8.0	2.0	.4	.3	.8	46	7
Perch (Ocean)	80	15.8	1.4	.2	.5	.4	36	91
Salmon								
Atlantic	125	16.8	5.4	.8	1.8	2.2	48	10
Chinook	153	17.1	8.9	2.1	3.8	1.8	56	19
Chinook (smoked)	91	15.5	3.7	.8	1.7	.8	20	9
Coho	157	23.3	6.4	1.2	2.2	1.9	42	25
Pink	99	16.9	2.9	.5	.8	1.2	44	34
Pink (canned)	118	16.8	5.1	1.3	1.5	1.7	43	182
Sockeye	143	18.1	7.3	1.3	3.5	1.6	53	5
Sockeye (canned)	130	17.4	6.2	1.4	2.4	1.9	37	204
Scallops	75	14.3	.6	0	0	.2	28	20
Shrimp	90	17.3	1.5	.3	.2	.6	129	44
Smelt	83	15.0	2.1	.4	.5	.8	60	51
Snapper	85	17.4	1.1	.2	.2	.4	32	27

NUTRIENT COMPARISON BEANS AND PEAS

½ cup cooked from dry	Calories	Gm Protein	Gm CHO*	Gm Fiber	mg Calcium	mg Sodium
Black Beans	75	5.0	13.5	5.1	16	0
Blackeyed Peas	65	4.4	11.7	6.8	14	2
Garbanzo	89	4.8	14.8	3.7	26	4
Great Northern	69	4.9	12.3	3.5	40	1
Kidney	74	5.1	13.3	5.0	17	1
(canned)	69	4.4	12.6	6.3	23	293
Lentils	76	5.9	13.2	3.3	12	1
Lima	72	4.9	13.0	5.9	11	1
(canned)	54	3.0	10.3	4.8	16	133
Navy	86	5.2	16.5	5.3	42	1
Pinto	78	4.6	14.5	6.4	27	1
Split Peas	76	5.4	13.7	3.3	9	1

NUTRIENT COMPARISON OF GRAIN PRODUCTS

½ cup cooked	Calories	Gm Protein	Gm Fiber	Gm CHO*	mg Calcium	mg Iron
Barley, Pearl	98	2.3	2.2	22	3	.6
Bulgar Wheat	123	4.8	5.3	22	14	1.4
Cornmeal	60	1.3	1.3	13	1	.7
Cornstarch	232	.2	.6	56	0	.3
Flour						
Buckwheat	170	3.2	3.0	39	6	.5
Light Rye	176	4.3	7.7	39	14	.6
Potato	314	7.2	1.0	22	30	15.4
Soy flour	185	25.4	6.0	17	83	2.6
White	227	6.6	1.7	48	10	2.8
Whole Wheat	200	8.0	7.6	43	25	2.6
Grits	73	1.8	2.3	16	1	.8
Masa Harina	203	5.3	7.4	41	115	4.4
Oats, rolled dry	155	6.5	4.4	27	21	1.7
Oatbran	107	8.4	7.6	32	25	2.3
Popcorn (dry, popped)	15	.5	.7	3	1	.1
Rice, Brown	116	2.5	1.7	25	12	.6
Rice, white	111	2.1	.4	25	10	1.4
Wheat Bran	38	2.9	7.6	11	21	2.0
Whole Wheat Berries	42	1.4	1.8	9	5	.5

* carbohydrates

NUTRIENT COMPARISON OF VEGETABLES

½ cup cooked	Calories	Gm Protein	Gm CHO*	Gm Fiber	RE Vit. A	mg Vit. C	mg Calcium	mg Sodium
Asparagus	23	2.3	4.0	1.5	75	25	22	4
Avocado	162	2.0	7.5	9.7	62	8	11	11
Beans, Green	22	1.2	4.9	1.6	42	6	29	2
Beets	26	.9	5.7	1.7	1	5	9	42
Broccoli	23	2.3	4.3	2.4	110	49	89	8
Brussel Sprouts	30	3.0	6.8	3.4	56	48	28	9
Cabbage	16	.8	3.8	1.7	9	33	32	12
Carrots	35	.9	8.2	2.7	1915	2	24	52
Cauliflower	24	2.0	4.9	2.5	2	72	28	14
Celery	19	.8	4.4	2.0	15	8	44	106
Corn	89	2.7	20.6	4.3	18	5	2	14
Eggplant	22	.7	5.3	3.0	5	1	5	2
Leeks	16	.4	4.0	1.7	2	2	16	5
Mushrooms	18	1.5	3.3	1.3	0	2	4	3
Okra	24	1.9	5.4	1.6	43	12	47	4
Onions	54	1.9	11.7	2.6	0	13	40	3
Peas	67	4.3	12.5	3.8	69	11	22	2
Pepper, Green	18	.6	3.9	1.2	39	95	4	2
Potato, Baked	93	1.9	21.5	2.0	0	11	9	7
Pumpkin	25	1.0	6.0	2.2	132	6	19	2
Spinach	21	2.7	3.4	2.2	875	20	122	6
Squash, Summer	15	.6	3.5	1.8	22	4	12	3
Squash, Winter	42	.9	10.7	2.9	717	15	42	4
Sweet potato, baked	88	1.5	20.7	2.6	1856	21	24	9
Tomatoes	34	1.1	5.3	1.8	139	22	9	10
Turnips	14	.6	3.8	1.6	0	9	18	39

* carbohydrate

DIABETIC EXCHANGES

	Serving Size	Calories	Gm Protein	Gm CHO*	Gm Fat

Fats	1 tsp. oil
	1 Tbsp. margarine
	   dressing
	   nuts
		45			5

Fruit	½ cup fresh ½ cup juice ¼ cup dried	60		15	
Meat					
lean	1 ounce	55	7		3
medium fat	1 ounce	75	7		5
high fat	1 ounce	100	7		8
Milk					
skim/very low fat	1 cup skim milk, 1%, ½% ½ cup evaporated skim ⅓ cup dry nonfat 8 oz. plain yogurt	90	8	12	trace
lofat	1 cup 2% 8 oz. lowfat yogurt	120	8	12	5
whole	1 cup whole milk ½ cup evaporated whole 8 oz. whole plain yogurt	150	8	12	8
Starch	½ cup cereal, grain ½ cup pasta 1 ounce bread ⅓ cup rice	80	3	15	trace
Vegetables	½ cup cooked 1 cup raw	25	2	5	

* carbohydrates

NUTRIENT COMPARISON OF FRUITS

½ cup fresh	Calories	Gm Fiber	RE Vit. A	mg Vit. C	mg Calcium	mg Iron
Apples	32	1.4	3	3	4	.1
Apricots	37	1.5	121	8	11	.4
Banana (½)	53	1.2	5	5	4	.2
Blackberries	37	4.9	12	15	23	.4
Blueberries	41	2.0	7	10	5	.1
Casaba Melon	23	.9	3	14	5	.3
Cherries	52	1.1	16	5	11	.3
Figs (each)	19	.9	4	.5	9	.1
Gooseberries[1]	93	3.0	17	13	20	.4
Grapefruit (½)	20	.8	.6	20	7	0
Grapes	70	1.2	8	11	11	.3
Kiwi	46	2.6	13	75	20	.3
Lemon	17	1.2	2	31	15	.4
Mandarin Orange[1]	78	2.1	106	25	9	.5
Mango	54	2.9	321	23	9	1.1
Cantelope	29	.8	258	34	9	.2
Honeydew	30	.9	3	21	5	.1
Watermelon	25	.3	29	8	7	.1
Orange	60	3.1	27	70	52	.1
Papaya	59	2.6	306	94	36	.2
Peaches	37	1.5	47	6	4	.1
Pears	98	4.6	3	7	19	.4
Pineapple	38	1.1	2	12	6	.3
Plums	36	1.3	21	6	3	.1
Prunes	57	2.3	16	2	12	.6
Raspberries	30	3.8	8	15	16	.4
Rhubarb[2]	139	2.6	8	4	174	.3
Strawberries	23	1.9	2	42	11	.3
Tangerine	37	1.7	77	25	12	.1

[1]canned
[2]sugar, cooked

Appetizers

♥ The configuration of the oil in macadamia and pistachio resembles the configuration of olive oil. Watch out, though, macadamia nuts are sometimes cooked in coconut oil.

♥ Peanut oil seems to have an affinity for coronary arteries.

♥ Fish oil capsules usually don't lower cholesterol. In **resistant** high triglyceride conditions, it sometimes works.

♥ If you continue to smoke, your benefits from a controlled fat diet will be curtailed to non—existent.

♥ Nuts that are high in monounsaturates are filbert, hickory, macadamia, pistachio, almonds and pecans.

APPETIZERS

ANTIPASTO PLATTER

This is a good prelude to an Italian meal. Save the sauce to use on other vegetables. Vary the vegetables to your taste. If you must limit your sodium intake, this is not for you.

1 cup catsup*
1 cup chili sauce*
1 cup water
½ cup olive oil
½ cup wine vinegar
½ cup lemon juice
1 clove garlic, minced
2 tablespoons brown sugar
1 tablespoon Worcestershire
   sauce*
1 tablespoon horseradish

salt to taste
dash hot pepper sauce
2 cups cauliflower flowerettes
1 ½ cups carrot slices
1 cup celery slices
½ pound small whole mushrooms
1 (8 oz.) jar pepperocini*
2 (6.5 oz.) cans water packed tuna
1 (2 oz.) tin anchovies*
pimento-stuffed olives for garnish

Combine the catsup, chili sauce, water, oil, vinegar, lemon juice, garlic, brown sugar, Worcestershire, horseradish, salt and hot pepper in a large saucepan. Bring to a boil and simmer a few minutes. Add the prepared vegetables to the sauce and simmer, covered, for about 20 minutes or until the vegetables are tender-crisp. Drain the tuna and add it to the sauce, taking care to keep it in as large pieces as possible. Simmer just until heated through. Divide among individual dishes, keeping each kind of vegetable and fish separated. Cool and chill as long as overnight. Garnish with anchovies and sliced olives.

Serves 15		167 calories per ½ cup serving		
Fat .... 8.7 G	Cholesterol .... 19 mg	Fiber .... 1.9 G	Diabetic exchanges:
saturated . 1.3 G	Protein .... 9.0 G	Vitamin C .. 20 mg	3 vegetable, 1 lean
mono .... 5.7 G	Carbohydrate .. 15.0 G	Calcium ... 49 mg	meat, 1 fat
poly ...... 1.0 G		Sodium .... 765 mg	

*Indicates high sodium content

ANCHOVY-CHEESE DIP

This is a quickie--only for those who love anchovies!

1 cup 1% cottage cheese*
1 tablespoon Butter Buds®*
2 minced anchovies or 2 teaspoons
   anchovy paste*
1 small onion or shallot, minced

1½ teaspoons capers
¾ teaspoon paprika
1 teaspoon Worcestershire sauce*
skim milk to correct consistency

Combine all ingredients in the bowl of the food processor and process until smooth. Add skim milk to correct consistency. Serve as a dip with fresh vegetables.

Serves 5		46 calories per ¼ cup serving					
Fat	.6 G	Cholesterol ...	3 mg	Fiber	.1 G	Diabetic exchanges:	
saturated .	.3 G	Protein	6.3 G	Vitamin C ..	1 mg	1 lean meat without	
mono	.2 G	Carbohydrate ..	2.2 G	Calcium ...	43 mg	the fat	
poly	.1 G			Sodium	265 mg		

SANDWICH SPREAD OR PARTY DIP

This gives you both protein and oat bran.

3-4 tablespoons water
1 beef bouillon cube*
¾ cup 1% cottage cheese*
½ teaspoon Dijon mustard
¾ teaspoon lemon juice

10 twists black pepper
3 tablespoons oat bran
skim milk to consistency
1 scallion, finely diced
½ stalk celery, finely diced

Dissolve the bouillon cube in the hot water, cool. Combine remaining ingredients, except the onion and celery in the blender and blend on low speed until smooth and slightly runny since the oat bran will absorb moisture and thicken the spread. Add onions and celery, stir. Serve either as a sandwich spread or a dip for vegetables.

Makes 1 cup		19 calories per 2 tablespoons					
Fat	.3 G	Cholesterol ...	1 mg	Fiber	.3 G	Diabetic exchanges:	
saturated .	.2 G	Protein	2.6 G	Vitamin C ..	0 mg	2 tablespoons free!	
mono	.1 G	Carbohydrate ..	2.0 G	Calcium ...	16 mg		
poly	.0 G			Sodium	176 mg		

*Indicates high sodium content

SEAFOOD COCKTAIL SAUCE

Our favorite cocktail sauce for shrimp; adjust the horseradish and hot pepper sauce to your taste.

1½ cups catsup*
¼ cup finely chopped celery
2 teaspoons horseradish
2 teaspoons Worcestershire sauce*

2 teaspoons fresh lemon juice
½ teaspoon onion salt*
dash hot pepper sauce

Combine all ingredients in a blender container and process until smooth. Chill.

Serves 8	56 calories per ¼ cup serving		
Fat .... .2 G	Cholesterol ... 0 mg	Fiber .... 1.0 G	Diabetic exchanges:
saturated .. 0 G	Protein .... 1.0 G	Vitamin C .. 9 mg	2 vegetables
mono ..... 0 G	Carbohydrate .. 13.4 G	Calcium ... 15 mg	
poly ...... .1 G		Sodium .... 671 mg	

MARINATED COCKTAIL MUSHROOMS

Easy to prepare and delicious to eat. Try other vegetables, such as artichokes.

1 pound small fresh mushrooms
¼ cup olive oil
2 tablespoons white wine vinegar

1 small onion, chopped
1 clove garlic, minced
dash sugar

Clean mushrooms and cook them in boiling salted water for 10 minutes. Drain well. Combine remaining ingredients, add mushrooms. Marinate for 12 hours or overnight. Serve on cocktail picks.

Serves 6	104 calories per serving		
Fat .... 9.0 G	Cholesterol ... 0 mg	Fiber .... 1.7 G	Diabetic exchanges:
saturated . 1.2 G	Protein .... 1.7 G	Vitamin C .. 3 mg	1 vegetable, 2 fat (not
mono .... 6.7 G	Carbohydrate .. 5.0 G	Calcium ... 6 mg	all the fat will
poly ...... 0.9 G		Sodium .... 2 mg	be consumed)

*Indicates high sodium content

DEVILED EGGS

Now you can go to picnics!

4 hardboiled eggs   **1-2 teaspoons prepared mustard**
¼ cup Egg Beaters®

Peel the hardboiled eggs and slice into halves. Discard the yolks. Put the Egg Beaters® in a double boiler over hot water and cook, stirring constantly until the Egg Beaters® are completely cooked. Cool; stir in the mustard, mashing the mixture well. Pack into egg white halves. Sprinkle with paprika. Chill.

Serves 4	35 calories per 2 halves		
Fat .... .6 G	Cholesterol ... 0 mg	Fiber .... .0 G	Diabetic exchanges:
saturated . .1 G	Protein .... 5.3 G	Vitamin C ... 0 mg	½ lean meat
mono ...... .2 G	Carbohydrate ... .6 G	Calcium ... 13 mg	
poly ...... .2 G		Sodium ..... 94 mg	

SHRIMP DIP

A quick, low fat dip for your vegetable platter.

9 cooked, peeled, deveined shrimp   **skim milk (to correct consistency)**
1 cup 1% cottage cheese*   **1 tablespoon capers**
2 tablespoons commercial chili sauce* **1 chopped shallot or small onion**
1-2 teaspoons onion powder   **1 tablespoon Butter Buds®***
1 tablespoon lemon juice

Combine all ingredients in the bowl of the food processor and process until smooth. Adjust consistency with skim milk. Serve as a dip for fresh vegetables.

Serves 6	68 calories per ½ cup serving		
Fat .... .8 G	Cholesterol ... 60 mg	Fiber .... .2 G	Diabetic exchanges:
saturated . .3 G	Protein .... 11.0 G	Vitamin C .. 3 mg	1¼ lean meat
mono .... .2 G	Carbohydrate .. 4.0 G	Calcium ... 48 mg	(light on fat)
poly ...... .2 G		Sodium .... 300 mg	

*Indicates high sodium content

GARLIC SHRIMP

For a hot appetizer when serving a light meal. The garlic is not subtle.

2-4 cloves garlic, thinly sliced
½ teaspoon dried red pepper flakes
1 bay leaf
2 tablespoons olive oil

¾ pound medium shrimp,
  shelled and deveined
2 tablespoons fresh lemon juice
1-2 tablespoons chopped fresh parsley

Cook the garlic, pepper flakes and bay leaf in the olive oil in a large skillet over medium high heat until the garlic is golden, about 3-4 minutes. Add the shrimp and cook just until they turn pink, about 2-4 minutes. Remove the bay leaf, transfer the shrimp to a serving dish, sprinkle with lemon juice and parsley and serve immediately.

Serves 6	100 calories per serving		
Fat .... 5.1 G	Cholesterol ... 111 mg	Fiber .... .1 G	Diabetic exchanges:
saturated . .1 G	Protein .... 12.0 G	Vitamin C .. 4 mg	1½ lean meat
mono .... 3.4 G	Carbohydrate .. 1.0 G	Calcium ... 26 mg	
poly ...... .1 G		Sodium .... 128 mg	

SPICED SHRIMP APPETIZER

This is a cold appetizer for those hot summer meals or serve as a luncheon main dish.

2 pounds shrimp
1 lemon, thinly sliced
1 onion, thinly sliced
½ cup pitted black olives, sliced*
2 tablespoons chopped pimento
½ cup fresh lemon juice
¼ cup olive oil

1 tablespoon white wine vinegar
1 clove garlic, minced
½ bay leaf
1 tablespoon dry mustard
¼ teaspoon cayenne
1 teaspoon salt*
freshly ground pepper to taste

Boil shrimp, drain, peel and devein. Combine shrimp, lemon slices, onion slices, olives and pimento in a large bowl. Toss. In a second bowl, combine the remaining ingredients and pour over the shrimp. Refrigerate overnight, stir occasionally.

Serves 8	208 calories per serving		
Fat .... 11.0 G	Cholesterol ... 221 mg	Fiber .... 1.1 G	Diabetic exchanges:
saturated . 1.8 G	Protein .... 24.2 G	Vitamin C .. 16 mg	3 lean meat (a plus
mono .... 7.3 G	Carbohydrate .. 3.9 G	Calcium ... 70 mg	on protein and fat)
poly ...... 1.4 G		Sodium .... 628 mg	

*Indicates high sodium content

SHRIMP APPETIZER

This cold appetizer has a thick, spicy sauce.

5 tablespoons hot mustard*
2 tablespoons paprika
1 tablespoon horseradish
⅓ cup vinegar
⅔ cup olive oil
1 cup minced scallions
½ cup minced celery

2 cloves garlic, minced
¼ cup minced fresh parsley
salt and freshly ground pepper to taste*
dash hot pepper sauce
1 pound cooked, peeled,
deveined shrimp

Combine the mustard, paprika, horseradish and vinegar in a glass bowl. Slowly add the olive oil, whisking constantly until all is incorporated. Stir in the scallions, celery, garlic and parsley. Add salt, pepper and hot pepper sauce to taste. Fold in shrimp and marinate in the refrigerator overnight. Serve on a bed of shredded lettuce as an appetizer.

Serves 8	106 calories per ½ cup serving		
Fat .... 4.7 G	Cholesterol ... 111 mg	Fiber ...... 1 G	Diabetic exchanges:
saturated . .6 G	Protein .... 12.9 G	Vitamin C .. 9 mg	1½ lean meat,
mono .... 3.0 G	Carbohydrate .. 3.7 G	Calcium ... 49mg	½ vegetable, (not all fat
poly ...... .7 G		Sodium .... 260 mg	will be consumed)

POTATO PEEL CHIPS

Don't throw away the potato peelings. Dry them on towels, sprinkle with garlic powder and fry them in olive oil until brown and crisp. Drain well on paper towels, salt to taste and keep your cotton picking hands off until the guests get a chance!

Serves 1	148 calories per 20 chips serving		
Fat .... 10.1 G	Cholesterol ... 0 mg	Fiber .... 1.4 G	Diabetic exchanges:
saturated . 2.6 G	Protein .... 1.6 G	Vitamin C .. 12 mg	1 starch, 2 fat
mono .... 5.1 G	Carbohydrate .. 14.7 G	Calcium ... 7 mg	
poly ...... 1.8 G		Sodium .... 133 mg	

*Indicates high sodium content

CEREAL PARTY MIX

Choose cereals with no added fats, devise your own combination. This recipe keeps the usual saturated fat out of the seasoning, but keep in mind that this is definitely high in sodium.

¼ cup olive oil
4 teaspoons Worcestershire sauce*
1 teaspoon seasoned salt*

7 cups mixed cereal of your choice
1 cup pretzels*
2 teaspoons Butter Buds®*

Preheat the oven to 250 degrees. Combine the oil, Worcestershire sauce and seasoned salt. Pour over cereal and pretzels, toss to coat. Add Butter Buds®, toss. Bake for 1 hour, stirring every 15 minutes. Spread on paper towels to cool. Store in an airtight container.

Serves 12	154 calories per ½ cup serving		
Fat .... 5.3 G	Cholesterol ... 0 mg	Fiber .... 1.5 G	Diabetic exchanges:
saturated . .8 G	Protein .... 2.8 G	Vitamin C .. 11 mg	1½ starch, 1 fat
mono .... 3.6 G	Carbohydrate .. 24.0 G	Calcium ... 12 mg	
poly ...... .8 G		Sodium .... 490 mg	

CLAM CANAPE

If you like clams, this is for you. Find a cracker with little saturated fat if you wish to use crackers.

1 cup 1% cottage cheese*
1 can (6 ounces) clams, drained
¼ teaspoon dry mustard
1 teaspoon onion powder

1 tablespoon Worcestershire sauce*
salt to taste*
skim milk to correct consistency

Combine all ingredients in the bowl of the food processor and process until smooth. Add skim milk to correct consistency. Serve on crackers or with fresh vegetable sticks.

Serves 8	39 calories per 1 Tbsp. serving		
Fat .... .5 G	Cholesterol ... 9 mg	Fiber .... .2 G	Diabetic exchanges:
saturated . .2 G	Protein .... 7.0 G	Vitamin C .. 1 mg	1 lean meat (light on fat)
mono .... .1 G	Carbohydrate ..... 1.8 G	Calcium ..... 35 mg	
poly .... .1 G		Sodium ...... 218 mg	

*Indicates high sodium content

HOMEMADE PRETZELS

Low salt, if you don't sprinkle on the Kosher salt. There's a beverage that goes with these—if only I could remember!

1 package yeast
½ teaspoon sugar
1½ cups warm beer
   (105-115 degrees)

½ teaspoon salt*
4½ cups flour
1 egg white, beaten
Kosher or rock salt*

Dissolve yeast and sugar in warm beer in a large mixing bowl. Add flour and salt; mix until blended. Turn out onto a very lightly floured surface and knead dough 8-10 minutes or until smooth and elastic.

Place dough in a greased bowl, turning to grease top. Cover and let rise in a warm place (85 degrees), free from drafts, 1 hour or until doubled in bulk.

Using kitchen shears dipped in flour, cut dough into 24 pieces; roll each into a ball. With floured hands, roll each ball between hands to form a rope 14 inches long. Twist each into pretzel shape, placing on greased foil-lined baking sheets, about 1½ inches apart. Brush each pretzel with egg white; sprinkle with Kosher salt. Bake at 475 degrees 12-15 minutes or until golden brown. Remove pretzels to wire rack. Serve warm.

Makes 24	93 calories per pretzel		
Fat .... .2 G	Cholesterol ... 0 mg	Fiber .... .8 G	Diabetic exchanges:
saturated ... 0 G	Protein .... 2.7 G	Vitamin C .. 0 mg	1 starch
mono ...... 0 G	Carbohydrate .. 18.6 G	Calcium ... 5 mg	
poly .... .1 G		Sodium .... 48 mg	

*Indicates high sodium content

Breads

♥ There is some similarity between the oils in 80% hard margarine and peanut oil.

♥ Evaluate the polyunsaturated fat content as well as saturated fat in your food.

♥ In the morning, a diurnal variation in your serum cortisone causes an elevation of blood sugar.

♥ I have an inexpensive machine in my office that gives me a good idea of diabetic compliance...it's called a scale.

BREADS

BISCUITS

These taste the same as the regular biscuits but have fewer calories.

2 cups flour
½ teaspoon salt*
1 tablespoon baking powder*

¼ teaspoon soda*
¾ cup buttermilk
1 tablespoon olive oil

Mix dry ingredients together. Add buttermilk and oil. Stir just until all dry ingredients are incorporated. Turn onto a lightly floured board and knead 7-8 times. Roll dough to ½ inch thickness, cut with 2½ inch cutter and place on cookie sheet which has been sprayed with pan spray. Bake at 400 degrees for 8 minutes or until lightly browned.

Makes 9	140 calories per biscuit		
Fat .... 2.2 G	Cholesterol ... 1 mg	Fiber .... .8 G	Diabetic exchanges:
saturated . .4 G	Protein .... 4.0 G	Vitamin C .. 0 mg	1¾ starch
mono .... 1.3 G	Carbohydrate .. 25.0 G	Calcium ... 54 mg	
poly ...... .3 G		Sodium .... 307 mg	

CORN MUFFINS

Surprisingly versatile, try them with jam or jelly.

1 cup all-purpose flour
¾ cup yellow cornmeal
2½ teaspoons baking powder*
½ teaspoon salt*

2 tablespoons sugar
¼ cup Egg Beaters®
1 cup skim milk
2 tablespoons olive oil

Preheat the oven to 400 degrees. Sift the dry ingredients together into a mixing bowl. Combine the Egg Beaters®, milk and olive oil and stir into the dry ingredients, stirring just until well combined. Do not beat. Spray muffin tins with pan spray and fill each cup ⅔ full. Bake for 20 minutes or until golden brown.

Makes 12	110 calories per muffin		
Fat .... 2.7 G	Cholesterol ... 0 mg	Fiber .... .9 G	Diabetic exchanges:
saturated . .4 G	Protein .... 3.1 G	Vitamin C .. 0 mg	1 starch, ½ fat
mono .... 1.8 G	Carbohydrate .. 18.0 G	Calcium ... 43 mg	
poly ...... .4 G		Sodium .... 177 mg	

*Indicates high sodium content

CORNBREAD DUMPLINGS

When you eat beans, you get a partial amino acid supply. Add corn and you have a total protein. They must be eaten at the same meal to be utilized as a complete protein. To cook the dumplings, you need a chicken or beef broth or even the soup of the bean soup.

½ cup flour
½ cup cornmeal
½ teaspoon baking powder*

½ teaspoon salt*
½ cup skim milk

Combine all ingredients to make a stiff dough. Drop by ½ teaspoonful into the hot broth and simmer until done-about 15 minutes.

Serves 5		105 calories per serving (serving size 4 dumplings)			
Fat	.3 G	Cholesterol ...	0 mg	Fiber .... 1.4 G	Diabetic exchanges:
saturated .	.1 G	Protein	3.0 G	Vitamin C .. 0 mg	1¼ starch
mono	.1 G	Carbohydrate ..	22.0 G	Calcium ... 40 mg	
poly	.1 G			Sodium .... 259 mg	

CORNMEAL BISCUITS

Just like the cornmeal muffins, these will go with just about anything. Try them with sausage and gravy (see recipe).

2 cups sifted all-purpose flour
1 tablespoon baking powder*
1 teaspoon soda*
½ teaspoon salt*
1 teaspoon sugar

½ cup yellow cornmeal
2 tablespoons olive oil
½ cup Egg Beaters®
¾ cup buttermilk

Sift together the flour, baking powder, soda, salt and sugar. Blend in the cornmeal. Combine the Egg Beaters®, buttermilk and oil and add to the dry ingredients. Mix until dough follows the fork around bowl. Turn out onto lightly floured board and knead 8-10 times. Roll ½ inch thick and cut with floured biscuit cutter. Bake at 400 degrees for about 15 minutes.

Makes 12		128 calories per biscuit			
Fat	3.0 G	Cholesterol ...	1 mg	Fiber .... .9 G	Diabetic exchanges:
saturated .	.5 G	Protein	4.2 G	Vitamin C .. 0 mg	1 starch, ½ fat
mono	1.8 G	Carbohydrate ..	21.0 G	Calcium ... 42 mg	
poly	.5 G			Sodium .... 274 mg	

*Indicates high sodium content

MUFFINS

The good smell of your mother's baking arises.

2 cups sifted all-purpose flour
½ teaspoon salt*
2½ teaspoons baking powder*
3 tablespoons sugar

¼ cup Egg Beaters®
1 cup skim milk
¼ cup olive oil

Preheat oven to 400 degrees. Spray muffin pan with pan spray. Combine flour, salt, baking powder and sugar. Add the Egg Beaters®, skim milk and olive oil and mix only until blended. Do not beat. Fill muffin cups ⅔ full and bake for 20-25 minutes.

Makes 12	134 calories per muffin		
Fat . . . . 4.9 G	Cholesterol . . . 0 mg	Fiber . . . . .5 G	Diabetic exchanges:
saturated . .7 G	Protein . . . . 3.0 G	Vitamin C . . 0 mg	1 starch, 1 fat
mono . . . . 3.4 G	Carbohydrate . . 19.0 G	Calcium . . . 44 mg	
poly . . . . . . .5 G		Sodium . . . . 178 mg	

WHOLE WHEAT ENGLISH MUFFINS

For the English muffin addict, you *know* what's in this one.

2 packages yeast
2¾ to 3 cups flour
1½ cups whole wheat flour
½ cup cracked wheat
¼ cup wheat germ
½ cup oat bran

2 cups skim milk
1 tablespoon olive oil
1 teaspoon sugar
2 teaspoons salt*
cornmeal

Combine yeast, ¾ cup all-purpose flour, whole wheat flour, cracked wheat, wheat germ and oat bran. Heat milk, oil, sugar and salt to 115-120 degrees, stirring constantly. Add to dry mixture. Beat at low speed on electric mixer for ½ minute, beat 3 minutes at high speed. Stir in enough flour by hand to make a moderately stiff dough. Knead 8-10 minutes, place in bowl, let rise until doubled in size. Punch dough down and let rest 10 minutes.

On lightly floured surface, roll dough to just less than ½ inch thick. Cut with 2½ inch round cutter, dip both sides of muffin in cornmeal, cover, let rise 30 minutes or until very light. Bake at medium-low heat on ungreased griddle or in ungreased skillets about 25-28 minutes or until done. Turn muffins frequently. Cool on wire racks.

Makes 24	104 calories per muffin		
Fat . . . . 1.1 G	Cholesterol . . . 0 mg	Fiber . . . . 2.0 G	Diabetic exchanges:
saturated . .2 G	Protein . . . . 4.1 G	Vitamin C . . 0 mg	1 starch
mono . . . . .5 G	Carbohydrate . . 20.3 G	Calcium . . . 35 mg	
poly . . . . . . .3 G		Sodium . . . . 190 mg	

*Indicates high sodium content

OAT BRAN MUFFINS

Another variant on a common theme these days.

2¼ cups oat bran
¼ cup raisins or chopped dates
  or chopped dried apricots
¼ cup brown sugar
1 tablespoon baking powder*

1¼ cups skim milk
2 egg whites
2 tablespoons olive oil
1 teaspoon cinnamon
½ teaspoon nutmeg

Combine all ingredients. Spoon mixture into muffin tins which have been sprayed with pan spray or use paper liners. Bake at 425 degrees for 15-17 minutes.

Makes 12	100 calories per muffin		
Fat .... 3.1 G	Cholesterol ... 0 mg	Fiber .... 3.0 G	Diabetic exchanges:
saturated . .5 G	Protein .... 4.7 G	Vitamin C .. 0 mg	1 starch
mono .... 2.0 G	Carbohydrate .. 20.5 G	Calcium ... 64 mg	
poly...... .5 G		Sodium .... 110 mg	

GARLIC DILL BREAD

This was my first bread recipe developed several years ago.

3 cups flour
2 teaspoons salt*
1 tablespoon yeast
½-1 teaspoon garlic powder

1-2 tablespoons dry dill weed
1 cup nonfat dry milk
3 teaspoons potato starch
hot water to consistency

Mix all above ingredients together, add enough hot water to reach the desired consistency. Knead, let rise until double. Punch down and shape into loaf, place in 9 x 5 x 3 bread pan; let rise for 30 minutes. Bake at 350 degrees for 30-35 minutes or until done.

Makes 1 loaf	104 calories per slice (18 slices/loaf)		
Fat .... .3 G	Cholesterol ... 1 mg	Fiber .... .8 G	Diabetic exchanges:
saturated . .1 G	Protein .... 4.0 G	Vitamin C .. 0 mg	1¼ starch
mono ..... 0 G	Carbohydrate .. 21.0 G	Calcium ... 61 mg	
poly...... .1 G		Sodium .... 291 mg	

*Indicates high sodium content

WATER BAGELS

There are those who say they'll kill for these.

4-5 cups flour
3 tablespoons sugar
1 tablespoon salt*
1 package yeast

1½ cups very hot tap water
1 egg white, beaten
1 tablespoon cold water

In large bowl thoroughly mix 1½ cups flour, sugar, salt and yeast. Gradually add very hot tap water to dry ingredients and beat 2 minutes at medium speed of electric mixer, scraping bowl occasionally.

Add ½ cup flour or enough to make thick batter. Beat at high speed 2 minutes, scraping bowl occasionally. Stir in enough additional flour to make soft dough.

Turn out onto lightly floured board. Knead until smooth and elastic, about 8-10 minutes. Place in ungreased bowl. Cover and let rise in warm place, free from draft, 20 minutes. Dough will not be doubled in bulk. Punch dough down. Turn out onto lightly floured board. Roll dough into 12 by 10 inch rectangle. Cut into 12 equal 10 by 1 inch strips. Pinch ends of strips together to form circles. Place on ungreased baking sheet. Cover and let rise in warm place, free from draft, 20 minutes. Dough will not be doubled in bulk.

In large shallow pan, bring water 1¾ inches deep, to boil. Lower heat and add a few bagels at a time. Simmer 3 minutes. Remove from water and place on towel to cool. Cool 5 minutes. Place on ungreased baking sheet. Bake at 375 degrees 10 minutes.

Remove from oven. Lightly beat egg white with cold water. Brush bagels with this mixture. Return to oven and bake about 20 minutes longer or until done. Remove from baking sheet and cool on wire racks.

Makes 12		167 calories per bagel			
Fat	.4 G	Cholesterol ... 0 mg	Fiber .... 1.3 G	Diabetic exchanges:
saturated .	.1 G	Protein .... 4.9 G	Vitamin C .. 0 mg	2 starch
mono	0 G	Carbohydrate .. 35.0 G	Calcium ... 12 mg	
poly	.2 G		Sodium .... 539 mg	

*Indicates high sodium content

FLAT CORNBREAD

This is only about ½ inch thick when baked.

¼ cup yellow cornmeal
¼ cup all-purpose flour
¾ teaspoon baking powder*
½ teaspoon salt*

½ teaspoon sugar
1 egg white
6 tablespoons skim milk
1 tablespoon olive oil

Combine all the dry ingredients in a bowl. Mix the egg white, skim milk and oil together and add to the dry ingredients, stirring until the mixture is combined. Spread the batter in a 9 inch round cake pan which has been sprayed with pan spray. Bake at 450 degrees for 15-20 minutes or until done. Invert on a cutting board and slice into wedges.

Serves 6	70 calories per wedge		
Fat .... 2.4 G	Cholesterol ... 0 mg	Fiber .... .6 G	Diabetic exchanges:
saturated . .3 G	Protein .... 2.1 G	Vitamin C .. 0 mg	¾ starch
mono .... 1.7 G	Carbohydrate .. 9.8 G	Calcium ... 29 mg	
poly ...... .3 G		Sodium .... 235 mg	

FOUR GRAIN BREAD

This is a relatively high protein bread.

1 package yeast
¼ cup bran
1 cup whole wheat flour
½ cup rye flour
¼ cup cornmeal
1 cup all-purpose flour
¼ cup oatmeal

1 tablespoon salt*
3 cups water
½ cup nonfat dry milk
2 tablespoons honey
3-4 cups all-purpose flour
3 heaping tablespoons potato starch

Mix yeast and honey with warm water. Mix all dry ingredients except the last 3-4 cups flour. Add the water-yeast mixture and beat until smooth. Work in enough flour to make the dough easy to handle. Knead for 20 minutes until smooth and elastic. Put in a bowl and cover with damp cloth, let rise until doubled. Punch dough down, turn onto floured surface and shape into 2 loaves. Put into bread pans sprayed with pan spray. Let rise again for about 30 minutes. Bake in 350 degree oven for 25-30 minutes or until done.

Makes 2 loaves	84 calories per slice (18 slices/loaf)		
Fat .... .3 G	Cholesterol ... 0 mg	Fiber .... 1.0 G	Diabetic exchanges:
saturated . .1 G	Protein .... 3.0 G	Vitamin C .. 0 mg	1 starch
mono .... .1 G	Carbohydrate .. 18.0 G	Calcium ... 18 mg	
poly ...... .1 G		Sodium .... 184 mg	

*Indicates high sodium content

HOMEMADE HAMBURGER BUNS

This makes your sandwich a meal, almost.

½ cup instant mashed potatoes
1 cup boiling water
1 package yeast
1 cup 1% cottage cheese*
2 tablespoons sugar
2 tablespoons olive oil

½-1 teaspoon salt*
¼ cup Egg Beaters®
4½ cups (about) flour
¼ cup sesame seed or instant toasted onion

In a large bowl, combine potatoes and 1 cup boiling water; stir with a fork until evenly moistened. Set aside to cool for at least 5 minutes.

In a small bowl, sprinkle yeast over ¼ cup warm water and let stand until softened, about 5 minutes.

To the instant mashed potatoes, add the cheese, sugar, oil, salt, Egg Beaters® and yeast mixture; stir to blend. (Combining the ingredients in the food processor makes the mixture very smooth.)

Stir 2 cups flour into the potato mixture and beat with a heavy spoon until batter is stretchy, about 5 minutes. Stir in 2½ cups more flour until evenly moistened. Scrape dough onto well-floured board and knead until dough is springy and no longer sticky. Place dough in an oiled bowl and turn dough over so top is oiled; cover bowl with plastic wrap.

Set dough in a warm place until doubled, about 1½ hours. Knead dough on a lightly floured board to expel air bubbles. Cut dough into 12 equal pieces. Lightly oil your hands. Pick up 1 piece of dough at a time and gently pull top surface under until top is smooth. Set tucked side down on lightly oiled 12x15 inch baking sheet. Repeat to shape remaining dough, setting pieces at least 2 inches apart. Cover lightly with plastic wrap and let stand in a warm place until puffy, about 30 minutes. Brush tops of buns with Egg Beaters®. Sprinkle with sesame seeds or toasted onion.

Bake in 350 degree oven until golden brown, 20-25 minutes. Transfer to racks to cool; serve warm or cool. If made ahead, package cooled buns airtight up to overnight; freeze to store longer. Slice buns in half to fill.

Makes 12	245 calories per bun		
Fat .... 5.0 G	Cholesterol ... 1 mg	Fiber .... 1.9 G	Diabetic exchanges:
saturated . 1.0 G	Protein .... 8.8 G	Vitamin C .. 1 mg	2¾ starch, 1 fat
mono .... 2.5 G	Carbohydrate .. 40.5 G	Calcium ... 56 mg	
poly ...... 1.1 G		Sodium .... 161 mg	

*Indicates high sodium content

GARLIC HERB BREAD

To lure you away from "butter lust."

2 tablespoons olive oil
¼ teaspoon oregano, hand rubbed
⅛ teaspoon basil, hand rubbed

1 small garlic clove, pressed
    through garlic press
6 slices French style bread

Combine first 4 ingredients and brush onto bread slices. Toast until lightly brown; serve at once.

Serves 6	41 calories per tsp. seasoning (calculations for seasoning)		
Fat .... 4.5 G	Cholesterol ... 0 mg	Fiber .... 0 G	Diabetic exchanges:
saturated . .6 G	Protein .... 0 G	Vitamin C .. 0 mg	1 fat (add 1 starch
mono .... 3.3 G	Carbohydrate .. 0.2 G	Calcium ... 3 mg	for bread)
poly ...... .4 G		Sodium .... 0 mg	

SODA BREAD

This is quicker and more predictable than yeast bread.

2 cups self rising flour
1 egg white
1 cup skim milk

1 tablespoon sugar
1 tablespoon olive oil

Combine all ingredients except olive oil in a medium bowl. Mix until well combined. Turn out onto floured board and knead until it is no longer sticky. Put olive oil in bottom of 8x4x2½ inch bread pan. Press dough into pan to force oil up sides. Bake in preheated 400 degree oven for 20-25 minutes. Cool on rack.

Serves 10	115 calories per slice		
Fat .... 1.6 G	Cholesterol ... 0 mg	Fiber .... .7 G	Diabetic exchanges:
saturated . .3 G	Protein .... 3.6 G	Vitamin C .. 0 mg	1½ starch
mono .... 1.0 G	Carbohydrate .. 21.1 G	Calcium ... 97 mg	
poly .... 0 G		Sodium .... 287 mg	

BRAN BRAN BREAD

Oat bran is an effective cholesterol lowering agent. I use no oil, eggs, milk or sugar in bread. The secret ingredient is potato starch. It emulsifies and makes the bread smoother and the crust softer. Using the potato water saved from cooking potatoes is not a screwy idea, it improves the texture of the bread. A thick slice of the bread, toasted, makes a meal.

2½ cups white flour
½ cup oat bran
¼ cup wheat bran (optional)
1 tablespoon dry yeast

2 teaspoons salt*
1½ cups warm water
3 heaping teaspoons potato starch

Dissolve yeast in warm water. Combine dry ingredients in food processor, add yeast-water mixture and process until mass forms into a ball. Turn out into a bowl, cover with a damp towel or plastic wrap and allow to rise until doubled. Punch down dough, form into loaf and place in 9x5x3 bread pan. Allow to rise in warm oven until almost double. Bake at 350 degrees for 35 minutes or until done. (I always start with a slightly warm or cold oven.)

Variation: Raisin Bread
Combine ¼ cup sugar with 1 tablespoon Butter Buds®. After punching down the dough after the first rise, flatten the dough, spread with raisins, cinnamon, and part of the sugar mixture; fold and knead. Repeat at least 4 times, be generous. Shape into loaf and bake as above. (Remember, the calories will be increased.) Analysis does not include this variation.

Makes 1 loaf		73 calories per slice (18 slices/loaf)				
Fat	.3 G	Cholesterol ...	0 mg	Fiber .... 1.2 G	Diabetic exchanges:
saturated .	.1 G	Protein	2.5 G	Vitamin C .. 0 mg	1 starch
mono	.1 G	Carbohydrate ..	16.0 G	Calcium ... 7 mg	
poly......	.1 G			Sodium .... 239 mg	

*Indicates high sodium content

NOODLES

If you like the taste of homemade egg noodles, but not the cholesterol, try making them with Egg Beaters®.

2 cups all-purpose flour
⅓ teaspoon salt or to taste*

½ cup Egg Beaters®
1-2 tablespoons water (as necessary)

Combine the flour and salt in a medium bowl. Add the Egg Beaters® and mix with a fork until the dough forms a ball. Add a small amount of water, as necessary, for the dough to shape. Turn out onto a well floured surface and knead until smooth. Roll out very thin; let dry slightly and cut.

Serves 6	169 calories per ½ cup serving		
Fat .... 1.1 G	Cholesterol ... 0 mg	Fiber .... 1.1 G	Diabetic exchanges:
saturated . .2 G	Protein .... 6.9 G	Vitamin C .. 0 mg	1 starch
mono .... .2 G	Carbohydrate .. 32.0 G	Calcium ... 18 mg	
poly...... .5 G		Sodium .... 127 mg	

GRANOLA

Commercial granola usually is loaded with fat and sugar. This has more acceptable oils, sugar input, plus lots of protein and fiber. In addition, it is low in sodium.

3 cups uncooked rolled oats
1½ cups wheat germ
½ cup oat bran
½ cup nonfat dry milk
½ cup sesame seeds
½ cup sunflower seeds

½ cup olive oil
2 tablespoons honey
1 cup raisins
½ cup chopped dates
½ cup chopped dried apricots

Toast the oatmeal in a 300 degree oven for 15 minutes, stirring occasionally. Cool. Combine the wheat germ, oat bran, dry milk, seeds and oatmeal. Combine the olive oil and honey, heat until warm and add to the oatmeal mixture. Toast at 300 degrees for 15 minutes. Cool and stir in fruit.

Serves 16	271 calories per ½ cup serving		
Fat .... 13.5 G	Cholesterol ... 0 mg	Fiber .... 5.2 G	Diabetic exchanges:
saturated . 1.9 G	Protein .... 8.4 G	Vitamin C .. 1 mg	2 fruit, 1 lean
mono .... 6.9 G	Carbohydrate .. 34.0 G	Calcium ... 60 mg	meat, 2 fat
poly...... 4.1 G		Sodium .... 17 mg	

*Indicates high sodium content

AMERICAN CHAPPATI

The Far Eastern Indians make a flat bread and so do we, but we call it "pizza dough." Bake one and tear off a piece now and then while you're eating.

2 cups all-purpose flour
1 package yeast

½ teaspoon salt (optional)*
1 cup warm water (or skim milk or whey)

Dissolve yeast in warm water, allow to proof. Add flour and salt (if you are using it), mixing well. Knead. Allow to rise. Punch down and flatten onto an 8 inch pizza pan which has been sprayed with pan spray. Allow to rise for 20-30 minutes. Bake 15 minutes in 350 degree oven or until slightly browned.

Serves 8	116 calories per 1/8 slice		
Fat .... .3 G	Cholesterol ... 0 mg	Fiber .... 1.1 G	Diabetic exchanges:
saturated .. 0 G	Protein .... 3.6 G	Vitamin C .. 0 mg	1¼ starch
mono ..... 0 G	Carbohydrate .. 23.8 G	Calcium ... 7 mg	
poly...... .1 G		Sodium .... 135 mg	

BANANA OATMEAL PANCAKES

This is not low calorie, but high in fiber and protein.

¾ cup quick rolled oats
⅔ cup whole wheat flour
¼ cup oat bran
¼ teaspoon salt*
1 teaspoon baking powder*

½ teaspoon baking soda*
1 medium, ripe banana, mashed
1 cup buttermilk
¼ cup Egg Beaters®
2 tablespoons olive oil

Combine the oats, flour, salt, baking powder, baking soda and oat bran. Combine the mashed banana and Egg Beaters®; stir in buttermilk and olive oil, mix until smooth. Add dry ingredients and stir until blended. Brush a griddle lightly with olive oil, pour ¼ cup batter onto griddle and bake until browned on both sides.

Makes 6	175 calories per cake		
Fat .... 6.4 G	Cholesterol ... 2 mg	Fiber .... 4.0 G	Diabetic exchanges:
saturated . 1.1 G	Protein .... 6.9 G	Vitamin C .. 2 mg	1¾ starch, 1 fat
mono .... 3.8 G	Carbohydrate .. 25.0 G	Calcium ... 77 mg	
poly...... 1.0 G		Sodium .... 275 mg	

*Indicates high sodium content

GRIDDLE CAKES

A basic pancake.

½-¾ cup skim milk (the less,
  the thicker)
2 tablespoons olive oil
2 egg whites
1 cup all-purpose flour

2 teaspoons baking powder*
1 tablespoon Butter Buds®*
1 package sweetener (do not use
  aspartame)
1 teaspoon sugar

Beat the milk, egg whites and oil, add the dry ingredients and stir enough to mix, but do not overbeat. Pour onto hot griddle sprayed with pan spray. Turn once.

Makes 6	136 calories per cake		
Fat .... 4.8 G	Cholesterol ... 0 mg	Fiber .... 0.6 G	Diabetic exchanges:
saturated . .7 G	Protein .... 4.0 G	Vitamin C .. 0 mg	1 starch, 1 fat
mono .... 3.3 G	Carbohydrate .. 18.0 G	Calcium ... 49 mg	
poly ...... .5 G		Sodium .... 187 mg	

YOGURT PANCAKES

Calcium, protein and taste. Cover it with strawberries.

¼ cup Egg Beaters®
1 cup low fat yogurt
2 tablespoons olive oil
¾ cup unsifted flour
2 tablespoons oat bran

1 tablespoon sugar
1 teaspoon baking powder*
½ teaspoon baking soda*
¼ teaspoon salt*
¼ teaspoon cinnamon (optional)

Combine the Egg Beaters®, yogurt and oil, stir until smooth. Add the dry ingredients, stirring until smooth. On lightly oiled hot griddle pour ¼ cup batter, bake until browned on both sides.

Makes 6	143 calories per cake		
Fat .... 5.7 G	Cholesterol ... 3 mg	Fiber .... .8 G	Diabetic exchanges:
saturated . 1.1 G	Protein .... 5.2 G	Vitamin C .. 0 mg	1¼ starch, 1 fat
mono ...; 3.6 G	Carbohydrate .. 18.3 G	Calcium ... 90 mg	
poly ...... .7 G		Sodium .... 258 mg	

*Indicates high sodium content

OVERNIGHT YEAST WAFFLES

These light, crispy waffles will start your day!

2 cups all-purpose flour
1 package dry yeast
¼ teaspoon cardamom
2 cups skim milk
2 tablespoons olive oil

1 teaspoon sugar
1 teaspoon salt*
¼ cup Egg Beaters®
2 stiffly beaten egg whites

In a large bowl, stir together the flour, yeast and cardamom. In a saucepan, heat the milk, oil, sugar and salt just until warm, stirring constantly, to about 115 degrees. Add to the flour mixture and beat well. Cover and refrigerate overnight or let stand at room temperature for 1½-2 hours. Just before baking, whip the egg whites to stiff peaks. Stir the Egg Beaters® into the flour mixture then fold in the beaten egg whites. Bake in a preheated waffle baker.

Makes 12		120 calories per waffle					
Fat	2.7 G	Cholesterol ...	1 mg	Fiber	.8 G	Diabetic exchanges:
saturated .	.4 G	Protein	5 G	Vitamin C ..	0 mg	1¼ starch, ½ fat,
mono	1.8 G	Carbohydrate ..	18 G	Calcium ...	59 mg	
poly	.4 G			Sodium	217 mg	

RAISIN BRAN PANCAKES

This is a high fiber, high protein, high carbohydrate, low fat breakfast.

1 cup whole wheat flour
⅔ cup all-purpose flour
2 tablespoons sugar
1 tablespoon baking powder*
½ teaspoon salt*

¼ cup Egg Beaters®
2 cups skim milk
¼ cup oat bran
2 tablespoons olive oil
1 cup raisin bran cereal

Stir together the flours, sugar, baking powder and salt. Set aside. In a mixing bowl, stir together the Egg Beaters®, milk, oil, oat bran and cereal. Let stand 5 minutes. Stir again and add flour mixture, stirring only until combined. Bake pancakes on griddle sprayed with pan spray or a non-stick skillet until browned on both sides.

Makes 12		124 calories per cake					
Fat	2.9 G	Cholesterol ...	1 mg	Fiber	2.3 G	Diabetic exchanges:
saturated .	.5 G	Protein	4.9 G	Vitamin C ..	0 mg	1½ starch
mono	1.8 G	Carbohydrate ..	21.0 G	Calcium ...	77 mg	
poly	.5 G			Sodium	227 mg	

*Indicates high sodium content

Notes

Soups

♥ We use the words "stock" or "broth" interchangeably.

♥ Black pepper, caraway seed and dill weed are relatively high in calcium. Poppyseed contains 100 mg per tablespoon.

♥ New products are being engineered to remove the cholesterol. I see no mention of what is being done to the fats in those products.

♥ The enigma of obesity is the frequent presence of a normal cholesterol mechanism. On the other hand, some of the worst cholesterol problems are found in skinny people.

♥ Weight loss diets are simple, really, but no one wants to believe that weight is related to fat intake. If you have paid a lot of money for a formal diet program, get it out and look at it. You'll see where the fat is reduced to absent.

SOUPS

BEEF STOCK

A rich stock is essential to making a hearty soup. Here's how:

4-6 beef knuckle bones   **1-2 onions, cut into fourths**
1-2 carrots, cut into thirds   **1-2 stalks celery, cut into thirds**

Place bones and vegetables in open roasting pan, add only enough water to cover the bottom of the pan to prevent juices from burning. Roast in 375 degree oven until the bones are well browned, not burned. Remove from oven and put bones and vegetables and any juices from the roasting pan in a large stock pot. Rinse the roasting pan with water, scrape to remove brown residue and add all to the stock pot. Add water to cover and bring to boil. Reduce heat and simmer for 12-14 hours, until liquid is reduced by half. Remove bones and vegetables and discard. (Any meat from the bones usually has much fat in it and very little flavor, so we discard it, too.)

Quickly cool stock by setting pan in ice water and cool the stock to room temperature then chill so that fat can be easily removed from the top of the broth. Refrigerate for up to 3 days or freeze for longer storage.

We calculated this as gelatin - 24 calories, 6 grams protein per cup.

CHICKEN BROTH

We buy our chickens whole, cut them up, separating the meaty pieces for chicken recipes and freeze the bony parts and skin until needed for making broth.

bony chicken parts and   **1 onion, halved**
**   skin of 3-4 chickens**   **1 stalk celery, cut into chunks**
1 carrot, cut into chunks   **water to cover**

Put all ingredients in a large soup pot, bring to boil, reduce heat and simmer for 2-3 hours. Remove chicken and vegetables from pot and set aside. Quickly cool broth by putting pot in ice water then chill so that fat may be removed. Cooked chicken may be removed from the bony parts and used for chicken salad, chicken noodles, etc. Discard vegetables and fat.

This is calculated the same as gelatin - 24 calories, 6 grams protein per cup.

MINESTRONE

An Italian soup designed by peasants to sustain them in their heavy work. There are as many variants as there are cooks, but don't say "minestrone soup."

2 cups beef or chicken stock
  (see recipe)*
4 ounces chicken or meat
1 cup chopped celery
½ cup cooked red or navy beans
¾ cup peas
1 cup spinach leaves
¼-½ cup chopped onion
1 carrot, diced
1 cup chopped Savoy cabbage

1 cup diced tomatoes
1 clove garlic, minced
1 tablespoon sage
1 tablespoon parsley
½ cup uncooked macaroni
½ cup freshly grated
  parmesan cheese*
salt and freshly ground pepper
  to taste*

Saute the chopped spinach leaves, onion, carrot, cabbage, and tomato in olive oil until vegetables are tender. Add chicken or meat and pasta; simmer for 25 minutes. Add sage, parsley and garlic. Add salt and freshly ground pepper to taste, stir. Ladle into individual soup bowls and sprinkle with parmesan cheese. Serve with homemade bread.

Variation
Use weiners (see recipe) pork tenderloin, chicken or turkey. Keep the fatty meats out. Add the meat at the end of cooking, if it is already cooked, and simmer the soup for 10 additional minutes.

Note: feel free to improvise in making this soup with whatever vegetables you have on hand. This is just my version.

Serves 6	224 calories per 1 cup serving		
Fat .... 8.7 G	Cholesterol ... 16 mg	Fiber .... 4.9 G	Diabetic exchanges:
saturated . 1.4 G	Protein .... 11.3 G	Vitamin C .. 17 mg	1½ starch, 1 lean
mono .... 5.5 G	Carbohydrate .. 25.9 G	Calcium ... 50 mg	meat, 1 fat
poly ...... 1.1 G		Sodium .... 451 mg	

*Indicates high sodium content

CIOPPINO

This seafood soup was first tasted by us in Sausalito and the memory lingers. It is different from bouillibase, being more robust and Italian. It usually is more robust than this and is modified for this book. We prefer to have the cook remove the shells from the seafood and let the diners eat rather than operate.

¼ cup olive oil, extra virgin
   if you like it
1 cup chopped onion
⅓ cup shredded carrot (this takes
   the sharpness out of the soup)
2 cloves garlic (save one for the end)
1 tablespoon chopped parsley
1½ cups tomato sauce*
2 cups tomatoes*
4 cups chicken broth (see recipe)*
3 chicken bouillon cubes*
1 bay leaf
½ to 1 teaspoon oregano,
   hand rubbed

1½ to 1 teaspoon thyme leaves,
   hand rubbed
½ teaspoon basil leaves, hand rubbed
1 cup water
½ cup dry white wine
½ pound shrimp, peeled or unpeeled
   (if peeled, use the shells to
   make a broth)
½ pound cod or monkfish, cubed
1 large king crab leg or a
   Dungeness, if you can get it
½ pound scallops
salt and freshly ground pepper to taste*
   (I use 20 twists fresh ground pepper)

Sauté onions and 1 of the garlic cloves in olive oil until onions are soft. Add all ingredients except the seafood, simmer 20 minutes. Add shrimp, crab, scallops and fish and simmer 5-7 minutes or until fish is cooked. Remove from heat, put remaining garlic clove into garlic press and squeeze into stew.

Serve in soup bowls and float a slice of lemon on top. Salad and bread is about all you will be able to add to this meal. Invite the neighbors!!!

Serves 8		230 calories per 2 cup serving		
Fat	8.9 G	Cholesterol ... 102 mg	Fiber .... 1.8 G	Diabetic exchanges:
saturated .	1.3 G	Protein .... 26.0 G	Vitamin C .. 18 mg	3 lean meat,
mono	5.5 G	Carbohydrate .. 10.1 G	Calcium ... 77 mg	2 vegetable
poly	1.5 G		Sodium .. 1418 mg	

*Indicates high sodium content

BOUILLABAISSE

Most people cook this with the shells left on the seafood. I prefer to remove the shells, boil them separately in water and add the strained broth to the soup. This leads to more flavorful eating and less fiddling around.

Group I

3-4 potatoes

2 carrots

2 onions

1-3 garlic cloves, minced

2 cups tomatoes*

Group II

chicken broth (see recipe)*

1 bottle clam juice

1 teaspoon caraway seeds

pinch saffron

1 tablespoon lemon juice

¼-½ cup chopped parsley

2 tablespoons olive oil

salt and pepper to taste*

Group III

2 medium lobster tails

12 shrimp

12 oysters, shucked or 1 can oysters

½ pound each of 3 kinds of white fish

Cut vegetables from Group I into bite-sized chunks and cook in broth and seasonings from Group II. Add Group III so that cooking time coincides with the doneness of the vegetables. Serve in bowls with a slice of lemon floating on top.

Serves 12	187 calories per 1 ½ cup serving		
Fat .... 4.5 G	Cholesterol ... 103 mg	Fiber .... 1.6 G	Diabetic exchanges:
saturated . .8 G	Protein .... 25.8 G	Vitamin C .. 15 mg	2 vegetable,
mono .... 2.1 G	Carbohydrate .. 10.2 G	Calcium .... 71 mg	3 lean meat
poly ...... .9 G		Sodium .... 538 mg	

*Indicates high sodium content

OYSTER STEW

You may use fresh oysters, but try them this way and you will be able to make this more often with little or no change in taste. This recipe is high in sodium. The olive oil and Butter Buds®give it the old fashioned flavor.

1 cup minced onion
1 cup minced celery
3 tablespoons olive oil
2 cups skim milk
1 8 ounce can oysters

1 teaspoon celery seed
freshly ground pepper to taste
2 tablespoons Butter Buds®*
1 chicken bouillon cube*
½ teaspoon cornstarch

Sauté onions and celery in olive oil. Add oyster liquid from can and the skim milk. Stir in Butter Buds®, bouillon cube, celery seed, and pepper. Heat to barely simmering and simmer 10 minutes. Add oysters and cornstarch which has been dissolved in a small amount of water. Simmer an additional 3-4 minutes to thicken slightly.

Serves 4	186 calories per 1 cup serving		
Fat .... 11.7 G	Cholesterol ... 28 mg	Fiber .... 0.3 G	Diabetic exchanges:
saturated . 1.9 G	Protein .... 7.8 G	Vitamin C .. 4 mg	1 low fat milk, 2 fat
mono .... 7.7 G	Carbohydrate .. 12.3 G	Calcium ... 180 mg	
poly ...... 1.3 G		Sodium .... 525 mg	

HUNGARIAN FISH SOUP

This is a variant on an old recipe.

3 onions, sliced
1 clove garlic, minced
1 green pepper, thinly sliced
2 tablespoons paprika
3 cups chicken broth (see recipe)*

1 cup fish pieces (white fish)
1-2 teaspoons lemon juice
salt and pepper to taste*
cayenne pepper to taste
2 tablespoons olive oil

Cook onions, garlic and green pepper in olive oil until soft. Stir in paprika, fish and chicken broth. Add seasonings to taste and cook until fish is done-about 5-10 minutes. This may also be prepared with shrimp or chicken pieces. Be sure to cook long enough to cook the meat thoroughly.

Serves 4	146 calories per 1½ cup serving		
Fat .... 8.1 G	Cholesterol ... 27 mg	Fiber .... 1.9 G	Diabetic exchanges:
saturated . 1.1 G	Protein .... 12.0 G	Vitamin C .. 25 mg	1 lean meat, 1 fat,
mono .... 5.2 G	Carbohydrate .. 7.5 G	Calcium ... 34 mg	1½ vegetable
poly ...... 1.2 G		Sodium .... 49 mg	

*Indicates high sodium content

CRAB-CLAM CHOWDER

This is a very rich tasting chowder that satisfies.

1 medium onion, chopped
2 tablespoons olive oil
2 potatoes, peeled and cut
   into ½ inch cubes
2 cups peeled, seeded and chopped
   tomatoes (fresh is best,
   canned will do)*
1 bay leaf
½ teaspoon thyme leaves,
   hand rubbed

several twists freshly ground pepper
1 bottle clam juice
1 can (6.5 ounce) minced clams
   with juice
1 can (6.5 ounce) canned crab meat
   with juice
chicken bouillon cubes(1 cube per
   cup) or equivalent low salt bouillon*
1 tablespoon Butter Buds®*
2 cups skim milk

Heat olive oil in soup pot, add onions and saute until translucent. Add potatoes and clam juice and cook for 10 minutes. Stir in tomatoes, bay leaf, Butter Buds®, thyme and pepper. Cook another 10 minutes. Check potatoes for doneness. If done, add bouillon cubes and cook another 5 minutes. Add crab, clams and milk and cook another 5 minutes. The soup may be thickened, if desired, with potato flour or cornstarch. Serve with good crusty bread.

Serves 8	138 calories per 1 cup serving		
Fat .... 4.4 G	Cholesterol ... 30 mg	Fiber .... 1.4 G	Diabetic exchanges:
saturated . .7 G	Protein .... 11.4 G	Vitamin C .. 12 mg	1 starch, 1 lean meat
mono .... 2.7 G	Carbohydrate .. 13.4 G	Calcium ... 126 mg	
poly...... .6 G		Sodium .... 491 mg	

CARROT SOUP

The flavor of oranges and carrots blends well.

2 carrots, sliced
1 small onion, chopped
1 clove garlic, minced
1 cup orange juice

1 chicken bouillon cube*
1 teaspoon low salt chicken bouillon
freshly ground pepper

Combine all ingredients in saucepan and cook until carrots and onion are tender. Cool. Put in blender and puree. Serve hot or cold.

Serves 2	110 calories per 1 cup serving		
Fat .... .8 G	Cholesterol ... 1 mg	Fiber .... 3.2 G	Diabetic exchanges:
saturated . .2 G	Protein .... 2.7 G	Vitamin C .. 59 mg	1 starch, ½ fruit
mono .... .2 G	Carbohydrate .. 24.7 G	Calcium ... 48 mg	
poly...... .3 G		Sodium .... 600 mg	

*Indicates high sodium content

LEAFY GREENS SOUP

This is a nice light soup which is deliciously different. It is loaded with vitamins and minerals and contains the seeds of fortune. "Use what others throw away."

2 tablespoons olive oil
1 cup chopped onions
6 cups loosely packed greens
   (radish tops, spinach, chard)
2 cups diced peeled potatoes

6 cups water or chicken broth
1 chicken bouillon cube*
salt to taste*
freshly ground pepper to taste

Heat the olive oil in a large saucepan, add onions and cook until soft. Stir in leaves, cover pan and cook over low heat until wilted, about 10 minutes.

Meanwhile, cook potatoes until soft in the water or broth along with the bouillon cube. Combine mixtures and continue to cook for 5 minutes to combine flavors. Puree if desired in food processor or blender. Season to taste with salt and pepper. If desired, a spoonful of yogurt may be placed on each serving.

Serves 6		86 calories per 1½ cup serving			
Fat.........	4.9 G	Cholesterol ...	0 mg	Fiber .... 2.1 G	Diabetic exchanges:
saturated .	.7 G	Protein	2.4 G	Vitamin C .. 19 mg	2 vegetable,1 fat,
mono	3.4 G	Carbohydrate ..	9.3 G	Calcium ... 53 mg	
poly......	.5 G			Sodium ....261 mg	

SPLIT PEA SOUP

This is a tasty high fiber addition to your diet. Serve with a whole grain bread and you have a complete protein.

1 cup split peas
1 quart water
1½ teaspoons salt
   or 2 chicken bouillon cubes*

½ cup chopped onion
½ cup chopped celery
2 tablespoons olive oil

Soak split peas overnight. Drain, rinse. Put peas and water in saucepan. Saute onions and celery in olive oil until soft, add to peas. Bring to boil, reduce heat and simmer until peas are soft-about 1½ hours. Puree in blender or food processor. Serve.

Serves 6		158 calories per 1 cup serving			
Fat.........	4.9 G	Cholesterol ...	0 mg	Fiber .... 5.1 G	Diabetic exchanges:
saturated .	.7 G	Protein	8.3 G	Vitamin C .. 2 mg	½ starch,
mono	3.4 G	Carbohydrate 21.2		Calcium ... 31 mg	½ high fat meat
poly......	.6 G			Sodium .... 463 mg	

*Indicates high sodium content

CABBAGE AND BEET SOUP

Cooked cabbage usually is very low on my want list and borscht has always eluded my taste, but this combination I look forward to.

1 quart beef stock (see recipe)*
2 cups uncooked beets (they may be
   cooked separately and added later)
1 onion, chopped
2 cups coarsely chopped cabbage

freshly ground pepper
4 tablespoons vinegar
½ cup lowfat sour cream or yogurt
salt to taste (unless bouillon
   cubes are used)

Combine all ingredients except the sour cream and simmer for about 30 minutes. Float a spoonful of sour cream on each bowl of soup.

Serves 6		45 calories per 1 cup serving					
Fat	.7 G	Cholesterol ...	2 mg	Fiber	1.5 G	Diabetic exchanges:	
saturated .	.4 G	Protein	3.7 G	Vitamin C ..	14 mg	2 vegetable	
mono	.2 G	Carbohydrate ..	6.8 G	Calcium ...	63 mg		
poly	.1 G			Sodium	557 mg		

SAVOY CABBAGE SOUP

This soup is made with Savoy cabbage, however regular green cabbage may be substituted.

3 tablespoons olive oil
1 large clove garlic, minced
1 large onion, chopped
½ teaspoon rubbed sage
1 cup chopped celery leaves
2 tablespoons chopped parsley
1 carrot, shredded
2 stalks celery, chopped

2 tablespoons tomato sauce
freshly ground pepper to taste
1 slice lemon
4 cups beef stock (see recipe)*
1 head Savoy cabbage, shredded
1 beef bouillon cube*
1 tablespoon Butter Buds®*
freshly grated parmesan cheese

Heat the olive oil in a large soup pot, add the garlic and onion and cook slowly for 10 minutes. Add sage, parsley, celery leaves, carrot and celery and cook 5 minutes more. Add tomato sauce, pepper, lemon, and Butter Buds®. Stir well, add broth and cook slowly for 1 hour. Stir occasionally. Add cabbage and bouillon cube. Cook for 20 minutes. Taste for seasoning. Ladle into individual soup bowls and top with cheese.

Serves 6		120 calories per 1½ cup serving					
Fat	7.4 G	Cholesterol ...	1 mg	Fiber	3.5 G	Diabetic exchanges:	
saturated .	1.1 G	Protein	4.2 G	Vitamin C ..	3 mg	2 vegetable, 1½ fat	
mono	5.2 G	Carbohydrate ..	10.5 G	Calcium ...	68 mg		
poly	.7 G			Sodium	678 mg		

*Indicates high sodium content

HEARTY VEGETABLE SOUP

Even without meat, this soup is rich in protein because of the vegetables.

2 cups beef stock (see recipe)*   1 cup diced onion
1 cup white soup beans   1 cup chopped celery
   (precooked from dry)   1 cup canned tomatoes*
1 cup lima beans, frozen   1 cup tomato sauce*
1 cup peas, frozen   1 cup cut green beans, frozen
1 cup corn, frozen   1 clove garlic, minced
1 cup diced potatoes

Simmer all ingredients together for 1½ hours, then add 1 clove minced garlic, several twists pepper. Serve.

Serves 10		104 calories per 1 cup serving			
Fat.........	.5 G	Cholesterol ...	0 mg	Fiber .... 5.7 G	Diabetic exchanges:
saturated .	.1 G	Protein	5.8 G	Vitamin C .. 14 mg	1¼ starch,
mono	.1 G	Carbohydrate ..	20.8 G	Calcium ... 49 mg	1 vegetable
poly......	.2 G			Sodium ....377 mg	

HEARTY POTATO SOUP

This one is a "sleeper." I really did not expect it to taste as rich and good as it does.

1 tablespoon olive oil
1 cup water   ¾ cup frozen peas
1 cup chopped onions   ¾ cup frozen green lima beans
¾ cup chopped celery   ¼ teaspoon freshly ground pepper
1 potato, peeled, cut into ½ inch cubes 1 clove garlic, minced
¾ cup frozen corn   2 cups skim milk

Heat olive oil, saute onions and celery in oil until soft. Add water and remaining ingredients except milk and simmer until vegetables are tender, about 20 minutes. Add skim milk and warm just to a boil (do not boil) and serve garnished with parsley, if desired.

Serves 6		122 calories per 1 cup serving			
Fat.........	2.6 G	Cholesterol ...	7 mg	Fiber .... 4.7 G	Diabetic exchanges:
saturated .	.4 G	Protein	5.4 G	Vitamin C .. 9 mg	1½ starch
mono	1.7 G	Carbohydrate ..	20.6 G	Calcium ... 78 mg	
poly......	.3 G			Sodium .... 62 mg	

*Indicates high sodium content

SPINACH-RICE SOUP

Can you imagine mint, nutmeg and allspice in one soup?

2 tablespoons olive oil
3 cloves garlic, minced
1 large onion, minced
¼ cup uncooked rice
1 teaspoon fresh mint leaves,
   minced or ¼ teaspoon dried
1½ cups spinach leaves, chopped
3 green onions, minced

⅛ teaspoon freshly ground
   black pepper
dash nutmeg
dash allspice
5 cups hot chicken broth
   (see recipe)*
freshly grated parmesan cheese

Heat the oil in a large soup pot, cook the garlic and onion slowly for 10 minutes, do not brown. Add rice, stir well, and fry the rice lightly. Add mint, spinach and green onion, stir, cover and simmer for 10 minutes. Add pepper, spices and broth. Simmer 15 minutes or until rice is tender. Taste for seasoning. Remove from heat and allow to stand 5 minutes, covered. Ladle into individual serving bowls, top with freshly grated parmesan cheese.

Serves 6	98 calories per 1 cup serving		
Fat .... 5.6 G	Cholesterol ... 1 mg	Fiber .... 1.0 G	Diabetic exchanges:
saturated . .9 G	Protein .... 2.4 G	Vitamin C .. 8 mg	½ starch, 1 fat,
mono .... 3.7 G	Carbohydrate .. 10.1 G	Calcium ... 39 mg	½ vegetable
poly...... .7 G		Sodium .. 1249 mg	

HERB SOUP WITH CHEESE

A delicious low calorie first course soup.

1 tablespoon olive oil
2 tablespoons minced chives
2 tablespoons minced parsley
1 cup finely chopped celery
¼ teaspoon dried tarragon
1 quart beef stock (see recipe)*

1 beef bouillon cube*
freshly ground pepper to taste
dash nutmeg
⅓ cup white wine (optional)
freshly grated parmesan cheese

Heat the olive oil, add the minced chives, parsley and celery and cook slowly for 5 minutes. Stir well, add stock. Cover and bring to boil, let cook until vegetables are tender, about 20 minutes. Taste for seasoning, add pepper and nutmeg. Stir in wine if you are using it. Put a piece of toast in each serving bowl, ladle in the soup and top each with freshly grated parmesan cheese.

Serves 5	32 calories per 1 cup serving		
Fat .... 2.9 G	Cholesterol ... 0 mg	Fiber .... .5 G	Diabetic exchanges:
saturated . .4 G	Protein .... .4 G	Vitamin C .. 3 mg	½ vegetable, ½ fat
mono .... 2.0 G	Carbohydrate .. 1.4 G	Calcium ... 18 mg	(bread not calculated)
poly...... .3 G		Sodium .... 231 mg	

*Indicates high sodium content

SENEGALESE SOUP

A flavor of the East.

2 cups chicken stock (see recipe)*
½ chicken breast, boned
   and skin removed
1 onion, chopped
¾ cup chopped celery
2 tablespoons olive oil

1 tablespoon curry powder
1 teaspoon turmeric
2 tablespoons bottled mango chutney
2 chicken bouillon cubes*
salt and freshly ground pepper
   to taste*

In a small saucepan bring the stock plus bouillon cubes to a boil and poach the chicken, covered, until it is springy to touch, about 8 minutes. Meanwhile in another saucepan, cook the onion and celery in oil until the vegetables are softened. Stir in the curry powder and turmeric and cook, stirring, for 2 minutes. Remove the chicken from the broth and coarsely chop it. Add the broth from cooking the chicken to the vegetable mixture and bring the mixture to a boil, stirring, reduce the heat and simmer for 5 minutes. In a blender, puree the mixture with the chutney and half the chopped chicken until the mixture is very smooth. Pour the mixture into a metal bowl and set it over ice water, stir until it is cold. Stir in the remaining chicken and serve.

Serves 4	121 calories per ¾ cup serving		
Fat .... 8.5 G	Cholesterol ... 17 mg	Fiber .... 1.1 G	Diabetic exchanges:
saturated . 1.3 G	Protein .... 7.6 G	Vitamin C .. 3 mg	1 fat, 1 vegetable,
mono .... 5.7 G	Carbohydrate .. 4.1 G	Calcium ... 28 mg	1 lean meat
poly...... 1.0 G		Sodium .... 988 mg	

CREAM OF MUSHROOM SOUP

This may be used in other recipes calling for cream of mushroom soup with the assurance that you know what you are eating. To make it taste right, the olive oil is necessary.

3 tablespoons olive oil
½ cup chopped onion
½ cup chopped mushrooms
1 tablespoon flour

2 cups chicken broth (see recipe)*
½ cup evaporated skim milk
salt and pepper to taste*

Saute onions and mushrooms in olive oil, do not brown. Add flour to thicken. Add chicken broth, simmer 20 minutes, stirring. Add evaporated skim milk and salt and pepper to taste. Cook until heated through. Put in blender and process until creamy consistency.

Serves 6	91 calories per ½ cup serving		
Fat .... 7.3 G	Cholesterol ... 1 mg	Fiber .... .4 G	Diabetic exchanges:
saturated . 1.0 G	Protein .... 2.8 G	Vitamin C .. 2 mg	1 vegetable, 1½ fat
mono .... 5.2 G	Carbohydrate .. 3.6 G	Calcium ... 33 mg	
poly...... .7 G		Sodium .... 270 mg	

*Indicates high sodium content

MIDDLE EASTERN MUSHROOM BARLEY SOUP

Barley coupled with high monounsaturated fat should help to lower your cholesterol.

8-10 dried mushrooms, coarsely
  chopped (soak to soften)
3 tablespoons olive oil (1 for sauteeing
  vegetables, 2 for roux)
1/4 cup finely chopped onion
1/4 cup finely chopped carrots

1/4 cup finely chopped celery
2 quarts chicken stock*
1/2 cup pearl barley
2 level tablespoons flour
salt and freshly ground pepper to taste*
1 tablespoon Butter Buds®*

Heat 1 tablespoon olive oil in soup pot, saute onions, carrots and celery until soft. Add chicken broth and bring to boil. Reduce heat to simmer, add mushrooms, barley and Butter Buds®, cover and simmer one hour. Ten minutes before end of cooking time, make a roux with 2 tablespoons olive oil and flour. Add to soup, adjusting for thickness. Simmer a few minutes more, then serve.

Serves 6	155 calories per 1 cup serving		
Fat .... 7.2 G	Cholesterol ... 1 mg	Fiber .... 3.3 G	Diabetic exchanges:
saturated . 1.0 G	Protein .... 2.9 G	Vitamin C .. 2 mg	1 vegetable, 1 fat,
mono .... 5.1 G	Carbohydrate .. 20.7 G	Calcium ... 8 mg	1 starch
poly...... .7 G		Sodium .... 535 mg	

BEEF BARLEY SOUP

In this soup, the cumin and oregano cannot be identified, but they enhance the flavor of the soup. If you wish to lower the sodium, remember to use low sodium bouillon granules or cubes.

4 cups water (may use potato water)
1/4-1/2 cup pearled barley
3 beef bouillon cubes*
1 chicken bouillon cube*
1/4-1/2 teaspoon cumin
1/4-1/2 teaspoon oregano

3-4 twists freshly ground pepper
1 cup celery, cut on the diagonal
1 cup onion, slivered
1 package brown gravy mix*
1 small clove garlic

Bring the water to boil and add the barley, simmer 25-30 minutes. Add the bouillon cubes, cumin, oregano, pepper, celery and onion. Simmer 15 minutes more. Stir brown gravy mix into 1/4 cup cold water and stir into soup 10 minutes before serving time. Just before serving, press garlic through garlic press into soup.

Serves 6	69 calories per 1 cup serving		
Fat .... .9 G	Cholesterol ... 1 mg	Fiber .... 1.6 G	Diabetic exchanges:
saturated . .4 G	Protein .... 2.4 G	Vitamin C .. 4 mg	1 starch
mono .... .3 G	Carbohydrate .. 13.4 G	Calcium ... 35 mg	
poly...... .2 G		Sodium .... 910 mg	

*Indicates high sodium content

GAZPACHO

My wife's favorite summer soup.

1½ pounds tomatoes, peeled,
   seeded and chopped
1 medium cucumber, peeled,
   seeded and chopped
1 medium red onion, chopped
1 medium green pepper,
   seeded and chopped
1 clove garlic, minced

2 cups tomato juice*
¼ cup red wine vinegar
1-2 tablespoons olive oil
dash hot pepper sauce or to taste
dash Worcestershire sauce
salt to taste*
1 cup bread croutons

Combine all ingredients, except bread croutons, in a large bowl and refrigerate until thoroughly chilled. If you like a smoother soup, puree all or part of the soup in the food processor or blender. Stir the soup and ladle into chilled bowls, garnish with the croutons. Additional chopped green pepper, onion and cucumber may be used for garnish.

Serves 10	55 calories per ¾ cup serving		
Fat .... 1.7 G	Cholesterol ... 0 mg	Fiber .... 2.0 G	Diabetic exchanges:
saturated . .3 G	Protein .... 1.7 G	Vitamin C .. 33 mg	½ vegetable,
mono .... 1.1 G	Carbohydrate .. 9.6 G	Calcium ... 20 mg	½ starch
poly ...... .3 G		Sodium .... 223 mg	

CREAM OF TOMATO SOUP

You can still enjoy the good taste of cream of tomato soup with this lowfat version.

1 can (16 ounce) tomatoes*
1 cup beef broth (see recipe)*
1 small onion, stuck with
   2 whole cloves
1 teaspoon basil
freshly ground pepper to taste
1 tablespoon Butter Buds®*

1 tablespoon olive oil
1 cup evaporated skim milk
1 beef bouillon cube for every cup
   of soup (in this case 3-4 cubes)*
1 tablespoon flour or cornstarch
   in water to thicken

Combine all ingredients except the milk and cook together for 30 minutes. Remove onion and discard. Put the mixture into the blender and puree. Add milk. Serve with parsley garnish.

Serves 4	100 calories per 1 cup serving		
Fat .... 4.3 G	Cholesterol ... 2 mg	Fiber .... 1.5 G	Diabetic exchanges:
saturated . .8 G	Protein .... 4.6 G	Vitamin C .. 19 mg	½ starch, 1 fat,
mono .... 2.8 G	Carbohydrate .. 12.0 G	Calcium ... 124 mg	1 vegetable
poly ...... .4 G		Sodium .. 1270 mg	

*Indicates high sodium content

41

TOMATO-CARROT SOUP

With a light lunch.

2 leeks, white part only, chopped
½ pound carrots, peeled and
   sliced thin
3 tablespoons olive oil
2 tablespoons Butter Buds®*
2 pounds plum tomatoes or
   28 ounces canned tomatoes,
   drained*

1½ cups tomato juice*
4-5 cups chicken stock (see recipe)*
1½ tablespoons tomato paste*
½ teaspoon dried thyme
1 teaspoon freshly ground white pepper

In a large saucepan, cook leeks and carrots in 3 tablespoons olive oil over moderately low heat, stirring occasionally, until vegetables are soft. Stir in the tomatoes, tomato juice, 4 cups of the stock, tomato paste, thyme and salt to taste. Bring to a boil and simmer the mixture, covered, stirring occasionally, for 30-40 minutes, or until the vegetables are very tender. In a blender, puree the soup in batches, transfer to a saucepan and thin it to desired consistency with remaining stock. Stir in Butter Buds®, taste for seasoning and heat, stirring, until hot and serve.

Serves 6	155 calories per 1½ cup serving			
Fat .... 8.4 G	Cholesterol ... 1 mg	Fiber .... 3.4 G		Diabetic exchanges:
saturated . 1.3 G	Protein .... 6.3 G	Vitamin C .. 28 mg		1 starch, 1½ fat
mono .... 5.6 G	Carbohydrate .. 15.1 G	Calcium ... 72 mg		½ vegetable
poly ...... 1.1 G		Sodium .... 231 mg		

QUICK TOMATO BEAN SOUP

Pork and beans in a soup?

2 tablespoons chopped onion
2 tablespoons chopped green pepper
1 tablespoon olive oil
1 can (16 oz.) pork and beans,
   pork removed*

1 can (16 oz.) whole tomatoes,
   undrained*

Saute the onion and green pepper in the olive oil. Add the beans and tomatoes, stirring to break up the tomatoes. Simmer, covered, for 10-15 minutes or until heated through.

Serves 4	165 calories per 1 cup serving			
Fat .... 4.9 G	Cholesterol ... 8 mg	Fiber .... 7.6 G		Diabetic exchanges:
saturated . 1.0 G	Protein .... 7.0 G	Vitamin C .. 25 mg		1½ starch, ½ fat,
mono .... 3.0 G	Carbohydrate .. 27.4 G	Calcium ... 94 mg		1 vegetable
poly ...... .6 G		Sodium .... 683 mg		

*Indicates high sodium content

BLACK BEAN SOUP

This soup is high in fiber, low in fat.

1 pound black beans
2 cloves garlic, minced
1 cup canned tomatoes*
2 onions, finely diced
1/4 cup minced parsley
1 teaspoon basil
1/4 teaspoon ground cardamom
1/2 teaspoon ground cumin
2 teaspoons salt*

freshly ground pepper to taste
1 tablespoon vinegar
1 cup finely diced celery
1/2 cup diced carrots
3-4 drops hot pepper sauce
yogurt
diced bell pepper
diced tomato

Soak beans overnight. Drain and rinse. Put beans in 4 quart pot, add coldwater to cover by 2 inches. Bring to boil, reduce heat and simmer for 3-4 hours, adding water as necessary, until beans are tender. Add garlic, tomatoes and onions, cook 30 minutes. Add remaining ingredients through hot pepper sauce and cook 10 minutes. Spoon into soup bowls and garnish with yogurt, diced pepper and tomato.

Serves 6		177 calories per 1 cup serving			
Fat	.9 G	Cholesterol ... 0 mg	Fiber .... 11.8 G	Diabetic exchanges:
saturated .	.2 G	Protein .... 11.2 G	Vitamin C .. 13 mg	1/2 vegetable, 2 starch
mono	.1 G	Carbohydrate .. 33.0 G	Calcium ... 74 mg	
poly	.4 G		Sodium .... 800 mg	

WHITE BEAN SOUP

Out of Eastern lowland cooking, usually high in grease, comes this soup high in protein, calcium and cholesterol lowering fiber.

2 cups dry white beans
2 tablespoons olive oil
1/4 cup finely chopped carrot
1/4 cup finely chopped celery

1/4 cup finely chopped onion
4 chicken bouillon cubes*
freshly ground pepper to taste
1 quart water

Soak beans overnight, drain and rinse. Saute vegetables in 2 tablespoons olive oil. Combine beans and sauteed vegetables in large pan, cover with water, add bouillon cubes. Simmer 1 1/2 to 2 hours or until beans are done.

Potatoes cut into bean sized dice and cooked along with the soup add a touch.

A variant—cook a ham bone with the soup and discard the bone when the beans are done. Also ham flavoring may be added.

Serves 6		296 calories per 1 cup serving			
Fat	5.9 G	Cholesterol ... 1 mg	Fiber .... 2.3 G	Diabetic exchanges:
saturated .	1.0 G	Protein .... 16.0 G	Vitamin C .. 2 mg	3 starch, 1 lean meat
mono	3.6 G	Carbohydrate .. 47.0 G	Calcium ... 106 mg	
poly	.9 G		Sodium .... 763 mg	

*Indicates high sodium content

43

FIVE BEAN SOUP

Beans have a high place in lowering cholesterol.

½ cup dried navy beans
½ cup dried white beans
½ cup dried garbanzo beans
½ cup dried red beans
½ cup dried black beans
3½ cups water or beef stock
2 tablespoons olive oil
1 large onion, chopped
3 cloves garlic, minced
1 large green bell pepper,
   seeded and diced

1 large carrot, diced
1 stalk celery, diced
1½ teaspoons ground cumin
1 teaspoon coarsley ground
   coriander seeds
1 teaspoon grated orange peel
¼ teaspoon freshly ground pepper
¼ teaspoon dried red pepper flakes

Rinse and sort beans; place beans in a large pot, add enough cold water to cover by 3 inches and let stand overnight. Drain and rinse beans and return to pot. Add 3½ cups water or broth and bring to a boil. Reduce heat and simmer beans, covered, until they are tender, about 1½ hours. Season to taste with salt. Heat oil in a large skillet. Add onion and garlic. Cover and cook until onion is soft, stirring occasionally, about 15 minutes. Add bell pepper, carrot, celery, cumin and coriander. Cover and continue to cook until vegetables are tender, stirring occasionally, about 15 minutes. Add vegetable mixture to beans, stir in orange peel, pepper and red pepper flakes. Taste and add more red pepper flakes if desired.

Serves 8		235 calories per 1 cup serving		
Fat .... 4.8 G	Cholesterol ... 0 mg	Fiber .... 10.0 G	Diabetic exchanges:
saturated . .7 G	Protein .... 12.4 G	Vitamin C .. 16 mg	2 starch, 1 lean meat,
mono .... 2.7 G	Carbohydrate .. 37.5 G	Calcium ... 85 mg	1 vegetable
poly...... .9 G		Sodium .... 19 mg	

CONFETTI BEAN SOUP

A low calorie, low fat soup.

4 ounces dry black beans
4 ounces dry Great Northern beans
4 ounces dry red beans
4 ounces dry pinto beans
4 ounces dry green split peas
9 cups water
3 beef bouillon cubes*
3 tablespoons dried chopped chives

1 teaspoon salt*
1 teaspoon savory
½ teaspoon cumin
½ teaspoon freshly ground pepper
1 clove garlic, chopped
1 can (14 ½-16 ounces) stewed
  tomatoes*
5 cups water

Rinse beans. Cover beans with water; soak overnight. Drain and rinse beans. Return beans to pan, add seasonings and 5 cups water. Cover and simmer 1½ hours or until beans are tender, stirring occasionally. Add can of stewed tomatoes and its liquid. Heat to boiling over high heat. Reduce heat to low and cook, uncovered 15 minutes longer, stirring to break up tomatoes. Discard bay leaf.

Serves 10		126 calories per 1 cup serving				
Fat.........	.7 G	Cholesterol ...	0 mg	Fiber	7.5 G	Diabetic exchanges:
saturated .	.2 G	Protein	8.3 G	Vitamin C ..	8 mg	1½ starch
mono	.1 G	Carbohydrate .. 22.7 G		Calcium ...	50 mg	
poly......	.2 G			Sodium ....591 mg		

PORK, CABBAGE AND MUSHROOM SOUP

A winter soup. Even though pork tenderloin is low fat, skim off the pork fat.

4 ounces pork tenderloin(4 medallions)
1 small onion, diced
½ medium carrot, diced
½ stalk celery, diced
8 leaves cabbage, sliced thin
2 tablespoons Butter Buds®*

1 clove garlic, minced
1 tablespoon olive oil
3 cups water
2 chicken bouillon cubes*
freshly ground pepper to taste
12 mushrooms, sliced

Saute pork tenderloins in ½ tablespoon olive oil until browned on both sides; remove pork from pan and dice. Return pork to pan, add 1 cup water and 1 teaspoon onions. Simmer 15 minutes. Remove from heat, cool sufficiently so that fat can be skimmed from broth. Meanwhile, saute vegetables in remaining olive oil for about 10 minutes. Pour defatted pork broth through strainer into sauteed vegetables, add pork, simmer 5 minutes. Add 2 cups water, bouillon cubes, mushrooms, Butter Buds® and pepper. Simmer 15 minutes.

Serves 4		129 calories per 1 cup serving				
Fat.........	8.1 G	Cholesterol ...	30 mg	Fiber	1.0 G	Diabetic exchanges:
saturated .	2.0 G	Protein	10.5 G	Vitamin C ..	7 mg	1 vegetable, 1 fat,
mono	4.5 G	Carbohydrate ..	3.6 G	Calcium ...	24 mg	1 lean meat
poly......	1.0 G			Sodium ....593 mg		

*Indicates high sodium content

SOUP au PISTOU

This is a vegetable-bean soup; you'd better like garlic. Beans are high in calcium.

1 cup dry white beans
4 cups water
2 tablespoons olive oil
1 cup chopped onion
3 cups chopped fresh tomatoes
3 ½ quarts water
1 teaspoon salt*
1 ½ thinly sliced carrots
1 cup chopped leeks
½ cup chopped celery leaves

2 cups fresh cut green beans
½ cup uncooked vermicelli
⅛ teaspoon saffron
1 tablespoon chopped garlic
½ teaspoon salt*
½ cup fresh basil or
5 tablespoons dried
6 tablespoons tomato paste*
½ cup freshly grated parmesan cheese*
4 tablespoons olive oil

Soak the beans overnight, drain, rinse and cover with fresh water. Cook until the beans are tender but still hold their shape.

To make the pistou: mash the garlic in a mortar and pestle or food processor, add basil and 4 tablespoons olive oil alternately, mashing or processing until smooth. Stir in tomato paste and ¼ cup cheese. Set aside.

Cook the onions until transparent in 2 tablespoons olive oil. Add tomatoes and cook briskly for 2-3 minutes. Add 3 ½ quarts water and salt, bring to boil, add carrots, leeks and celery leaves and cook 10-15 minutes until vegetables are tender but not soft. Add cooked beans. Just before serving, mix half of the pistou with the soup. Pass the remaining pistou and parmesan cheese separately.

Serves 18		158 calories per 1 ½ cup serving			
Fat	8.6 G	Cholesterol ...	2 mg	Fiber .... 2.3 G	Diabetic exchanges:
saturated .	1.5 G	Protein	5.1 G	Vitamin C .. 13 mg	1 vegetable, 1 fat,
mono	5.8 G	Carbohydrate ..	16.6 G	Calcium ... 97 mg	1 starch
poly......	.8 G			Sodium .... 240 mg	

*Indicates high sodium content

MEATLESS CHILI

Most Americans eat chili con carne, this is chili sans carne. However, for those who must have their meat, use beef flavored turkey (see recipe) but remember there are 20 grams saturated fat per pound. Very high salt.

4 tablespoons olive oil
2 onions, chopped
½ green pepper, finely chopped
1 rounded teaspoon oregano,
   hand rubbed
1 teaspoon ground cumin
1 rounded tablespoon chili powder,
   more if desired

1 clove garlic, minced
1 (16 oz.) can tomatoes*
freshly ground pepper
2 (16 oz.) cans red beans*
4 beef bouillon cubes +
    4 teaspoons low salt beef bouillon*

Saute onion and green pepper in olive oil. Add oregano, cumin, chili powder, stir; add garlic at last moment. Add remaining ingredients and simmer 20 minutes.

Serves 6	236 calories per 1 cup serving		
Fat .... 10.2 G	Cholesterol ... 0 mg	Fiber .... 12.5 G	Diabetic exchanges:
saturated . 1.5 G	Protein .... 9.6 G	Vitamin C .. 20 mg	1 ½ starch, 2 fat,
mono .... 6.9 G	Carbohydrate .. 28.6 G	Calcium ... 76 mg	1 vegetable
poly...... 1.2 G		Sodium .. 1343 mg	

MEATLESS CHILI MAC

The catsup makes the difference. Serve catsup and Worcestershire sauce separately (⅔ catsup + ⅓ Worcestershire sauce) spooned over all.

2 large onions, diced
1 small green bell pepper, diced
2 tablespoons olive oil
½ cup catsup*
1 cup tomato juice, optional*
3 beef bouillon cubes*

2 heaping tablespoons low salt
   beef bouillon
1 tablespoon oregano, hand rubbed
1 teaspoon ground cumin
1 can red beans*
1 tablespoon chili powder

Saute the onions and bell pepper in olive oil until tender. Add the remaining ingredients and simmer 20 minutes. Serve over spaghetti. Top with grated parmesan if desired.

Serves 8	119 calories per ½ cup serving		
Fat .... 4.2 G	Cholesterol ... 0 mg	Fiber .... 5.6 G	Diabetic exchanges:
saturated . .7 G	Protein .... 4.4 G	Vitamin C .. 20 mg	1 starch, 1 fat
mono .... 2.7 G	Carbohydrate .. 17.4 G	Calcium ... 43 mg	
poly...... .6 G		Sodium .... 890 mg	

*Indicates high sodium content

TEXAS RED CHILI

My "Mexican Expert" says this is "mild" South of the Border. Don't believe it! Tone this down (or up?) as you desire. As written, this is HOT for most people.

1½ pound 1" turkey breast cubes
   or textured beef flavored
soy protein chunks (prepared
according to package directions)
4 tablespoons olive oil
¼ cup chili powder
2 teaspoons hand rubbed oregano
1½ teaspoons cumin powder

1 tablespoon cayenne pepper
   (or to taste)
3 cloves garlic, minced
1 quart beef stock*
2 beef bouillon cubes
   (or 2 teaspoons low salt bouillon)*
¼ cup cornmeal

Heat the olive oil in a 3 quart heavy saucepan. Saute the turkey cubes or textured protein cubes to firm consistency. Do this in portions, transferring done portions to bowl for later use. Saute garlic in last portion, take care not to brown the garlic. Return all meat or protein cubes to pan and add remaining ingredients except cornmeal. Simmer at least one hour, then sprinkle cornmeal over mixture, stirring constantly to avoid lumps. Simmer another 20 minutes. I like this served with coarsely chopped raw onions and a thick slice of bread. NOT for the faint of heart!

Analysis is for turkey breast: soy protein cubes are much lower in calories.

Serves 8	240 calories per 1 cup serving		
Fat .... 10.9 G	Cholesterol ... 60 mg	Fiber .... 2.0 G	Diabetic exchanges:
saturated . 2.2 G	Protein .... 27.4 G	Vitamin C .. 4 mg	¼ fat, ½ starch,
mono .... 5.8 G	Carbohydrate .. 7.9 G	Calcium ... 43 mg	3½ lean meat
poly ...... 1.7 G		Sodium .. 1028 mg	

*Indicates high sodium content

Salads

♥ Don't pay attention to the dietary habits of your skinny friends, those creeps!

♥ Plums have a fair amount of monounsaturated oil, as do avocados, coriander, curry powder and celery seed.

♥ If you jog 1½ miles, you use 120 calories.

♥ Although a cholesterol determination of 200 is an apparent goal, many authorities think 180 is a better goal. I think 150 is better.

SALADS

CAESAR SALAD

We don't use raw egg yolk—too much chance of salmonella.

⅓ cup olive oil
2 cloves garlic, coarsely chopped
2 tablespoons lemon juice
1 tablespoon Worcestershire sauce*
½ teaspoon salt*

¼ teaspoon freshly ground pepper
1 head Romaine lettuce
¼ cup grated parmesan cheese*
croutons
6 anchovy fillets*

Put the olive oil and garlic into a small bowl and let stand for 30 minutes. Add the lemon juice, Worcestershire, salt and pepper. Beat with a fork to mix well. Wash and dry the lettuce leaves, tear them into bite-size pieces and place them in a large salad bowl. Pour on the dressing and toss quickly. Add the cheese and toss again. Lastly, sprinkle with croutons and arrange the anchovies decoratively across the top. Serve immediately.

Anchovies not included in calculations.

Serves 6	77 calories per 1 tablespoon dressing		
Fat .... 7.8 G	Cholesterol ... 2 mg	Fiber .... .3 G	Diabetic exchanges:
saturated . 1.4 G	Protein .... 1.2 G	Vitamin C .. 6 mg	1½ fat, ½ vegetable
mono .... 5.4 G	Carbohydrate .. 1.0 G	Calcium ... 36 mg	
poly...... .6 G		Sodium .... 146 mg	

HOT SPINACH SALAD

An old friend revisited.

10 ounces fresh spinach
3 tablespoons olive oil
1 teaspoon red wine vinegar
½ garlic clove

½ teaspoon salt*
freshly ground pepper to taste
bacon bit substitute

Wash spinach leaves thoroughly and put into a microwave safe dish. Combine oil, vinegar, garlic pressed through a garlic press, salt and pepper; pour over spinach leaves. Cook in microwave for 1 minute on high power. Remove and toss with bacon bits. (The spinach leaves should be only slightly wilted-microwave ovens vary, so timing may have to be adjusted accordingly.)

Serves 4	90 calories per 1 tablespoon dressing		
Fat .... 10.1 G	Cholesterol ... 0 mg	Fiber ...... 0 G	Diabetic exchanges:
saturated . 1.4 G	Protein .... 0 G	Vitamin C .. 0 mg	1½ fat
mono .... 7.5 G	Carbohydrate .. .2 G	Calcium ... 3 mg	
poly...... .8 G		Sodium .... 267 mg	

*Indicates high sodium content

GREEK SALAD

Classic.

DRESSING
½ cup olive oil
2 tablespoons red wine vinegar
½ teaspoon salt*
½ teaspoon freshly ground
   black pepper

¾ teaspoon dried oregano leaves,
   crumbled
¼ teaspoon dried basil leaves,
   crumbled
1 clove garlic, minced

SALAD
4 ripe tomatoes, cut into wedges
1 red bell pepper, cut into strips
1 green bell pepper, cut into strips

1 small red onion, thinly sliced
¼ cup Calamata olives, pitted and sliced*
2 ounces Feta cheese*

In a bowl, combine the oil, vinegar, salt, black pepper, oregano, basil and garlic. Mix well. At this point, pour the dressing over the salad ingredients and serve on lettuce leaves. Most of the oil will drain off.

Dressing analysis

Makes ½ cup dressing	193 calories per 2 tablespoons			
Fat .... 21.6 G	Cholesterol ... 0 mg	Fiber .... .1 G	Diabetic exchanges:
saturated . 2.9 G	Protein .... 0 G	Vitamin C .. 0 mg	4¼ fat
mono .... 15.9 G	Carbohydrate .. .7 G	Calcium ... 9 mg	
poly ...... 1.8 G		Sodium .... 213 mg	

Salad ingredient analysis

Serves 5	45 calories per serving			
Fat .... 2.8 G	Cholesterol ... 6 mg	Fiber .... 1.4 G	Diabetic exchanges:
saturated . 1.3 G	Protein .... 1.9 G	Vitamin C .. 32 mg	1 vegetable, ½ fat
mono .... 1.0 G	Carbohydrate .. 4.9 G	Calcium ... 48 mg	
poly ...... .2 G		Sodium .... 120 mg	

*Indicates high sodium content

COLE SLAW

This cole slaw differs from the usual mayonnaise version in that a serving of this salad is "free" for diabetics.

2 cups shredded cabbage
¼ cup chopped celery
¼ cup chopped carrot
1 tablespoon chopped onion
¼ cup vinegar

¼ cup water
1-2 packages sweetener
1 teaspoon sugar
¼ teaspoon celery salt
freshly ground pepper to taste

Combine all ingredients, allow to set 15 minutes before serving to allow flavors to mingle.

Serves 5		16 calories per ½ cup serving					
Fat	.2 G	Cholesterol ...	0 mg	Fiber	1.0 G	Diabetic exchanges:	
saturated .	0 G	Protein	.5 G	Vitamin C ..	14 mg	1 serving is free	
mono	0 G	Carbohydrate ..	4.0 G	Calcium ...	25 mg		
poly	0 G			Sodium	13 mg		

SAUERKRAUT SALAD

This is surprisingly tasty for the small amount of calories. The price is the salt.

4 cups sauerkraut, rinsed and drained*
⅓ cup canned pimento, sliced
1 medium green pepper,
   cut into thin slices
1 small onion, thinly sliced

½ cup vinegar
½ cup water
2 tablespoons sugar
4 packages sweetener

Combine all ingredients, mix well. Chill. Will keep well in the refrigerator.

Note: The calculations have been based on undrained sauerkraut, rinsing and draining should lower the sodium somewhat.

Serves 10		32 calories per ½ cup serving					
Fat	.2 G	Cholesterol ...	0 mg	Fiber	2.0 G	Diabetic exchanges:	
saturated ..	0 G	Protein	.9 G	Vitamin C ..	29 mg	1¼ vegetable	
mono	0 G	Carbohydrate ..	7.9 G	Calcium ...	28 mg		
poly	0 G			Sodium .... 526 mg			

*Indicates high sodium content

BROCCOLI SALAD

This is for people who don't particularly like broccoli.

1 bunch broccoli, cut up
   into small pieces
1 small white onion
½ red bell pepper
½ yellow bell pepper
2 tablespoons white vinegar
1 teaspoon garlic powder

1 clove garlic, minced
1 tablespoon fresh dill weed
½ teaspoon salt*
freshly ground pepper to taste
½ cup olive oil
½ teaspoon sugar

Steam broccoli over hot water for 5 minutes. Plunge into cold water to cool; drain thoroughly. Cut peppers and onions into strips. Combine remaining ingredients and pour over vegetables. Refrigerate several hours before serving. Drain to remove excess oil and serve.

Serves 6	37 calories per ½ cup serving			
Fat .... 1.2 G	Cholesterol ... 0 mg	Fiber .... 2.3 G		Diabetic exchanges:
saturated . .2 G	Protein .... 2.3 G	Vitamin C .. 55 mg		1 vegetable, ¼ fat
mono .... .7 G	Carbohydrate .. 6.0 G	Calcium ... 88 mg		
poly ...... .2 G		Sodium .... 97 mg		

TABOOLI

Our version of this Middle Eastern salad. It is meant to be nutritious.

⅓ cup cracked wheat
½ cup finely chopped parsley
2 medium tomatoes,
   seeded and chopped

1 medium onion, chopped
½ cup olive oil
⅓ cup lemon juice
salt and freshly ground pepper to taste*

Soak the cracked wheat in water for 20 minutes, drain and put it in a clean towel and squeeze it dry. Combine the cracked wheat, parsley, tomato and onion. Mix together the oil and lemon juice and pour over the wheat mixture. Season with salt and pepper to taste. Serve as salad or in pita bread.

Serves 5	247 calories per ½ cup serving			
Fat .... 21.9 G	Cholesterol ... 0 mg	Fiber .... 2.1 G		Diabetic exchanges:
saturated . 3.0 G	Protein .... 2.0 G	Vitamin C .. 19 mg		2 vegetable, 4 fat
mono .... 15.9 G	Carbohydrate .. 12.4 G	Calcium ... 20 mg		
poly ...... 2.0 G		Sodium .... 10 mg		

*Indicates high sodium content

GARDEN VEGETABLE SALAD

A salad you can prepare a day ahead.

6 shredded wheat biscuits,
  coarsely crushed
2 medium tomatoes,
  seeded and chopped
1 medium cucumber,
  seeded and chopped
½ cup chopped green pepper

⅓ cup scallions, sliced
⅓ cup parsley, chopped
1 tablespoon snipped dill
2 cloves garlic, crushed
¼ teaspoon freshly ground pepper
¼ cup lemon juice
¼ cup olive oil

In a large bowl, combine all ingredients except the lemon juice and oil. Combine the juice and oil and pour over the vegetables. Toss to mix well. Cover with plastic wrap and refrigerate 6 hours or overnight.

Serves 8	127 calories per ½ cup serving		
Fat .... 7.0 G	Cholesterol ... 0 mg	Fiber .... 2.8 G	Diabetic exchanges:
saturated . 1.8 G	Protein .... 2.3 G	Vitamin C .. 21 mg	1 starch, 1¼ fat
mono .... 5.0 G	Carbohydrate .. 15.5 G	Calcium ... 25 mg	
poly...... 1.2 G		Sodium .... 7 mg	

GARBANZO BEAN SALAD

This is a high fiber, high monounsaturated fat, high protein salad. Serve with a grain for a complete protein.

2 tablespoons olive oil
1½ tablespoons red wine vinegar
¼ teaspoon ground cumin
1 15½ ounce can garbanzo beans

1 medium sized celery stalk, sliced
1 small red onion, sliced
2 canned roasted red peppers, sliced
2 tablespoons chopped parsley

Drain and rinse garbanzo beans to remove salt. Whisk together the olive oil, vinegar, and cumin. Add the remaining ingredients and toss to coat well. Cover and refrigerate at least 2 hours to develop flavors.

Serves 6	167 calories per ½ cup serving		
Fat .... 6.5 G	Cholesterol ... 0 mg	Fiber .... 5.5 G	Diabetic exchanges:
saturated . .8 G	Protein .... 6.8 G	Vitamin C .. 13 mg	1 starch, 1 fat,
mono .... 3.8 G	Carbohydrate .. 21.8 G	Calcium ... 45 mg	1½ vegetable
poly...... 1.3 G		Sodium .... 104 mg	

BLACK BEAN AND BELL PEPPER SALAD

The high fiber comes from beans which is good for lowering your cholesterol.

2 cups cooked black beans
1 large green bell pepper, diced
½ cup peeled, seeded and
  chopped tomato
2 scallions, thinly sliced

1 jalapeno pepper, seeded,
  deribbed and minced (optional)
1 tablespoon olive oil
1 tablespoon lime juice
salt and freshly ground pepper to taste*

Put beans in a medium bowl. Add bell pepper, tomato, scallions, jalapeno pepper; toss to mix. In a small bowl, combine the oil, lime juice, salt and pepper; pour the dressing over the bean mixture and toss well to coat.

Serves 6	127 calories per ½ cup serving			
Fat .... 2.8 G	Cholesterol ... 0 mg	Fiber .... 7.3 G	Diabetic exchanges:
saturated . .4 G	Protein .... 7.0 G	Vitamin C .. 19 mg	1 starch, ½ lean meat,
mono .... 1.7 G	Carbohydrate .. 19.8 G	Calcium ... 24 mg	¾ vegetable
poly...... .4 G		Sodium .... 3 mg	

GERMAN POTATO SALAD

Tastes suspiciously like the original.

1 tablespoon olive oil
1 small onion, chopped
2 tablespoons flour
⅔ cup white vinegar
1⅓ cups water

2 tablespoons sugar
1 beef bouillon cube*
freshly ground pepper
6 cups sliced cooked potatoes
1 tablespoon bacon chips substitute*

Heat the oil in a medium saucepan, saute the onion just until soft. Blend in the flour slowly, then stir in the vinegar and water. Cook until mixture boils and thickens slightly. Stir in sugar, bouillon cube and pepper. Simmer 10 minutes. Layer the potatoes, bacon substitute and sauce in top of a double boiler. Keep warm for 6-8 hours to allow flavors to blend. This also can be layered in a crockpot and cooked on low for 6-8 hours. Serve warm.

Serves 10	171 calories per ½ cup serving			
Fat .... 1.6 G	Cholesterol ... 1 mg	Fiber .... 2.6 G	Diabetic exchanges:
saturated . .3 G	Protein .... 3.1 G	Vitamin C .. 12 mg	2 starch
mono .... 1.0 G	Carbohydrate .. 37.6 G	Calcium ... 16 mg	
poly...... .2 G		Sodium .... 111 mg	

*Indicates high sodium content

POTATO-TUNA SALAD

This is the Cadillac of tuna salad.

4 large whole potatoes
1 7-ounce can white tuna in water,
   drained*
1 red onion, thinly sliced
1 green pepper, sliced into rings
2 ripe tomatoes, cut into wedges

2 hard boiled eggs, yolks discarded,
   whites sliced
½ cup small green olives*
salt and freshly ground pepper
   to taste*
salad dressing (recipe follows)

Boil the potatoes until tender and cool slightly, cut them into ⅛ inch slices. Spoon 2 tablespoons of the salad dressing into the bottom of a large salad bowl. Add a layer of sliced potatoes, sprinkle in some olives, sliced onions, sliced peppers and some of the tuna. Sprinkle with salt and pepper. Spoon more dressing over this layer. Continue to layer ingredients and dressing until all have been used except for 3 tablespoons of dressing. Arrange the egg white slices and tomato wedges on top of the salad, spoon over the remaining salad dressing. Refrigerate several hours but not overnight. Serve with crusty bread.

SALAD DRESSING

½ cup olive oil
½ cup red-wine vinegar
1 teaspoon Dijon mustard
1 clove garlic, chopped
¼ teaspoon sugar
¼ teaspoon basil

¼ teaspoon thyme
¼ teaspoon oregano
1 tablespoon grated parmesan cheese*
¼ teaspoon horseradish
salt to taste*
freshly ground pepper to taste

Combine all ingredients in a blender jar and blend until smooth.

Serves 12	158 calories per ½ cup serving		
Fat .... 10.0 G	Cholesterol ... 10 mg	Fiber .... 1.3 G	Diabetic exchanges:
saturated . 1.4 G	Protein .... 6.8 G	Vitamin C .. 13 mg	¾ starch, ½ fat,
mono .... 7.1 G	Carbohydrate .. 11.4 G	Calcium ... 22 mg	½ lean meat
poly...... .9 G		Sodium .... 179 mg	

*Indicates high sodium content

TUNA AND POTATO SALAD

This is a variant on the more complex preceding recipe. It is equally as good, but you'll eat it more because it's easier to make.

2 cups white potatoes,
  boiled and sliced
1 can tuna (if oil packed,
  reserve oil*)

½ onion, sliced
⅓ green pepper, sliced in rings
green olives
salt and pepper to taste*

Sauce:
2 tablespoons olive oil
1 tablespoon red wine vinegar
fresh ground pepper

1 teaspoon mustard, Dijon is best
Anchovy paste-squeeze 2 inches of
  paste from tube

Blend sauce ingredients together and pour over vegetables and tuna. Toss. Let set about ½ hour to allow flavors to mingle.

Serves 6	130 calories per ½ cup serving		
Fat......... 5.4 G	Cholesterol ... 19 mg	Fiber .... .9 G	Diabetic exchanges:
saturated . .7 G	Protein .... 11.0 G	Vitamin C .. 9 mg	2 vegetable, ½ fat
mono .... 3.8 G	Carbohydrate .. 9.8 G	Calcium ... 12 mg	1 lean meat
poly...... .5 G		Sodium .... 225 mg	

POTATO SALAD

Its simplicity is such that changing anything ruins it, especially the pimentos.

2 cups diced, peeled red potatoes
2 boiled eggs, discard yolks
½ cup diced celery
½ cup diced red onion
2 tablespoons diced pimento

3 tablespoons olive oil mayonnaise
  (see recipe)
salt and freshly ground pepper
  to taste*

Cook the ι toes just until tender; drain and cool. Add chopped egg white, celery, onion and pimento. Add enough mayonnaise to moisten well. Season with salt and pepper.

Note: There is some flavor of the egg yolk which is transferred to the egg white during the boiling of the whole egg.

Serves 6	83 calories per ½ cup serving		
Fat......... .9 G	Cholesterol ... 0 mg	Fiber .... .7 G	Diabetic exchanges:
saturated . .2 G	Protein .... 3.3 G	Vitamin C .. 16 mg	1 starch
mono .... .5 G	Carbohydrate .. 15.7 G	Calcium ... 18 mg	
poly...... .1 G		Sodium .... 54 mg	

*Indicates high sodium content

CARROT PINEAPPLE MOLD

An old favorite.

1-3 ounce package sugar free
  orange gelatin
1 cup boiling water
1 tablespoon lemon juice

½ cup pineapple juice
⅛ teaspoon salt (optional)*
1 cup shredded carrots
1 cup crushed pineapple, well drained

Dissolve gelatin and salt in boiling water. Add pineapple juice, chill until slightly thickened. Fold in carrots and pineapple and pour into individual molds or a 1 quart mold. Chill until firm.

Serves 6	46 calories per ½ cup serving					
Fat	.1 G	Cholesterol ...	0 mg	Fiber	1.2 G	Diabetic exchanges:
saturated ..	0 G	Protein	1.4 G	Vitamin C ..	8 mg	¾ fruit
mono	0 G	Carbohydrate ..	10.6 G	Calcium ...	16 mg	
poly	0 G			Sodium	9 mg	

SPARKLING BERRY SALAD

Spritzy!!

2 packages unflavored gelatin
2 cups cranberry-raspberry juice
2 tablespoons sugar
3 packages sweetener
1 cup club soda

1 teaspoon lemon juice
1 teaspoon grated orange peel
2 cups assorted fruit-blueberries,
  raspberries or strawberries

In a medium saucepan, sprinkle the gelatin over 1 cup cranberry-raspberry juice, let stand 1 minute. Stir over low heat until gelatin is completely dissolved, about 5 minutes. Stir in sugar until dissolved. In a large bowl, combine remaining juice, soda, gelatin mixture, lemon juice, orange peel and sweetener. Chill, stirring occasionally, until mixture is consistency of unbeaten egg white (about 1 hour). Fold in berries and chill until firm.

Serves 10	56 calories per ½ cup serving					
Fat	.1 G	Cholesterol ...	0 mg	Fiber	1.3 G	Diabetic exchanges:
saturated ..	0 G	Protein	1.4 G	Vitamin C ..	30 mg	1 fruit
mono	0 G	Carbohydrate ..	12.6 G	Calcium ...	7mg	
poly	0 G			Sodium	8 mg	

*Indicates high sodium content

SEVEN-UP SALAD

If you wish to add extra monounsaturated oil, stir in some chopped pecans.

1 package sugar free strawberry
or lime flavored gelatin
½ cup boiling water

½ cup 1% fat cottage cheese*
1 cup drained crushed pineapple
1 cup sugar free Seven-Up

Blend the cottage cheese until it is completely smooth. Combine the gelatin and boiling water, stirring until the gelatin is completely dissolved. Let cool. Stir in the well drained crushed pineapple and soft drink. Stir in the smooth cottage cheese. Pour into individual dishes or gelatin mold and chill until firm.

Serves 4		64 calories per ½ cup serving				
Fat	.3 G	Cholesterol ...	1 mg	Fiber	.8 G	Diabetic exchanges:
saturated .	.2 G	Protein	5.3 G	Vitamin C ..	6 mg	⅔ low fat milk, ⅛ fruit
mono	0 G	Carbohydrate ..	10.6 G	Calcium ...	27 mg	
poly	0 G			Sodium	118 mg	

SALSA

A serendipitous discovery—it "makes" tacos.

3 quarts tomatoes, peeled
and coarsely chopped
1 green pepper, cut into
½ inch squares
2 onions, coarsely chopped
tomato juice to consistency
(use what comes out of tomatoes
when cut up)
5 chicken bouillon cubes*
1 beef bouillon cube*
¼ cup white vinegar

3 tablespoons sugar
(or more to taste)
2 heaping teaspoons chili powder
2 heaping teaspoons ground cumin
1 tablespoon coriander seed,
ground in mortar and pestle
1 tablespoon red pepper seeds,
grated
½ teaspoon cayenne pepper
20 twists black pepper

Simmer all ingredients except tomatoes for 20 minutes. Add tomatoes and simmer 15 more minutes. This can be canned following current canning instructions. To make it hotter increase the cayenne pepper.

Makes 4 quarts		19 calories per 4 tablespoons				
Fat	.2 G	Cholesterol ...	0 mg	Fiber	1.0 G	Diabetic exchanges:
saturated .	0 G	Protein	.8 G	Vitamin C ..	13 mg	4 tablespoons are free!
mono	0 G	Carbohydrate	4.1 G	Calcium	8 mg	
poly	0 G			Sodium	131 mg	

*Indicates high sodium content

STRAWBERRY/ONION SALAD

Intriguing combination, isn't it?

⅓ cup olive oil
3 tablespoons vinegar
2 tablespoons water
1 package sweetener
1 tablespoon poppy seeds

½ teaspoon salt*
½ teaspoon paprika
¼ teaspoon freshly ground pepper
strawberries, red onion slices,
  butter lettuce

Combine all dressing ingredients in the blender and mix well. Chill. Pour the dressing over sliced strawberries and thinly sliced red onions on a bed of butter lettuce. Other fruits may be used (bananas, pineapple, melon.)

Analysis is for dressing only.

Makes 10 TBLS	115 calories per 2 tablespoons		
Fat......... 12.6 G	Cholesterol ... 0 mg	Fiber .... .2 G	Diabetic exchanges:
saturated . 1.7 G	Protein .... .3 G	Vitamin C .. 0 mg	2½ fat, (1¼ cup
mono .... 8.8 G	Carbohydrate .. 1.0 G	Calcium ... 24 mg	strawberries = 1 fruit)
poly...... 1.5 G		Sodium .... 178 mg	

MINT CITRUS MELON SALAD

A cool, refreshing salad for hot summer days.

3 cups melon (cantalope,
  watermelon, honeydew) balls
3-4 cardamom seeds
2 tablespoons chopped fresh mint

⅔ cup freshly squeezed orange juice
½ cup freshly squeezed lemon juice
1 teaspoon grated orange zest

Crush the cardamom seeds. Combine cardamom, mint, orange juice, lemon juice and orange zest. Mix thoroughly and pour over the melon balls. Chill at least 30 minutes before serving.

serves 4	68 calories per ¾ cup serving		
Fat......... .5 G	Cholesterol ... 0 mg	Fiber .... 1.3 G	Diabetic exchanges:
saturated . .1 G	Protein .... 1.2 G	Vitamin C .. 66 mg	1⅛ fruit
mono .... .1 G	Carbohydrate .. 17.0 G	Calcium ... 17 mg	
poly...... .2 G		Sodium .... 9 mg	

*Indicates high sodium content

ANCHOVY SALAD DRESSING

If you're reading this, you must be an anchovy lover. You won't be disappointed.

6 tablespoons olive oil
1 tablespoon wine vinegar
salt and pepper to taste
1 teaspoon minced chives
½ teaspoon minced chervil

½ teaspoon minced parsley
½ teaspoon minced thyme
2 inches anchovy paste squeezed
    from tube
1 small garlic clove, minced

Combine all ingredients in blender container and blend until smooth. Serve on salad greens.

Serves 8	90 calories per 1 tablespoon		
Fat........... 10.0 G	Cholesterol .... 0 mg	Fiber........ 0 G	Diabetic exchanges:
saturated... 1.4 G	Protein .... 0 G	Vitamin C ... 0 mg	2 fat
mono...... 7.5 G	Carbohydrate .... .3 G	Calcium.... 2mg	
poly .... .9 G		Sodium ..... 0 mg	

HERB SALAD DRESSING

This makes a large quantity which keeps well.

⅔ teaspoon dry mustard
⅔ teaspoon salt
¼ teaspoon freshly ground pepper
2 cups olive oil
⅔ cup red wine vinegar
3 dashes hot pepper sauce

2 cloves garlic, halved
½ teaspoon dried mint
½ teaspoon dried basil
2 tablespoons minced parsley
2 teaspoons sugar

Combine all ingredients in a jar. After 2 hours, remove the garlic halves. Put the dressing into the blender container and blend on low speed until the dressing is smooth. Shake well before each use.

Makes 2⅓ cups	193 calories per 2 tablespoons		
Fat......... 21.6 G	Cholesterol ... 0 mg	Fiber .... 0 G	Diabetic exchanges:
saturated . 2.9 G	Protein .... 0 G	Vitamin C .. 0 mg	4 fat
mono .... 15.9 G	Carbohydrate .. 1.0 G	Calcium ... 4 mg	
poly...... 1.8 G		Sodium .... 80 mg	

SPICY APPLE JUICE DRESSING

An oil free, low calorie dressing for salad greens. Note diabetics: a serving of 2 tablespoons is free!

¾ cup apple juice
½ cup apple cider vinegar
2¼ teaspoons garlic powder
2¼ teaspoons cornstarch
1½ teaspoons oregano leaves, crushed

¾ teaspoon powdered mustard
¾ teaspoon paprika
¼ teaspoon freshly ground pepper
1 package sweetener

In a small saucepan, combine all ingredients except sweetener. Bring to a boil and cook, stirring, until thickened. Remove from heat, cool and stir in sweetener. Cover and chill until ready to use. Beat with whisk before serving.

Makes 1¼ cups	14 calories per 2 tablespoons			
Fat .... 0 G	Cholesterol ... 0 mg	Fiber .... .1 G		Diabetic exchanges:
saturated .. 0 G	Protein .... .2 G	Vitamin C .. 0 mg		1 serving-free
mono ..... 0 G	Carbohydrate .. 3.7 G	Calcium ... 5 mg		
poly .... 0 G		Sodium .... 1 mg		

SUMPTUOUS RED DRESSING

Serve this and your friends will ask "Are you really sure this is good for you?"

½ cup olive oil
4 tablespoons red-wine vinegar
⅓ cup catsup*
1 teaspoon capers
1 tablespoon Worcestershire sauce*
2 dashes hot pepper sauce
1 clove garlic, minced

1 teaspoon sugar
½ teaspoon basil
¼ teaspoon oregano
¼ teaspoon ground cloves
¼ teaspoon salt*
freshly ground pepper to taste

Mix all ingredients in small blender container and blend at low speed for 1 minute. Allow to stand several hours or overnight.

Makes 1 cup	120 calories per 2 tablespoons			
Fat .... 12.0 G	Cholesterol ... 0 mg	Fiber .... .2 G		Diabetic exchanges:
saturated . 1.6 G	Protein .... .2 G	Vitamin C .. 2 mg		2 fat
mono .... 8.9 G	Carbohydrate .. 3.6 G	Calcium ... 6 mg		
poly ...... 1.1 G		Sodium .... 164 mg		

*Indicates high sodium content

OLIVE OIL MAYONNAISE

I don't know how long this will keep—it never lasts long enough to find out!

2 tablespoons olive oil
1 cup 1% fat cottage cheese*
2 tablespoons low fat
   cream cheese (for consistency)

freshly ground black pepper to taste
1-2 teaspoons lemon juice
1-3 teaspoons Dijon mustard

Blend all ingredients in the blender, store in covered jar in the refrigerator.

Makes 1¼ cups	51 calories per 2 tablespoons				
Fat......... 4.0 G	Cholesterol ... 4 mg	Fiber ...... 0 G	Diabetic exchanges:
saturated . 1.2 G	Protein .... 3.1 G	Vitamin C. 0 mg	1⅛ fat
mono .... 2.4 G	Carbohydrate .. .8 G	Calcium ... 17 mg	
poly...... .3 G		Sodium .... 107 mg	

DILL SAUCE

This is excellent on fish.

½ cup olive oil mayonnaise
   (see recipe)*
½ cup low fat yogurt
1 tablespoon Dijon mustard

½ teaspoon garlic powder
freshly ground white pepper
1 teaspoon onion powder
1 tablespoon dried dill weed

Combine all ingredients, mix well.

Makes 1 cup	34 calories per 2 tablespoons				
Fat........... 1.9 G	Cholesterol .... 1 mg	Fiber........ 0 G	Diabetic exchanges:
saturated ... .5 G	Protein .... 2.5 G	Vitamin C ... 0 mg	¼ low fat milk
mono .... 1.2 G	Carbohydrate .. 2.1 G	Calcium ... 43 mg	
poly...... .1 G		Sodium .... 85 mg	

MUSTARD CURRY SAUCE

The small amount of oil in mustard is mostly monounsaturated.

¼ cup prepared mustard
3-4 teaspoons mild curry powder
⅛ teaspoon garlic powder
⅛ teaspoon freshly ground black pepper

½ teaspoon celery salt*
⅛ cup white wine or to consistency
1½ teaspoons sugar

Combine all ingredients, adjusting consistency with the white wine. Use to baste meats or fish while cooking or use as a sauce at the table.

Makes ⅓ cup	18 calories per 1 tablespoon				
Fat......... .6 G	Cholesterol ... 0 mg	Fiber .... 0 G	Diabetic exchanges:
saturated .. 0 G	Protein .... 1.0 G	Vitamin C .. 0 mg	1 tablespoon free
mono .... .5 G	Carbohydrate .. 2.4 G	Calcium ... 14 mg	
poly....... 0 G		Sodium .... 131 mg	

*Indicates high sodium content

THOUSAND ISLAND DRESSING

Original taste, but more nutritious and fewer calories.

1 cup 1% fat cottage cheese*
¼ cup chili sauce*
¼ cup skim milk
2 tablespoons olive oil
1 teaspoon paprika

½ teaspoon salt*
2 tablespoons chopped celery
2 tablespoons chopped green pepper
1 tablespoon finely chopped onion
1-2 tablespoons sweet pickle relish*

In blender container, combine cheese, chili sauce, milk, oil, paprika and salt. Blend until smooth. Stir in chopped vegetables and relish. Chill. Serve over lettuce salad.

Makes 2 cups		35 calories per 2 tablespoons					
Fat	2.0 G	Cholesterol ...	1 mg	Fiber	1.5 G	Diabetic exchanges:	
saturated .	.4 G	Protein	2.2 G	Vitamin C ..	2 mg	¼ medium fat meat,	
mono	1.4 G	Carbohydrate ..	2.3 G	Calcium ...	17 mg	½ vegetable	
poly......	.2 G			Sodium	203 mg		

LO-FAT CREAMY SALAD DRESSING

This is quick and easy.

2 heaping tablespoons
  1% fat cottage cheese*
2 heaping tablespoons
  low fat yogurt
½ green onion, green part only
⅛ sweet red pepper
  (for color and taste)

¼ teaspoon garlic powder
¼ teaspoon Worchestershire sauce
¼ teaspoon oregano, hand rubbed
skim milk to consistency
salt and freshly ground pepper
  to taste

Put all ingredients in the blender and blend to creamy consistency.

Makes ½ cup		7 calories per 1 tablespoon					
Fat	.1 G	Cholesterol ...	0 mg	Fiber	0 G	Diabetic exchanges:	
saturated .	.1 G	Protein	.8 G	Vitamin C ..	2 mg	2 tablespoons free!	
mono	0 G	Carbohydrate ..	.7 G	Calcium ...	15 mg		
poly......	0 G			Sodium	19 mg		

*Indicates high sodium content

TARRAGON SAUCE

This Bearnaise look alike has a very similar taste and a longer refrigerator life because it has no egg yolks. Use it on meats, fish, potatoes, etc.

skim milk
¾ cup 1% fat cottage cheese*
2 tablespoons Butter Buds®*
2 tablespoons white vinegar

2 teaspoons chopped onion
¾ teaspoon dry tarragon
pepper to taste
½ teaspoon dry tarragon

Cook vinegar, onions, ¾ teaspoon tarragon and pepper until reduced by half. Cool. Strain into cottage cheese, add Butter Buds® and ½ teaspoon dry tarragon, hand rubbed. Blend and add skim milk (1-3 tablespoons) until the consistency is right. It's better the next day.

Makes ¾ cup	18 calories per 2 tablespoons						
Fat	.2 G	Cholesterol ...	1 mg	Fiber	0 G	Diabetic exchanges:	
saturated .	.1 G	Protein	2.8 G	Vitamin C ..	0 mg	2 tablespoons are free!	
mono	.1 G	Carbohydrate	1.1 G	Calcium	20 mg		
poly	0 G			Sodium	88 mg		

TARTAR SAUCE

The taste is traditional, the fat is not.

½ cup 1% fat cottage cheese*
6 tablespoons olive oil
2 teaspoons Dijon mustard

twist pepper (preferably white)
1 tablespoon white vinegar
1 tablespoon lemon juice

Combine all ingredients in the blender container and blend until smooth.

Add:

2 teaspoons pickle relish*
1 teaspoon capers

1 scallion, chopped fine

Stir into mixture and allow to set in refrigerator several hours to develop flavor.

Makes ¾ cup	103 calories per 2 tablespoons						
Fat	10.3 G	Cholesterol ...	1 mg	Fiber	.1 G	Diabetic exchanges:	
saturated .	1.5 G	Protein	1.9 G	Vitamin C ..	2 mg	2 fat, ½ vegetable	
mono	7.6 G	Carbohydrate ..	1.3 G	Calcium ...	11 mg		
poly	.9 G			Sodium	83 mg		

*Indicates high sodium content

Main Dishes

♥ A cholesterol lowering diet is a long–term endeavor. The beneficial changes in the arteries are slow to appear.

♥ Corn oil and soybean oil are quite similar in composition of saturated, monounsaturated and polyunsaturated fats.

♥ Low HDL is an independent risk for increased atherosclerosis and seems to be inherited. It is common in diabetes. We're not sure how to beat it, but nicotinic acid, olive oil, a glass of wine or beer a day, and regular exercise have been recommended to raise it. There are medicines your physician may recommend.

♥ The new no–calorie oils in the offing will not give the benefits of olive oil.

♥ Diabetes means "to siphon." There are two kinds: mellitus, having to do with sugar; and insipidus, having to do with the pituitary.

MAIN DISHES

SCALOPPINE WITH PEPPERS

Italian, even without pasta.

2 whole chicken breasts, boned,
   halved, skin removed
½ teaspoon salt*
¼ teaspoon pepper
flour
1 large green pepper

1 large red bell pepper
3 tablespoons olive oil
1 clove garlic, minced
¼ cup red wine
1 tablespoon red wine vinegar

Place the chicken breast halves between sheets of waxed paper and pound firmly with a meat mallet or rolling pin until they are ¼ inch thick. Sprinkle with salt and pepper, dust with flour. Halve the peppers, seed, cut lengthwise into ½ inch strips. Heat 2 tablespoons olive oil in a large skillet. Add the scaloppine and saute until golden brown on both sides, about 5 minutes. When the meat is done, remove to platter, keep warm. Add remaining oil to skillet and saute pepper strips until tender; add garlic and saute 1 minute. Stir in wine and vinegar, stirring to coat peppers with pan juices. Spoon peppers and juices over scaloppine and serve.

Serves 4	251 calories per 4 oz. serving		
Fat .... 14.2 G	Cholesterol ... 63 mg	Fiber .... .5 G	Diabetic exchanges:
saturated . 2.5 G	Protein .... 23.8 G	Vitamin C .. 40 mg	3 lean meat, 1 fat
mono .... 8.9 G	Carbohydrate .. 3.9 G	Calcium ... 18 mg	1½ vegetable
poly...... 1.8 G		Sodium .... 326 mg	

LIME SUPREME WITH DIJON

Made for grilling.

2 whole chicken breasts, boned,
   halved, skin removed
juice of 1 lime
1 tablespoon Dijon style mustard*
1 clove garlic, minced

freshly ground pepper
1 tablespoon dry white wine
1 teaspoon dried basil, hand rubbed
½ teaspoon dried tarragon, hand rubbed
¼ teaspoon dried rosemary, hand rubbed

Combine all ingredients and place chicken breasts in the mixture to marinate overnight in the refrigerator. The next day, remove breasts and broil them until done. Serve immediately, garnished with parsley if desired.

Serves 4	134 calories per 3 oz. serving		
Fat .... 3.4 G	Cholesterol ... 60 mg	Fiber .... .2 G	Diabetic exchanges:
saturated . .9 G	Protein .... 22.3 G	Vitamin C .. 4 mg	2½ lean meat
mono .... 1.3 G	Carbohydrate .. 1.9 G	Calcium ... 27 mg	
poly...... .7 G		Sodium .... 104 mg	

*Indicates high sodium content

CHICKEN WITH MARSALA

You may want to add mushrooms for a Sicilian flair.

2 whole chicken breasts, halved,
  boned and skin removed
¼ cup flour
salt and pepper*
2 tablespoons olive oil

2 tablespoons Marsala wine
½ cup chicken stock (see recipe)*
lemon juice
parsley

Put chicken breasts between sheets of waxed paper and pound to ¼ inch thickness. Sprinkle chicken with salt and pepper, dust with flour. Heat the olive oil in a skillet and saute the chicken until lightly browned and remove to a plate. Deglaze pan by adding Marsala and bring to a boil. Add the stock and bring to a boil again. Boil until it reaches a syrupy consistency. Return chicken to the skillet, reduce the heat to low, cover and simmer 2-3 minutes. To serve, arrange the chicken on a heated platter, add a few drops of lemon juice to the sauce in the skillet, pour sauce over the chicken, sprinkle with parsley.

Serves 4	211 calories per 4 oz. serving		
Fat .... 10.1 G	Cholesterol ... 51 mg	Fiber .... .2 G	Diabetic exchanges:
saturated . 1.8 G	Protein .... 19.6 G	Vitamin C .. 0 mg	2½ lean meat, ½ fat
mono .... 6.1 G	Carbohydrate .. 7.3 G	Calcium ... 13 mg	½ starch
poly ...... 1.4 G		Sodium .... 232 mg	

MARINATED CHICKEN BREASTS

A flavorful alternative to plain grilled chicken.

2 whole chicken breasts, boned,
  halved and skin removed
½ cup minced parsley
½ teaspoon rosemary
½ teaspoon savory
5 juniper berries

1 clove garlic
6 peppercorns
1 onion, minced
4 teaspoons olive oil
white wine to paste consistency

Place all ingredients except chicken in blender container and blend until smooth. Spread mixture over chicken breasts and wrap the breasts in plastic wrap. Refrigerate several hours. Remove wrapping and bake chicken, covered at 375 degrees until internal temperature is 185. Watch closely as the meat will dry out. May be grilled instead of baked.

Serves 4	249 calories per 5 oz. serving		
Fat .... 9.7 G	Cholesterol ... 97 mg	Fiber .... .7 G	Diabetic exchanges:
saturated . 2.1 G	Protein .... 35.5 G	Vitamin C .. 8 mg	4½ lean meat
mono .... 5.1 G	Carbohydrate .. 1.9 G	Calcium ... 33 mg	
poly ...... 1.5 G		Sodium .... 91 mg	

*Indicates high sodium content

CHICKEN WITH MORELS

In a "French" restaurant a variation of this is expensive. It tastes the same..

2 small leeks, chopped
  (or ½ cup onion, chopped)
½ cup fresh morels
2 whole chicken breasts, boned,
  halved, skin removed
salt and pepper*

2 tablespoons olive oil
½ cup white wine
½ cup chicken stock (see recipe)*
½ cup skim milk combined
  with 1 tablespoon flour
⅛ teaspoon nutmeg

Put chicken breasts between 2 sheets of waxed paper and pound to ¼ inch thickness. Sprinkle chicken with salt and pepper; saute in the olive oil until golden. Add the leeks and cook until the leeks are soft, about 3 minutes. Add the wine and stock and bring to a simmer. Cover the pan and gently simmer, turning the chicken once, until done, about 10 minutes. Remove chicken and keep warm. Add mushrooms to pan and cook over high heat until sauce is slightly thickened, about 1 minute. Lower heat and stir in skim milk mixture. Simmer gently until sauce thickens enough to coat the back of a spoon, about 3 minutes. Season with nutmeg and salt and pepper to taste. Spoon sauce over chicken.

If morels are unavailable, use other mushrooms but don't expect the same flavor.

Serves 4	206 calories per 6 oz. serving			
Fat .... 9.5 G	Cholesterol ... 44 mg	Fiber .... .9 G	Diabetic exchanges:
saturated . 1.7 G	Protein .... 18.6 G	Vitamin C .. 3 mg	2 lean meat, 1 fat,
mono .... 5.8 G	Carbohydrate .. 6.6 G	Calcium ... 59 mg	½ low fat milk
poly ...... 1.2 G		Sodium .... 243 mg	

*Indicates high sodium content

71

HERBED SCALOPPINE WITH WHITE BEANS

High protein, high fiber.

2 whole chicken breasts, boned,
 cut into thirds, skin removed
½ teaspoon oregano, hand rubbed
½ teaspoon basil, hand rubbed
½ teaspoon salt*
¼ teaspoon freshly ground pepper
2 cups cooked white beans
3 tablespoons olive oil

1 tablespoon red wine vinegar
1 clove garlic, halved
1 bay leaf
½ cup chicken stock (see recipe)*
½ cup dry white wine
2 green onions, thinly sliced
1 tablespoon tomato paste*
2 tablespoons chopped parsley

Place the chicken breasts between sheets of waxed paper and pound until ¼ inch thick. Combine the oregano, basil, salt and pepper in small bowl. Sprinkle mixture evenly on both sides of the chicken. Place the beans in a small saucepan with 1½ tablespoons olive oil and the wine vinegar. Heat the remaining 1½ tablespoons olive oil in a large skillet and add all the garlic and bay leaf, saute until both begin to turn brown then discard them. Add the chicken and saute until golden brown, about 5 minutes on each side. Combine the stock, wine and tomato paste in a small bowl. Pour over the scaloppine. Simmer, stirring up the browned bits on the bottom of the pan. Turn scaloppine to coat with sauce. Simmer until liquid is reduced to about ½ cup. Heat beans until hot; stir in green onions and pour into a shallow dish. Arrange scaloppine over the beans and cover with the sauce. Sprinkle with parsley.

Serves 6	238 calories per 5 oz. serving			
Fat .... 9.3 G	Cholesterol ... 34 mg	Fiber .... 5.7 G	Diabetic exchanges:
saturated . 1.6 G	Protein .... 18.0 G	Vitamin C .. 5 mg	1 starch, 1 vegetable,
mono .... 5.8 G	Carbohydrate .. 18.2 G	Calcium ... 60 mg	2 lean meat, ½ fat
poly ...... 1.2 G		Sodium .... 190 mg	

*Indicates high sodium content

SICILIAN CHICKEN

If you've never fried sweet potatoes, try this imaginative version.

1 whole chicken breast, boned, skin removed	2 tablespoons olive oil
1 garlic clove, minced	1 sweet potato
1 rounded teaspoon oregano	1 white potato
1 rounded teaspoon rosemary, crushed	salt and freshly ground pepper to taste

Cut the chicken breast into finger size pieces.

Peel and cube the potatoes into ½ inch cubes. Boil the white and sweet potatoes separately 5 minutes then remove from water to cool. The potatoes may be precooked in the microwave; be careful that they are not overcooked.

Combine the chicken pieces with the garlic, oregano and rosemary and marinate for at least one hour-longer is better. Saute the chicken in 1 tablespoon olive oil just until the edges start to brown, do not overcook. (Best in a non stick pan.)

Remove chicken from pan, add 1 tablespoon olive oil and fry the prepared potatoes until they start to turn brown, stirring frequently. It is best to cook the white potatoes first since the sweet potatoes tend to blacken easily. Add salt and pepper to taste. Extra rosemary and oregano may be added to the potatoes during cooking.

Serve with a bland side dish such as broiled tomatoes, fried zucchini, etc.

Serves 4	225 calories per 6 oz. serving		
Fat .... 9.0 G	Cholesterol ... 48 mg	Fiber .... 1.8 G	Diabetic exchanges:
saturated . 1.5 G	Protein .... 18.8 G	Vitamin C .. 10 mg	2 lean meat, 1 starch,
mono .... 5.7 G	Carbohydrate .. 16.7 G	Calcium ... 21 mg	½ fat
poly....... 1.1 G		Sodium .... 49 mg	

GREEK CHICKEN

Dimitris, the mother of my Greek childhood friends, often made this dish and I would stand and watch her and learn rather than play with my friends.

1 chicken, cut into serving pieces,
  skin removed
½ teaspoon nutmeg
½ teaspoon cinnamon
½ teaspoon thyme
juice of ½ lemon

1 small can tomato paste*
1 clove garlic
salt and pepper to taste*
½ cup grated Kessari or parmesan cheese*
½ pound spaghetti

Place chicken in heavy saucepan and barely cover with water. Add remaining ingredients except cheese and pasta and simmer 2-3 hours. Remove chicken from sauce and cook sauce down to thicker consistency.

Meanwhile, cook spaghetti. When ready to serve, put a layer of spaghetti in casserole, sprinkle with grated Kessari or parmesan cheese, ladle sauce over spaghetti, make another layer of spaghetti, cheese and sauce. Serve with chicken on top of spaghetti or in a separate dish.

This is an excellent dish for cooking all day in the crockpot. Just put all ingredients except the cheese and spaghetti in the crockpot and cook on high for 6-8 hours. Remove the chicken when the cooking is done and thicken the sauce in a saucepan on the stove. Finish as above.

Serves 6	329 calories per 7 oz. serving		
Fat .... 10.1 G	Cholesterol ... 99 mg	Fiber .... 1.9 G	Diabetic exchanges:
saturated . 3.5 G	Protein .... 37.1 G	Vitamin C .. 13 mg	4 lean meat, 1½ starch
mono .... 3.4 G	Carbohydrate .. 21.0 G	Calcium ... 127 mg	
poly ...... 2.0 G		Sodium .... 218 mg	

*Indicates high sodium content

ITALIAN CHICKEN

Great for crockpot cooking.

1 (2½-3 pound) fryer chicken,
   cut up, skin removed
1 cup sliced fresh mushrooms
¼ cup chopped onion
¼ cup chopped green pepper
½ small head cabbage,
   cut into wedges
8 ounces tomato sauce*

1 teaspoon dried oregano, hand rubbed
½ teaspoon dried basil, hand rubbed
1 clove garlic, minced
2 cups chicken stock (see recipe)*
1 chicken bouillon cube*
1 tablespoon cornstarch
parmesan cheese

Combine all ingredients except cornstarch and cheese in a large pot. Bring to boil, reduce heat and simmer until chicken starts to fall from bones—1½ to 2 hours. Remove chicken from pot, stir cornstarch into a little cold water then add to the cooking liquid. Stir until slightly thickened. Serve sauce and freshly grated parmesan cheese with chicken.

For crockpot cooking, combine all ingredients as above in crockpot and cook 6-8 hours on high. Finish with cornstarch as above.

Serves 6	240 calories per 4 oz. serving		
Fat .... 8.1 G	Cholesterol ... 95 mg	Fiber .... 1.9 G	Diabetic exchanges:
saturated . 2.2 G	Protein .... 32.8 G	Vitamin C .. 29 mg	4 lean meat,
mono .... 2.8 G	Carbohydrate .. 8.0 G	Calcium ... 48 mg	1 vegetable
poly...... 1.9 G		Sodium .... 765 mg	

LEMON BAKED CHICKEN

A diversion from fried chicken.

2 tablespoons olive oil
2 tablespoons fresh lemon juice
1 clove garlic, minced

½ teaspoon salt*
freshly ground pepper
1 fryer chicken, cut up, skin removed

Preheat oven to 350 degrees. Combine all ingredients except chicken. Arrange chicken in oven casserole dish, pour lemon and oil mixture over chicken, cover and bake about 45-60 minutes or until chicken is tender. Uncover chicken during last 10 minutes to allow chicken to brown. Sprinkle with chopped parsley before serving.

Serves 6	257 calories per 4 oz. serving		
Fat .... 12.9 G	Cholesterol ... 101 mg	Fiber .... 0 G	Diabetic exchanges:
saturated . 2.9 G	Protein .... 32.9 G	Vitamin C .. 2 mg	4½ lean meat
mono .... 6.3 G	Carbohydrate .. .6 G	Calcium ... 19 mg	
poly...... 2.3 G		Sodium .... 275 mg	

*Indicates high sodium content

TANGY CHICKEN

This is one of Charlie's favorites—it's easy to prepare, too.

1 medium onion, sliced
2 cloves garlic, minced
1 teaspoon dried rosemary leaves
½ teaspoon dried basil leaves
½ teaspoon dried thyme leaves
2 tablespoons olive oil
2 cups canned tomatoes,
   cut into pieces*

¾ cup catsup*
¼ cup vinegar
1 chicken bouillon cube*
freshly ground pepper to taste
2½-3 pound chicken, cut into pieces,
   skin removed
spaghetti
¼ cup parmesan cheese

In a large skillet, saute onion, garlic and herbs in olive oil until onion is softened. Stir in tomatoes, catsup, vinegar, bouillon and pepper. Add chicken. Bring to a boil, reduce heat and simmer, covered, for 45-60 minutes or until chicken is tender. Serve over spaghetti. Sprinkle with parmesan cheese.

Analysis is for chicken and sauce. ½ cup cooked spaghetti = 80 calories

Serves 8	227 calories per 7 oz. serving			
Fat .... 9.5 G	Cholesterol ... 71 mg	Fiber .... 1.2 G	Diabetic exchanges:
saturated . 2.1 G	Protein .... 24.5 G	Vitamin C .. 14 mg	2½ vegetable, 3 lean
mono .... 4.6 G	Carbohydrate .. 10.7 G	Calcium ... 42 mg	meat, (½ cup cooked
poly...... 1.7 G		Sodium .... 558 mg	spaghetti = 1 starch)

*Indicates high sodium content

CHICKEN WITH VEGETABLES

Good eating, easy preparation.

2 whole chicken breasts, boned,
   halved, skin removed
2 large potatoes,
   cut into ½ inch cubes
2 carrots, sliced
½ pound fresh green beans

1 onion, sliced
1 tablespoon chopped parsley
1 chicken bouillon cube*
freshly ground pepper
1 cup chicken stock (see recipe)*

Place all ingredients in an oven-going pot and bake at 350 degrees, covered tightly, for 2 hours or until the vegetables are tender.

Also, this makes a good crockpot dish. Place all ingredients in the crockpot and cook on alternating low/high for 8 hours.

Serves 4	204 calories per 10 oz. serving		
Fat .... 3.1 G	Cholesterol ... 48 mg	Fiber .... 3.9 G	Diabetic exchanges:
saturated . .8 G	Protein .... 20.9 G	Vitamin C .. 20 mg	2 lean meat, ½ starch,
mono .... 1.0 G	Carbohydrate .. 23.5 G	Calcium ... 54 mg	2 vegetable
poly ...... .8 G		Sodium .... 540 mg	

LEMON CHICKEN CASSEROLE

Think dill and lemon.

¼ cup flour
1 teaspoon dried dill weed
⅛ teaspoon freshly ground pepper
1 fryer chicken, cut up, skin removed
2 tablespoons olive oil
1 clove garlic, minced

2 cups chicken stock (see recipe)*
¼ cup fresh lemon juice
¼ teaspoon grated lemon peel
2 stalks celery, sliced
8 ounces small, whole fresh mushrooms
1 chicken bouillon cube*

Combine the flour, dill and pepper. Coat chicken with flour mixture. In a large skillet, heat the olive oil, add garlic and cook briefly, remove garlic, do not let it brown. Add chicken and brown on all sides. Remove chicken and set aside. Stir any remaining flour mixture into skillet, gradually add stock, scraping up any bits from the bottom of the pan. Stir in lemon juice, peel, celery, previously cooked garlic and chicken bouillon cube. Bring to boil; return chicken to skillet, cover and simmer 25 minutes until chicken is tender. Add mushrooms, cover and cook 10 minutes longer. Remove to serving platter, garnish with lemon slices and parsley sprigs.

Serves 6	214 calories per 9 oz. serving		
Fat .... 8.4 G	Cholesterol ... 80 mg	Fiber .... 1.0 G	Diabetic exchanges:
saturated . 1.0 G	Protein .... 26.0 G	Vitamin C .. 10 mg	2½ vegetable,
mono .... 4.4 G	Carbohydrate .. 7.7 G	Calcium ... 30 mg	4¼ lean meat
poly ...... 1.4 G		Sodium .... 557 mg	

*Indicates high sodium content

CURRIED CHICKEN WITH BANANAS

Let this dish introduce you to the endless possibilities of curry.

4 chicken thighs, skin and
  excess fat removed
1 banana
1 apple, peeled, cored, diced ½ inch
½ cup canned tomatoes*
1 medium onion, diced

1 clove garlic, minced
1½ cups water
1 chicken bouillon cube*
1 teaspoon salt free bouillon
½ teaspoon mild curry powder
½ cup yogurt

Combine chicken with all ingredients except apples, bananas, and yogurt and cook for approximately one hour. About 10 minutes before serving, add the banana and apple, since they tend to become mushy with prolonged cooking. When the cooking time is done, stir in the yogurt. Adjust the sweetness with lemon juice. Serve over brown rice.

Serves 4	229 calories per 1 cup serving		
Fat......... 7.5 G	Cholesterol ... 64 mg	Fiber .... 2.7 G	Diabetic exchanges:
saturated . 2.1 G	Protein .... 22.0 G	Vitamin C .. 23 mg	3 lean meat, 1 fruit
mono .... 2.6 G	Carbohydrate .. 19.1 G	Calcium ... 103 mg	
poly...... 1.7 G		Sodium .... 555 mg	

PETE'S HUNTER STEW

A variation on an old standard.

3 cups water
4 chicken legs, skin removed
2-3 carrots, cubed
2-3 onions, cut into eighths
2 stalks celery, coarsely sliced
2 potatoes, cubed
1 teaspoon rosemary leaves

1 teaspoon sage leaves
½ teaspoon lemon juice
1 chicken bouillon cube*
1 beef bouillon cube*
salt and pepper to taste*
1 package chicken gravy mix*

Cook the chicken in the water for 20-30 minutes, until done. Remove the chicken and add the vegetables; rub the herbs in the palms of your hands and add to the stew. Remove the chicken from the bones and add to the stew; cook for 20-25 minutes. Add lemon juice, bouillon cubes, salt and pepper. Stir chicken gravy mix into ½ cup cold water then add to the stew. Cook 5 minutes.

Serves 8	121 calories per 8 oz. serving		
Fat......... 2.9 G	Cholesterol ... 30 mg	Fiber .... 1.5 G	Diabetic exchanges:
saturated . .8 G	Protein .... 11.3 G	Vitamin C .. 7 mg	1 lean meat, ¾ starch,
mono .... 1.0 G	Carbohydrate .. 12.1 G	Calcium ... 30 mg	¼ vegetable
poly...... .7 G		Sodium .... 451 mg	

*Indicates high sodium content

ROSEMARY CHICKEN WITH LEMON

Lemon, rosemary and yogurt over chicken—an old favorite of ours.

2 whole chicken breasts, boned,
   halved and skin removed
½ teaspoon salt*
¼ teaspoon pepper
flour
zest from one whole lemon
1 tablespoon olive oil

½ teaspoon rosemary leaves
1 large clove garlic, minced
¼ cup dry white wine
1 cup chicken broth (see recipe)*
½ cup yogurt or low fat sour cream
1 tablespoon flour

Place chicken between sheets of waxed paper and pound thin. Season with salt and pepper and dust lightly with flour. Saute meat in oil until golden. Sprinkle rosemary and garlic over meat and cook about 30 seconds. Add wine and stock and cook uncovered until the pan liquid has reduced a little. Remove chicken to platter, stir half the lemon zest into the liquid in the skillet. Combine the yogurt or sour cream with the flour and add it to the liquid in the skillet. Heat gently over low heat, stirring constantly, until thickened. Pour sauce over meat and sprinkle with additional lemon zest.

Serves 4	215 calories per 6 oz. serving		
Fat .... 8.1 G	Cholesterol ... 65 mg	Fiber .... .2 G	Diabetic exchanges:
saturated . 1.9 G	Protein .... 25.6 G	Vitamin C .. 1 mg	3 lean meat,
mono .... 4.1 G	Carbohydrate .. 6.1 G	Calcium ... 73 mg	½ low fat milk
poly ...... 1.3 G		Sodium .... 721 mg	

*Indicates high sodium content

KABOB

This is not shish kabob. This is an Indian dish that can be formed into patties or rolls and sauteed. This is the answer to leftover turkey or chicken. The original recipe used lamb.

1 pound ground turkey or chicken,
   raw or cooked
1 cup lentils
1 teaspoon ground cinnamon
1 teaspoon ground cumin
¼ teaspoon red pepper-use your
   own discretion
½ teaspoon ground cloves

1 teaspoon salt*
1 teaspoon pepper
2-3 green onions, chopped
1 small green pepper, chopped
1 egg white, slightly beaten
1 cup fine bread crumbs
olive oil

Combine the meat, lentils and spices in a saucepan, add 2 cups water and cook until the lentils are tender and the water is evaporated. Remove from heat, add the green onions and the green pepper. Put entire mixture through a food chopper. Taste for seasonings. Form mixture into patties about 3 inches in diameter, ½ inch thick. Dip each patty into slightly beaten egg white and then into fine bread crumbs. Saute in olive oil until lightly browned, adding olive oil as needed.

Serves 10	211 calories per 3 oz. serving		
Fat .... 10.8 G	Cholesterol ... 38 mg	Fiber .... 2.7 G	Diabetic exchanges:
saturated . 2.8 G	Protein .... 18.1 G	Vitamin C .. 12 mg	2 lean meat, 1 starch
mono .... 5.9 G	Carbohydrate .. 14.2 G	Calcium ... 37 mg	1 vegetable
poly...... 2.0 G		Sodium .... 296 mg	

*Indicates high sodium content

BREAST OF CHICKEN FLAMBE

Flambe is not critical to the dish, but fun for the cook and a delight for the guests.

2 whole chicken breasts, boned,
   halved, skin removed
1 tablespoon dried tarragon
3 tablespoons flour
salt and pepper*
2 tablespoons fresh lemon juice

2 tablespoons olive oil
2 tablespoons cognac
1 cup chicken broth (see recipe)*
2 tablespoons Dijon-style mustard*
1 tablespoon capers
lemon zest strips

Combine flour, tarragon, salt and pepper. Dip the chicken breasts in the flour mixture and shake off excess. Heat the olive oil in saute pan; saute chicken breasts until lightly browned. Add chicken broth, mustard and lemon juice. Cover the pan, reduce the heat to low and simmer, turning once, until cooked through, about 25 minutes. Season to taste with salt and pepper. Warm the cognac in a small saucepan over medium heat, pour the cognac over the chicken, carefully ignite and shake until the flames subside. Arrange chicken on serving plate, strain sauce over and garnish with capers and fresh lemon zest strips.

Serves 4	257 calories per 5 oz. serving		
Fat .... 10.6 G	Cholesterol ... 51 mg	Fiber .... .6 G	Diabetic exchanges:
saturated . 1.8 G	Protein .... 21.2 G	Vitamin C .. 4 mg	3 lean meat, 1 starch
mono .... 6.4 G	Carbohydrate .. 14.3 G	Calcium ... 32 mg	½ vegetable
poly...... 1.4 G		Sodium .... 343 mg	

CHICKEN PAPRIKA

An unbelievably simple piquant sauce. Use Hungarian paprika for best flavor.

4 chicken thighs, skin removed
¼ teaspoon pepper
¼ cup flour
3 tablespoons olive oil

1 tablespoon paprika
1 cup water
1 tablespoon vinegar
1 chicken bouillon cube*

Combine the flour with pepper. Coat the chicken pieces with the flour mixture. Heat olive oil in medium skillet and saute the chicken pieces until browned. Add remaining ingredients and simmer, uncovered, until most of the liquid has evaporated. This makes a thick flavored coating on the chicken. Serve with noodles or potatoes.

Serves 4	226 calories per 4 oz. serving		
Fat .... 13.8 G	Cholesterol ... 55 mg	Fiber .... .6 G	Diabetic exchanges:
saturated . 2.8 G	Protein .... 17.6 G	Vitamin C .. 1 mg	2½ lean meat, 1 fat
mono .... 7.5 G	Carbohydrate .. 7.5 G	Calcium ... 19 mg	½ starch
poly...... 2.4 G		Sodium .... 336 mg	

*Indicates high sodium content

SAUTEED CHICKEN BREASTS

One of our stand-by recipes.

1 whole chicken breast, halved,
   boned and skin removed
freshly ground pepper
¼ cup flour
1 tablespoon olive oil

1 clove garlic, minced
¼ cup chopped shallots
½ cup fresh mushrooms
½ cup dry white wine
1 chicken bouillon cube*

Place chicken breast pieces between sheets of waxed paper and pound to ¼ inch thickness. Combine the flour and pepper, dust the chicken breasts lightly with flour mixture. Heat the olive oil in a skillet and saute the chicken until lightly browned. Add the garlic, shallots, mushrooms, wine and bouillon cube. Cover and cook gently about 30-40 minutes, or until the chicken is tender. Serve the chicken covered with the sauce. Garnish with parsley sprigs and cherry tomatoes.

Serves 2	316 calories per 8 oz. serving		
Fat .... 10.8 G	Cholesterol ... 80 mg	Fiber .... 0.8 G	Diabetic exchanges:
saturated . 2.0 G	Protein .... 34.7 G	Vitamin C .. 7 mg	4 lean meat,
mono .... 6.3 G	Carbohydrate .. 8.6 G	Calcium ... 38 mg	1½ vegetable
poly ...... 1.5 G		Sodium .... 632 mg	

OVEN BARBEQUED CHICKEN

You make your own barbeque sauce for this one.

1 frying chicken, cut into
   serving pieces, skin removed
¼ cup water
¼ cup vinegar
1 tablespoon olive oil
½ cup chili sauce*

3 tablespoons Worcestershire sauce*
1 tablespoon dry mustard
1 chicken bouillon cube*
½ teaspoon freshly ground pepper
1 clove garlic, minced
¼ cup chopped onion

Combine all ingredients except chicken in a saucepan and simmer for 10 minutes. Put chicken pieces in a baking pan and pour sauce over chicken. Bake in preheated 350 degree oven uncovered, for 50-60 minutes, baste frequently.

Serves 6	266 calories per 5 oz. serving		
Fat .... 10.9 G	Cholesterol ... 101 mg	Fiber .... .5 G	Diabetic exchanges:
saturated . 2.7 G	Protein .... 33.7 G	Vitamin C .. 4 mg	4 lean meat, ½ starch
mono .... 4.7 G	Carbohydrate .. 7.2 G	Calcium ... 28 mg	
poly ...... 2.2 G		Sodium .... 588 mg	

*Indicates high sodium content

BEEF FLAVORED TURKEY

For use as ground beef substitute.

½ pound ground turkey
1 teaspoon olive oil
¼ cup chopped onions, if desired

1 teaspoon low sodium beef bouillon
water to cover

Saute the turkey in the olive oil, adding onions, if desired. Cover with water and add the bouillon and cook until the water is evaporated. For hamburger sandwich: Fry turkey patty in olive oil until done. Add low sodium beef bouillon, half cover with water and cook until the water is evaporated.

Serves 2	275 calories per 4 oz. serving		
Fat .... 17.0 G	Cholesterol ... 95 mg	Fiber .... 0 G	Diabetic exchanges:
saturated . 5.4 G	Protein .... 29.5 G	Vitamin C .. 0 mg	4 medium fat meat
mono .... 7.8 G	Carbohydrate .. 0 G	Calcium ... 33 mg	
poly ...... 3.8 G		Sodium .... 130 mg	

ITALIAN BEEFLESS

This is the best Italian beef recipe I have ever seen. Cooked this way, the turkey flavor is not present and nobody will know, unless you tell them.

½ whole turkey breast (2½ pounds)
1 package brown gravy mix
   (get a good one, not all are tasty)*
¼ cup white vinegar
1 medium onion, chopped
1 green pepper, seeded and chopped

1 clove garlic, minced
1 teaspoon oregano
1 tablespoon Worcestershire sauce*
hot pepper sauce to taste
beef bouillon cubes*
water to cover

Simmer the turkey breast in water to cover, add 1 bouillon cube for each cup water, bring to boiling, reduce heat and simmer for several hours (4-5 hours). Remove the turkey from the broth and string the meat. Add remaining ingredients, except the gravy mix, to the broth. Return the turkey to the broth and cook another 2-3 hours. Stir the brown gravy mix into ½ cup water and add it to the broth, cook 20 minutes. Serve on buns accompanied with fresh sliced onion and pepperocini.

Serves 12	172 calories per 7 oz. serving		
Fat .... 5.0 G	Cholesterol ... 73 mg	Fiber .... .1 G	Diabetic exchanges:
saturated . 1.7 G	Protein .... 28.0 G	Vitamin C .. 6 mg	3 lean meat,
mono .... 1.1 G	Carbohydrate .. 2.1 G	Calcium ... 36 mg	½ vegetable
poly ...... 1.4 G		Sodium .... 342 mg	

*Indicates high sodium content

TURKEY LOAF

Served cold, this spicy loaf could be used as a very lowfat luncheon meat.

1 pound ground turkey breast
2 green onions, minced
1 clove garlic, minced
1 teaspoon basil
¼ teaspoon lemon zest
⅛ teaspoon thyme

dash freshly ground pepper
1 egg white, slightly beaten
1 slice whole wheat bread
⅓ cup chicken broth (see recipe)*
½ chicken bouillon cube*
dissolved in the broth

Heat oven to 350 degrees. Make crumbs of the slice of bread. Combine all ingredients and pack mixture into a 1½ pint loaf pan. Put the loaf pan into a larger pan which has about 1 inch of hot water in it. Bake at 350 degrees for about 1 hour or until internal temperature is 180 degrees. Cool, serve warm or cold, thinly sliced.

Serves 6	140 calories per 4 oz. serving		
Fat .... 2.8 G	Cholesterol ... 53 mg	Fiber .... .6 G	Diabetic exchanges:
saturated . .9 G	Protein .... 24.0 G	Vitamin C .. 2 mg	2½ lean meat
mono .... .5 G	Carbohydrate .. 3.5 G	Calcium ... 30 mg	
poly...... .7 G		Sodium .... 230 mg	

SWEET AND SOUR TURKEY

A stir fry dish.

2 cups cubed, cooked turkey
2 tablespoons olive oil
1 clove garlic, minced
1 large onion, halved and sliced
1 green pepper, seeded, cut in squares
1 cup chicken stock (see recipe)*
1 teaspoon sugar

1 tablespoon vinegar
1 tablespoon cornstarch
1 tablespoon soy sauce*
1 tablespoon catsup*
1 cup cubed pineapple
1 tomato, seeded, cubed
3 cups cooked rice

Fry the turkey cubes in olive oil until lightly browned, remove from oil and drain. Add garlic and onion to oil and saute briefly, stir in peppers, stock, sugar and vinegar. Mix cornstarch with 2 tablespoons water, stir mixture into vegetables; cook and stir until thickened. Add soy sauce and catsup. Stir in turkey, pineapple and tomatoes. Cook just until hot. Serve immediately over rice.

Analysis is for sauce only. For ⅓ cup cooked rice add 80 calories.

Serves 8	129 calories per 5 oz. serving		
Fat .... 5.3 G	Cholesterol ... 27 mg	Fiber .... .9 G	Diabetic exchanges:
saturated . 1.1 G	Protein .... 11.0 G	Vitamin C .. 15 mg	1 vegetable, ¼ fruit
mono .... 2.9 G	Carbohydrate .. 9.5 G	Calcium ... 20 mg	1 lean meat, ¼ fat,
poly...... .9 G		Sodium .... 276 mg	(⅓ cup rice =
			1 starch)

*Indicates high sodium content

CURRIED TURKEY

Toasting the spices is essential. For sodium watchers, no salt is added. This curry is made for the dish.

1¼ pounds turkey breast 1" cubes
1 inch cinnamon stick
½ teaspoon cardamom seeds
1 teaspoon cumin seeds
1 teaspoon coriander seeds
3 cloves

1 teaspoon peppercorns
1 clove garlic, minced
2 tablespoons olive oil
2 cups onion rings
2 cups cooked rice

Put spices into a heavy skillet and cook over low heat, shaking frequently, until the spices are fragrant and lightly toasted, about 5 minutes. Watch carefully, as the spices burn easily. Grind the spices in the blender. Rub the ground spice into the turkey cubes, cover and refrigerate at least one hour. Heat the olive oil in a skillet and saute the turkey cubes until turkey is cooked through. Add garlic to skillet and cook briefly. Remove turkey from skillet and add more oil as needed. Saute onions just until transparent. Serve turkey and onions immediately over rice.

Analysis is for curried turkey. For ⅓ cup rice add 80 calories.

Serves 6		204 calories per 5 oz. serving			
Fat	7.8 G	Cholesterol ...	66 mg	Fiber .... .8 G	Diabetic exchanges:
saturated .	1.6 G	Protein	28.9 G	Vitamin C .. 4 mg	1 vegetable, 3¼ lean
mono	3.9 G	Carbohydrate ..	3.4 G	Calcium ... 35 mg	meat, (⅓ cup cooked
poly......	1.2 G			Sodium .... 62 mg	rice = 1 starch)

TURKEY WITH OLIVES AND TOMATOES

The flavor is more complex than it appears.

2 cups turkey cubes
1 cup black olives, pitted and halved*
1 cup peeled, seeded, chopped tomato
½ teaspoon grated orange zest
2 teaspoons tarragon
2 tablespoons olive oil

⅓ cup flour
1 cup white wine
1 chicken bouillon cube*
pepper to taste
2 tablespoons minced parsley

Heat the olive oil in a frying pan, dust the turkey with flour and cook in the hot oil until golden brown, about 5 minutes. Stir in the tarragon, tomatoes, orange zest, bouillon cube and wine. Cover and cook over low heat, stirring occasionally and adding water if necessary, until the turkey is very tender, about 1 hour. Stir in olives and season to taste with pepper. Sprinkle the parsley over the stew and serve.

Serves 5	255 calories per 6 oz. serving		
Fat .... 13.6 G	Cholesterol ... 43 mg	Fiber .... 1.7 G	Diabetic exchanges:
saturated . 2.5 G	Protein .... 18.0 G	Vitamin C .. 8 mg	2½ lean meat, 1 fat,
mono .... 7.9 G	Carbohydrate .. 9.4 G	Calcium ... 59 mg	¾ starch
poly ...... 1.9 G		Sodium .... 440 mg	

*Indicates high sodium content

WEINER SAUSAGE

Do you miss hot dogs? Here they are. The olive oil and oat bran redeems this somewhat. In spite of turkey meat being less fat, it is still saturated. If you have the equipment and the patience, these can be made into sausages with casings.

2 teaspoons freshly ground pepper
1 teaspoon coriander seeds
½ teaspoon thyme leaves
¼ teaspoon nutmeg
⅛ teaspoon cayenne pepper
¼ teaspoon cumin seed
½ teaspoon turmeric
1 teaspoon dry mustard
2 teaspoons onion powder
¼ teaspoon garlic powder

¼ teaspoon cinnamon
2 teaspoons salt*
1 teaspoon sugar
3 teaspoons paprika (for color)
1 pound ground turkey meat
2 tablespoons white vinegar
¼ cup olive oil
⅓ cup oat bran
1 egg white

Put all seeds and leaves in the blender, blend for 4 minutes. Shake the ground spices through a tea strainer, discard the residue remaining in the strainer. Add remaining herbs and spices and mix in blender for about 1 minute.

Process turkey meat in food processor in small batches, add olive oil, vinegar, egg white and spices, process, scraping down sides frequently. Add oat bran and process again. Transfer mixture to a bowl (by now the mixture is warm), cover with plastic wrap and refrigerate several hours or overnight.

Fill a shallow pan (I use a skillet) ⅔ full of cold water. Extrude the sausage mixture with a cookie press fitted with a cream puff attachment so that a ½ to ¾ inch diameter coil is formed. Place skillet on stove and heat water to simmering, simmer for about 40 minutes. About half way through cooking, cut the sausages into desired lengths. Cool and refrigerate or freeze.

Serves 10	166 calories per 2 oz. serving		
Fat .... 11.6 G	Cholesterol ... 38 mg	Fiber .... .9 G	Diabetic exchanges:
saturated . 2.8 G	Protein .... 13.0 G	Vitamin C .. 1 mg	1½ lean meat, 1½ fat
mono .... 6.5 G	Carbohydrate .. 4.0 G	Calcium ... 26 mg	¼ starch
poly ...... 2.0 G		Sodium .... 485 mg	

*Indicates high sodium content

HOT DOGS

Another version of hot dogs.

2 pounds ground turkey
2 egg whites
2 tablespoons vinegar

½ cup olive oil
2 teaspoons mustard (ball park type)
¼ teaspoon red food color (for better color)

Combine all ingredients in the bowl of the food processor and process for 5 minutes.

2 teaspoons black peppercorns
2 teaspoons coriander seeds

1 teaspoon whole thyme leaves
1 teaspoon cumin seeds

Combine spices in the blender jar and blend on highest speed for 4 minutes. Strain through a tea strainer. Set aside strained spices, discard residue.

1 teaspoon mace
1 teaspoon cinnamon
½ teaspoon cayenne pepper
1 tablespoon dry mustard
2 tablespoons paprika (for color)

2 tablespoons onion powder
½ teaspoon garlic powder
4 teaspoons salt*
4 teaspoons sugar

Combine spices, adding the strained spices also and add to the meat mixture in the food processor and process until well blended, stopping to scrape sides occasionally. Transfer mixture to a bowl, cover securely with plastic wrap and refrigerate several hours or overnight.

If you have a sausage stuffer, make weiners. If not, use a cookie press with the cream puff attachment and squeeze the meat mixture into a skillet of cold water. Have the water just deep enough to cover the weiners. Bring to just under a simmer and cook for 40 minutes. Remove from water and cool. Serve or store in the refrigerator to be used in a few days or store in the freezer for longer periods.

A simpler version of spices:
1 teaspoon freshly ground pepper
1 teaspoon cinnamon
1 teaspoon nutmeg
2 teaspoons onion powder

½ teaspoon garlic powder
4 teaspoons salt*
4 teaspoons sugar

Substitute this combination for the two lists of spices above.

Serves 20	160 calories per 2 oz. serving		
Fat .... 11.5 G	Cholesterol ... 38 mg	Fiber .... .3 G	Diabetic exchanges:
saturated . 2.8 G	Protein .... 12.0 G	Vitamin C .. 1 mg	2 lean meat, 1 fat
mono .... 6.5 G	Carbohydrate .. 2.2 G	Calcium ... 25 mg	¼ vegetable
poly ...... 2.0 G		Sodium .... 491 mg	

*Indicates high sodium content

TURKEY BREAKFAST SAUSAGE

Country sausage flavor.

½ pound ground turkey
1 heaping teaspoon dried sage

½ teaspoon freshly ground pepper
1 tablespoon olive oil

Combine all ingredients. Use fresh, refrigerate, or freeze in patties. Fry in a non stick skillet; most of the olive oil will fry out.

Serves 3	211 calories per 3 oz. serving		
Fat .... 14.4 G	Cholesterol ... 64 mg	Fiber .... .1 G	Diabetic exchanges:
saturated . 4.0 G	Protein .... 19.7 G	Vitamin C .. 0 mg	2¾ lean meat
mono .... 7.4 G	Carbohydrate .. .4 G	Calcium ... 27 mg	
poly ...... 2.8 G		Sodium .... 87 mg	

SAUSAGE GRAVY AND BISCUITS

The secret of good gravy is long simmering.

4 biscuits (see recipe)
4 ounces turkey breakfast sausage
  (see recipe)
1 tablespoon flour

1 cup skim milk
freshly ground pepper
salt to taste

Saute sausage, crumbling it into small pieces. Combine flour and skim milk and add to the cooked sausage. Simmer, stirring constantly. Add salt and pepper to taste. The longer it simmers, the better. Serve over biscuits.

Analysis does not include biscuit.

Serves 4	123 calories per ½ cup serving		
Fat .... 7.2 G	Cholesterol ... 25 mg	Fiber .... 0 G	Diabetic exchanges:
saturated . 1.8 G	Protein .... 9.7 G	Vitamin C .. 1 mg	1 lean meat, 1 fat,
mono .... 4.1 G	Carbohydrate .. 4.7 G	Calcium ... 88 mg	¼ low fat milk
poly ...... 1.5 G		Sodium .... 64 mg	

SHRIMP-SCALLOP SPAGHETTI

Right out of Mediterranean cooking.

1 tablespoon olive oil
½ pound fresh spinach
salt and pepper to taste*
1 clove garlic
1 tablespoon olive oil
8 small shrimp, peeled and deveined
½ cup bay scallops
¼ cup chopped red bell pepper

1 teaspoon oregano
1 clove garlic
2 tablespoons white wine
1 chicken bouillon cube in ⅓ cup water*
½ cup skim milk
1 teaspoon flour
parmesan cheese
spaghetti

Cook spaghetti according to package directions, drain and arrange on plate.

While spaghetti is cooking, heat 1 tablespoon olive oil in saute pan, add spinach, garlic, salt and pepper and saute until spinach is wilted. Arrange over spaghetti on plate.

Heat 1 tablespoon olive oil in saute pan, saute shrimp, scallops, pepper, oregano and garlic until shrimp is pink and scallops are opaque. Add white wine to deglaze pan. Add chicken bouillon in water, cook briefly. Stir flour into milk and add to pan, cook until thickened. Pour over spinach/spaghetti.Sprinkle with freshly grated parmesan cheese.

Analysis is for sauce only.

Serves 6	117 calories per ½ cup serving		
Fat .... 5.4 G	Cholesterol ... 67 mg	Fiber .... 1.4 G	Diabetic exchanges:
saturated . .8 G	Protein .... 12.6 G	Vitamin C .. 19 mg	1¾ lean meat,
mono .... 3.5 G	Carbohydrate .. 4.1 G	Calcium ... 88 mg	1 vegetable, (½ cup
poly ...... .7 G		Sodium .... 331 mg	spaghetti = 1 starch)

*Indicates high sodium content

CURRIED SCALLOPS

If you liked your introduction to curry, (see Curried Chicken with Bananas) try it now with seafood.

2 tablespoons olive oil
1 pound sea or bay scallops
2 teaspoons curry powder (or to taste)
¼ cup dry white wine or chicken broth*

1 tablespoon lemon juice
1 tablespoon chopped parsley
2 cups cooked rice

Dry the scallops; if using sea scallops, cut them into quarters. Heat the olive oil, add the scallops and cook 2-3 minutes, stirring constantly. Add curry and mix well, cooking a few minutes more. Remove scallops and keep warm. Add wine or broth, lemon juice and parsley to the same skillet. Stir, scraping any particles from the bottom of the pan, mixing sauce together. Pour sauce over scallops and serve at once over hot rice.

Analysis does not include rice; for ⅓ cup cooked rice add 80 calories

Serves 4		202 calories per 4 oz. serving		
Fat .... 8.1 G	Cholesterol ... 50 mg	Fiber .... .4 G	Diabetic exchanges:
saturated . 1.0 G	Protein .... 26.0 G	Vitamin C .. 3 mg	3½ lean meat, ¼ fat,
mono .... 5.1 G	Carbohydrate .. 4.5 G	Calcium ... 42 mg	(⅓ cup cooked rice
poly...... 1.0 G		Sodium .... 225 mg	= 1 starch)

SEAFOOD SALSA

Real Italian sauces don't contain meat. They are more like this.

12 bay scallops (4 ounces)
12 shrimp, peeled (4 ounces)
½ pound white fish
1 lobster tail
1 large onion, diced
12 mushrooms, sliced

1 rounded teaspoon basil, hand rubbed
freshly ground pepper to taste
3 tomatoes, peeled
1 tablespoon olive oil
salt to taste*

Saute the onions and mushrooms in olive oil, add tomatoes, basil, salt and pepper. Simmer for 20 minutes then add the seafood; cook 10 minutes. Serve over spaghetti.

Analysis does not include pasta. For ½ cup cooked pasta add 80 calories.

Serves 6		158 calories per 7 oz. serving		
Fat .... 4.2 G	Cholesterol ... 81 mg	Fiber .... 1.4 G	Diabetic exchanges:
saturated . .6 G	Protein .... 23.4 G	Vitamin C .. 13 mg	1 vegetable, 2½ lean
mono .... 2.1 G	Carbohydrate .. 5.2 G	Calcium ... 22 mg	meat, (½ cup pasta
poly...... .8 G		Sodium .... 219 mg	= 1 starch)

*Indicates high sodium content

PETE'S SHRIMP

This was put together one night in Florida because everyone else was going to boil shrimp in beer—then they wanted mine.

12 shrimp, peeled and deveined
1 tablespoon olive oil
1 teaspoon oregano
juice of ½ lemon

1 clove garlic, minced
2 canned tomatoes*
1 chicken bouillon cube*

Saute shrimp in olive oil with oregano and lemon juice. Add ½ of the minced garlic clove, tomatoes and bouillon cube. Cook shrimp just until done, then remove them and cook the sauce to thicken. Lastly, stir in the remaining minced garlic and the cooked shrimp. Serve over pasta or rice.

Serves 3		153 calories per 6 oz. serving			
Fat.........	6.0 G	Cholesterol ... 174 mg	Fiber .... .8 G	Diabetic exchanges:
saturated .	1.0 G	Protein .... 19.7 G	Vitamin C .. 19 mg	2½ lean meat,
mono	3.6 G	Carbohydrate .. 5.3 G	Calcium ... 65 mg	½ vegetable
poly......	1.0 G		Sodium .... 669 mg	

MARINATED FISH STEAK

Most of the marinade will drain off, but the flavor remains.

4 fresh fish steaks (swordfish, tuna, halibut, etc. at least ¾ inch thick)

Marinade:
2 tablespoons soy sauce*
2 tablespoons fresh orange juice
1 tablespoon olive oil
1 tablespoon tomato paste*
1 tablespoon minced fresh parsley

1 clove garlic, crushed
½ teaspoon fresh lemon juice
¼ teaspoon dried oregano
¼ teaspoon freshly ground pepper

Whisk together the marinade ingredients until they are well combined. Put the fish in a shallow dish so that it is in one layer. Pour the marinade ingredients over, cover and allow it to set for 1 hour, turning it once. Remove the fish steaks and broil or grill them according to your preference, until they flake easily.

Analysis is for the marinade which will drain off, mostly.

Makes ½ cup		29 calories per 2 teaspoons			
Fat.........	2.3 G	Cholesterol ... 0 mg	Fiber .... .2 G	Diabetic exchanges:
saturated .	.3 G	Protein .... .5 G	Vitamin C .. 5 mg	½ fat, ¼ vegetable
mono	1.7 G	Carbohydrate .. 2.0 G	Calcium ... 6 mg	
poly......	.2 G		Sodium .... 345 mg	

*Indicates high sodium content

BROILED FISH WITH SESAME SEEDS

Sesame seeds add flavor, not calories.

4 (3 ounce) 1 inch thick fish steaks   **olive oil**
lemon juice   **sesame seeds**

Choose fish filets or steaks which are at least 1 inch thick; thicker may not get done on inside, thinner will dry out. Drizzle with lemon juice, coat well with olive oil. Broil 5 minutes on each side, depending upon the distance from broiler. Coat the fish with sesame seeds after broiling the fish and broil until the seeds are brown, about 1 minute more.

Analysis is for haddock.

Serves 4	119 calories per 3 oz. serving		
Fat .... 3.1 G	Cholesterol ... 63 mg	Fiber .... 0 G	Diabetic exchanges:
saturated . .4 G	Protein .... 22.8 G	Vitamin C .. 1 mg	3 lean meat
mono .... 1.8 G	Carbohydrate .. 0 G	Calcium ... 36 mg	
poly ...... .4 G		Sodium .... 74 mg	

BROILED FISH WITH TERMINAL GARLIC

Garlic added at the end enhances the flavor of most dishes, especially this one.

4 (4 ounce) fish fillets   **freshly ground pepper**
  (cod, haddock, etc.)   **olive oil**
lemon juice   **1 clove garlic**

Drizzle lemon juice on fish fillets. Sprinkle with freshly ground pepper and brush with olive oil. Broil until it flakes; turn once. Do not overcook. Put a clove of garlic in the garlic press and distribute it evenly over fish after broiling is done. Serve immediately with lemon wedges and salt to taste at the table.

Analysis is for cod.

Serves 4	142 calories per 4 oz. serving		
Fat .... 3.2 G	Cholesterol ... 62 mg	Fiber .... 0 G	Diabetic exchanges:
saturated . .5 G	Protein .... 26.0 G	Vitamin C .. 2 mg	3½ lean meat
mono .... 1.8 G	Carbohydrate .. .7 G	Calcium ... 17 mg	
poly ...... .5 G		Sodium .... 89 mg	

BROILED SCROD FILLETS

Fresh scrod has a "pungent" odor which disappears when cooked.

1 pound scrod fillets
¼ cup olive oil
2 teaspoons Worcestershire sauce

2 teaspoons lemon juice
dash hot pepper sauce
¼ teaspoon garlic powder

Place fish fillets on broiler rack. Combine remaining ingredients and brush on fillets. Broil until fish flakes; turn once. Do not overcook. Brush once during broiling.

Since fish is brushed with sauce, analysis is just for cod.

Serves 6		89 calories per 3 oz. serving					
Fat	.7 G	Cholesterol ...	47 mg	Fiber	0 G	Diabetic exchanges:	
saturated .	.1 G	Protein	19.0 G	Vitamin C ..	1 mg	3 lean meat	
mono	.1 G	Carbohydrate ..	0 G	Calcium ...	12 mg		
poly......	.2 G			Sodium	66 mg		

FISH FILLETS WITH ANCHOVY DRESSING

If you're watching your sodium, avoid this sauce.

1 cup olive oil
¼ cup fresh lemon juice
4 anchovy fillets*
2 cloves garlic
freshly ground pepper to taste
½ cup packed fresh parsley leaves
¼ cup snipped fresh chives

¼ cup minced fresh basil
flour
6 (3 ounce) ocean perch fillets
olive oil
1 pound spinach, washed and stemmed, patted dry

Combine the first 5 ingredients in the blender and process until smooth. Add parsley and blend until chopped very fine. Add chives and basil and blend until just incorporated. Dust the fish with flour. Heat a small amount of olive oil in a skillet and cook the fish until golden brown on both sides about 2½ minutes per side. Transfer to a heated platter. In the microwave, cook the spinach just until wilted. Divide the spinach among plates, top with fish. Sprinkle fish with pepper. Spoon dressing over fish and serve immediately.

Analysis is for sauce only.

Makes 1¼ cup		97 calories per 1 tablespoon					
Fat.........	10.8 G	Cholesterol ...	0 mg	Fiber	.1 G	Diabetic exchanges:	
saturated .	1.5 G	Protein	.1 G	Vitamin C ..	3 mg	2 fat	
mono	8.0 G	Carbohydrate ..	.7 G	Calcium ...	7 mg		
poly......	.9 G			Sodium ....227 mg			

*Indicates high sodium content

POACHED SALMON

A fish poaching pan is best, but a large enough pan with a rack will do if cheesecloth is wrapped around the fish so it will hold its shape.

whole fresh salmon fillet
2 cups dry white wine
4 carrots, sliced
3 onions, sliced
bay leaf
parsley, 10-12 sprigs

10 peppercorns
chicken bouillon cubes
(usually 1 cube to 1 cup water,
but in this recipe I use 1 cube
for 2 cups of water.)
water to cover

Combine all ingredients (except the fish) and simmer for 20-30 minutes to blend, remove the vegetables and peppercorns. Place the cheesecloth wrapped fish in the prepared poaching liquid and simmer gently for 25-30 minutes or until the fish flakes easily. Allow the fish to remain in the poaching liquid for up to 45 minutes until served. Serve with dill sauce. (see recipe)

Analysis is for coho salmon.

244 calories per 4 oz. serving			
Fat .... 8.6 G	Cholesterol ... 56 mg	Fiber .... 0 G	Diabetic exchanges:
saturated . 1.6 G	Protein .... 31.0 G	Vitamin C .. 1 mg	4 lean meat
mono .... 3.0 G	Carbohydrate .. 0 G	Calcium ... 33 mg	
poly...... 2.5 G		Sodium .... 67 mg	

BROILED SALMON

All salmon taste good, but have nutritional differences. See tables in this book.

4 (4 ounce) salmon steaks
2 teaspoons olive oil

pepper
2 teaspoons lemon juice

Drizzle lemon juice over steaks. Brush olive oil over steaks. Broil 5 minutes on each side or until done. Add salt and pepper at table. Serve with dill sauce. (see recipe)

Analysis is for pink salmon.

Serves 4	152 calories per 4 oz. serving		
Fat .... 6.2 G	Cholesterol ... 59 mg	Fiber .... 0 G	Diabetic exchanges:
saturated . .9 G	Protein .... 22.6 G	Vitamin C .. 3 mg	3 lean meat
mono .... 2.7 G	Carbohydrate .. .2 G	Calcium ... 46 mg	
poly...... 1.7 G		Sodium .... 76 mg	

BATTER FRIED FISH

There are beer batter aficionados who swear by their favorite brew, but I have found that any carbonated beverage will do. I even used orange pop once and couldn't tell the difference! Keep in mind that flour holds the oil.

4 fish fillets (4 ounces each)   ⅔ cup carbonated beverage
½ cup flour   garlic powder (optional)
½ teaspoon salt*

Mix batter ingredients to thick liquid consistency. Dip fish in flour before dipping them in batter so the batter will stick. Fry in olive oil, of course. Salt at table.

Analysis is for perch.

Serves 4	224 calories per 4 oz. serving		
Fat......... 8.8 G	Cholesterol ... 48 mg	Fiber .... .4 G	Diabetic exchanges:
saturated . 1.2 G	Protein .... 22.8 G	Vitamin C .. 3 mg	3 lean meat, ¾ starch
mono .... 5.7 G	Carbohydrate .. 12.0 G	Calcium ... 128 mg	
poly...... 1.1 G		Sodium .... 360 mg	

FRIED FISH OR SMELTS

Frozen smelt have an odor that says you got there too late, but this method will surprisingly eradicate the smell. We do this with cut up bits of fish also.

1 lb. smelts   ½ cup flour
1 teaspoon garlic powder   2 tablespoons olive oil
freshly ground pepper

Sprinkle the fish with garlic powder and pepper to taste. Put flour in a bag, add the fish and shake to coat. Fry the fish in the olive oil until crisp. At the table, sprinkle with vinegar and salt, if desired.

Analysis is for smelt.

Serves 4	200 calories per 4 oz. serving		
Fat......... 9.6 G	Cholesterol ... 79 mg	Fiber .... 0 G	Diabetic exchanges:
saturated . 1.4 G	Protein .... 20.0 G	Vitamin C .. 0 mg	3 lean meat, ½ starch
mono .... 5.7 G	Carbohydrate .. 6.5 G	Calcium ... 70 mg	
poly...... 1.6 G		Sodium .... 68 mg	

*Indicates high sodium content

PAN FRIED HALIBUT

This recipe compares favorably with the best prepared halibut I have ever tasted. I like it straight, but tartar sauce or dill sauce goes well. (See recipes.)

fresh halibut steaks
   ¾ to 1 inch thick
garlic powder

flour
1-2 tablespoons olive oil
lemon juice

Drizzle a little lemon juice on fish steaks. Sprinkle with garlic powder and allow to set 20 minutes. Put olive oil in non stick skillet and heat. Lightly flour fish steaks and pan broil until browned.

125 calories per 3 oz. serving							
Fat	5.2 G	Cholesterol	24 mg	Fiber	.1 G	Diabetic exchanges:	
saturated	.7 G	Protein	16.0 G	Vitamin C	2 mg	¼ starch, 2 lean meat	
mono	3.0 G	Carbohydrate	2.7 G	Calcium	37 mg		
poly	.9 G			Sodium	41 mg		

MACKEREL PATTIES

Canned mackerel can be used in patties in place of salmon and since it has a high EPA level, there is good reason to use it. This has EPA, olive oil and oat bran: you can't get much better than that!

1 can mackerel (or salmon)
1 small onion, diced finely
1 egg white
½ teaspoon celery seed
oat bran to consistency

1 teaspoon low sodium
   chicken bouillon granules
1 teaspoon lemon juice
1 tablespoon olive oil

Drain mackerel, reserving liquid. Put mackerel into bowl and break it up with a fork. Stir in onion, egg white, bouillon, celery seed and lemon juice and mix thoroughly. Add reserved liquid, stir well; add enough oat bran so that the mixture can be shaped into patties. Fry the patties in olive oil until browned.

Serves 6		**137 calories per patty**					
Fat	6.4 G	Cholesterol	48 mg	Fiber	1.4 G	Diabetic exchanges:	
saturated	1.4 G	Protein	16.0 G	Vitamin C	1 mg	2 lean meat	
mono	3.5 G	Carbohydrate	6.0 G	Calcium	155 mg		
poly	.4 G			Sodium	239 mg		

PORK TENDERLOIN MARINADE I

Battuto is Italian for "pound." In this case, you pound the flavoring in a mortar and pestle.

1-2 pound pork tenderloin (or turkey breast)

BATTUTO

2 tablespoons parsley
2 tablespoons green onion, with tops
½ bay leaf, crumbled
2 tablespoons fresh thyme
¼ teaspoon black pepper
¼ teaspoon mace

½ teaspoon dry mustard
½ teaspoon dry lemon peel
4 tablespoons olive oil
1 tablespoon lemon juice or vinegar
1 clove garlic, minced

Make tiny slashes on meat. Using a mortar and pestle or blender, make a paste of the battuto ingredients. Smear battuto paste over meat. Wrap meat in plastic wrap and put in the refrigerator several hours or overnight for the flavor to penetrate. Remove, place in an oven roasting bag, insert meat thermometer through a hole in the bag and roast the meat at 325 degrees until internal temperature is 170 degrees.

Analysis is for marinade, most of which will run off. For pork analysis, see roast pork recipe.

Makes ¼ cup	173 calories per 2 tablespoons		
Fat .... 18.0 G	Cholesterol ... 0 mg	Fiber .... .9 G	Diabetic exchanges:
saturated . 2.5 G	Protein .... .5 G	Vitamin C .. 7 mg	4 fat
mono .... 13.3 G	Carbohydrate .. 32.0 G	Calcium ... 63 mg	
poly ...... 1.6 G		Sodium .... 3 mg	

PORK TENDERLOIN MARINADE II

The combination of herbs and spices is limited only by your imagination.

1-2 pound pork tenderloin
1 teaspoon grated lemon peel
½ teaspoon cumin seed
1 teaspoon marjoram

½ teaspoon ground ginger
4 tablespoons olive oil
4 tablespoons lemon juice
1 clove garlic, minced

Make several small slashes in the meat. Combine remaining ingredients and spread over meat. Wrap with plastic wrap and then with foil. Refrigerate overnight. Place meat in an oven roasting bag, place meat thermometer through hole in bag and roast at 325 degrees until internal temperature is 170 degrees. Let set at room temperature for 15 minutes, slice and serve.

Analysis is for marinade, most of which will run off. See roast pork recipe for pork analysis.

Makes ½ cup	126 calories per 2 tablespoons			
Fat .... 13.6 G	Cholesterol ... 0 mg	Fiber .... .1 G	Diabetic exchanges:
saturated . 1.8 G	Protein .... .2 G	Vitamin C .. 8 mg	2½ fat, ½ vegetable
mono .... 9.9 G	Carbohydrate .. 1.9 G	Calcium ... 7 mg	
poly...... 1.2 G		Sodium .... 0 mg	

DRY MARINADE FOR PORK TENDERLOIN

This powdery addition sticks to the meat because the meat has been rubbed with olive oil.

1-2 pound pork tenderloin
olive oil
1 teaspoon garlic powder
½ teaspoon celery seed
½ teaspoon curry powder

1 teaspoon ground ginger
¼ teaspoon cayenne pepper
½ teaspoon lemon peel
2 heaping tablespoons fine bread crumbs

Rub the meat with olive oil. Combine the remaining ingredients and sprinkle over meat. Allow to stand for 1 hour. Place the meat in an oven baking bag, insert a meat thermometer through one of the holes and bake the roast at 325 degrees until the internal temperature is 170 degrees.

Analysis is for pork marinade, most fat will run off.

Makes ⅓ cup	303 calories per recipe			
Fat .... 28.0 G	Cholesterol ... 0 mg	Fiber .... 1.1 G	Diabetic exchanges:
saturated . 3.9 G	Protein .... 2.2 G	Vitamin C .. 2 mg	5½ fat, ¾ starch
mono .... 20.2 G	Carbohydrate .. 12.2 G	Calcium ... 36 mg	
poly...... 2.5 G		Sodium .... 95 mg	

CHINESE PORK AND BROCCOLI

If you are watching your sodium intake, using a low sodium soy sauce will reduce sodium only a small amount.

1 bunch broccoli
4 (2 oz.) pork tenderloin medallions
1 clove garlic, minced
2 teaspoons cornstarch
½ teaspoon sugar
2 tablespoons soy sauce*
2 tablespoons water
2 tablespoons olive oil

4 scallions, sliced
2 teaspoons grated fresh ginger
2 tablespoons soy sauce*
1 tablespoon cornstarch
½ cup chicken broth (see recipe)*
¼ cup water
3 cups cooked rice

Wash and trim broccoli, cut into bite size pieces. Cut meat into strips, 1 x ½ inch. In a small bowl, combine the 2 teaspoons cornstarch, sugar, 2 tablespoons soy sauce, garlic and 2 tablespoons water; add pork strips and toss to coat, set aside. Heat the 1 tablespoon olive oil in a large skillet or wok; stir pork and marinade mixture; brown in the hot oil; remove from skillet and set aside. Add 1 tablespoon olive oil to skillet and saute scallions and ginger, stir fry about a minute. Combine the remaining soy sauce, cornstarch, chicken broth and water; add to skillet and stir until thickened. Add pork and heat through. Serve over rice.

Analysis does not include rice. ⅓ cup cooked rice = 80 calories.

Serves 6	169 calories per 5 oz. serving		
Fat .... 10.2 G	Cholesterol ... 40 mg	Fiber .... .9 G	Diabetic exchanges:
saturated . 2.5 G	Protein .... 14.0 G	Vitamin C .. 23 mg	2 medium fat meat,
mono .... 5.8 G	Carbohydrate .. 5.4 G	Calcium ... 21 mg	½ vegetable, (⅓ cup
poly ...... 1.1 G		Sodium .... 791 mg	cooked rice = 1 starch)

*Indicates high sodium content

PORK WITH SWEET RED PEPPERS

The tenderloin of pork is very low in fat.

3 large cloves garlic
½ teaspoon salt*
½ teaspoon freshly ground pepper
4 teaspoons olive oil
6 pork tenderloin slices,
   about ½ inch thick (3 ounces)

4 red peppers, seeded
   and cut into ¼ inch strips
½ cup dry white wine
½ cup chicken stock (see recipe)*
1-2 teaspoons finely shredded lemon zest

Blend the garlic cloves, salt, pepper and 2 teaspoons olive oil in the blender until the garlic is finely chopped. Place the pork in a single layer on waxed paper and spread the garlic mixture over it. Cover with waxed paper and marinate overnight in the refrigerator or for 2-3 hours at room temperature. Heat 2 teaspoons olive oil in a large skillet over moderate heat and saute the pork until it is deeply golden (4-6 minutes on each side.) Remove the pork and saute the pepper strips for about 5 minutes and remove them from the skillet. Add the wine and broth to the skillet and bring to a boil. Return the pork and peppers to the skillet and reduce the heat to low. Simmer until the pork is tender, 15-20 minutes. Remove the pork and peppers to a heated plate and keep warm. Boil the remaining liquid until it is reduced to ¾ cup. Spoon it over the pork and peppers, sprinkle with lemon zest and serve hot.

Serves 6	288 calories per 5 oz. serving		
Fat .... 15.7 G	Cholesterol ... 90 mg	Fiber .... 1.0 G	Diabetic exchanges:
saturated . 4.7 G	Protein .... 28.6 G	Vitamin C .. 1 mg	½ fat, 1 vegetable,
mono .... 7.8 G	Carbohydrate .. 3.6 G	Calcium ... 17 mg	2½ lean meat
poly ...... 1.9 G		Sodium .... 132 mg	

POLYNESIAN BARBECUED PORK TENDERLOIN

Pork tenderloin is low fat meat.

1 pound tenderloin of pork, sliced
¼ cup barbecue sauce (commercial)*
2 tablespoons soy sauce*

1 teaspoon ground ginger
1 tablespoon brown sugar or
   ½ teaspoon brown sugar substitute

Combine meat and remaining ingredients in sauce pan and simmer one hour. Let set overnight in the refrigerator. Reheat and serve. This may be served right after cooking, but the flavor is better the next day.

Serves 6	152 calories per 4 oz. serving		
Fat .... 4.2 G	Cholesterol ... 71 mg	Fiber .... .1 G	Diabetic exchanges:
saturated . 1.5 G	Protein .... 22.3 G	Vitamin C .. 1 mg	3 lean meat, 1 vegetable
mono .... 1.8 G	Carbohydrate .. 4.9 G	Calcium ... 8 mg	
poly ...... .6 G		Sodium .... 565 mg	

*Indicates high sodium content

PORK MARSALA

If you use a non stick pan, you can eliminate 240 calories of olive oil or 40 per serving.

6 pork tenderloin medallions 　(3 oz. ea.) 2 tablespoons olive oil 1 clove garlic, minced 1 tablespoon tomato paste*	¼ cup Marsala ½ cup beef stock (see recipe)* 1 cup sliced mushrooms 1 teaspoon chopped parsley

Pound tenderloin slices to ¼ inch thickness. Heat oil in saute pan, brown pork slices on both sides, remove from pan. Add garlic and saute briefly (do not brown), mix tomato paste with Marsala and beef broth, add to pan along with mushrooms. Stir to blend with pan juices, simmer 3-5 minutes. Return pork slices to pan and heat through. Sprinkle with chopped parsley and serve immediately.

Serves 6	268 calories per 4 oz. serving		
Fat .... 15.6 G	Cholesterol ... 80 mg	Fiber .... .3 G	Diabetic exchanges:
saturated . 4.4 G	Protein .... 25.4 G	Vitamin C .. 2 mg	3 medium fat meat,
mono .... 8.3 G	Carbohydrate .. 2.5 G	Calcium ... 11 mg	½ fat, 1 vegetable
poly...... 1.8 G		Sodium .... 156 mg	

ROAST PORK TENDERLOIN WITH GARLIC

Many flavorings for pork are used; we like this one because it's not only tasty, but simple, too.

1-2 pound pork tenderloin 1-2 cloves garlic, slivered	freshly ground pepper to taste

With the point of a paring knife, cut deep punctures in the pork tenderloin and insert a sliver of garlic into the holes. Make insertions about 1½ inches apart. Sprinkle pepper to taste on the roast. Allow to sit for about an hour. Put the roast in an oven cooking bag, insert a meat thermometer through one of the holes and roast at 325 degrees until internal temperature is 170 degrees. Allow to rest for 15 minutes after removing from oven. Slice and serve.

Serves 4-8	141 calories per 3 oz. serving		
Fat .... 4.1 G	Cholesterol ... 79 mg	Fiber .... 0 G	Diabetic exchanges:
saturated . 1.4 G	Protein .... 24.0 G	Vitamin C .. 0 mg	3 lean meat
mono .... 1.8 G	Carbohydrate .. 0 G	Calcium ... 5 mg	
poly...... .5 G		Sodium .... 57 mg	

*Indicates high sodium content

PORK AND CABBAGE CASSEROLE

This was developed by a famous chef in the late 1800's, adapted here.

8 cabbage leaves
6 pork tenderloin medallions
   (3 oz. each)
water
freshly ground pepper

1 cup evaporated skim milk
1 tablespoon olive oil
¼-½ cup white wine
large pinch sage
2 tablespoons Butter Buds®*

Take the outer leaves of a young cabbage and slice them fine. Boil them in salted water for 7 minutes. Drain. Add salt, pepper and milk and barely simmer 25-30 minutes. Saute well trimmed pork in olive oil about 15 minutes until well browned and cooked through. Remove from pan. Add white wine and sage to pan and deglaze, add this to the cabbage mixture along with the Butter Buds®. Simmer a couple of minutes. Spread ½ cabbage mixture over bottom of oven proof casserole, layer pork and then the rest of the cabbage. Bake in 350 degree oven for 20 minutes.

Since the milk in this dish will curdle, remove the pork from the casserole, put remaining ingredients in the blender and puree to sauce and serve over pork.

Serves 6	214 calories per 3 oz. serving		
Fat .... 10.4 G	Cholesterol ... 60 mg	Fiber .... .4 G	Diabetic exchanges:
saturated . 3.1 G	Protein .... 21.5 G	Vitamin C .. 5 mg	3 lean meat, ½ fat,
mono .... 5.3 G	Carbohydrate .. 5.8 G	Calcium ... 135 mg	1 vegetable
poly...... 1.2 G		Sodium .... 94 mg	

BSLT

Not exactly BLT, but close enough so that you don't go mad in the summer.

2 toasted bread slices
2 tomato slices
1 tablespoon olive oil mayonnaise
   (see recipe)

1 lettuce leaf
1 tablespoon bacon bit substitute*

Assemble the sandwich by shaking the bacon bit substitute pieces onto the mayonnaise so they will stick. Add lettuce and tomato slices.

Serves 1	227 calories per sandwich		
Fat .... 5.8 G	Cholesterol ... 2 mg	Fiber .... 1.8 G	Diabetic exchanges:
saturated . 1.2 G	Protein .... 9.6 G	Vitamin C .. 7 mg	2 starch, ½ fat
mono .... 2.0 G	Carbohydrate .. 33.4 G	Calcium ... 85 mg	
poly...... .7 G		Sodium .... 460 mg	

*Indicates high sodium content

TACOS WITH BEANS

Commercially prepared tortilla shells can add fat. Check the label. There are some made only with ground corn and water. Until you put on the cheese, this is very low fat.

1 16 oz. can red beans, drained*
2 teaspoons onion powder
¼ teaspoon garlic powder
2 tablespoons green pepper,
  chopped fine
¾ cup canned tomatoes, chopped*

¼ teaspoon cumin
½ teaspoon oregano, hand rubbed
24 coriander seeds, crushed
  in a mortar and pestle
1 beef bouillon cube*
hot sauce to taste

Combine and cook all ingredients except the tortilla shells for 20 minutes.

Fill shells with a spoonful of the bean sauce, chopped tomato, chopped lettuce and low fat shredded cheese, if desired. Top with salsa (see recipe).

Analysis is for the filling.

Makes 10		57 calories per taco			
Fat	.3 G	Cholesterol ...	0 mg	Fiber .... 3.6 G	Diabetic exchanges:
saturated .	.1 G	Protein	3.8 G	Vitamin C .. 4 mg	⅔ starch,
mono	.1 G	Carbohydrate ..	10.0 G	Calcium ... 18 mg	(taco shell =
poly	.1 G			Sodium .... 126 mg	1 starch,1 fat)

"BEEFLESS" STROGANOFF

If done right, your guests will believe they are eating beef.

20 beef flavored soy protein cubes
12 mushrooms, sliced
1 can evaporated skim milk
garlic powder
nutmeg to taste
  (be careful, not too much)

2 tablespoons olive oil
salt and pepper to taste*
1 beef bouillon cube*
1-2 teaspoons low salt beef bouillon

Cover cubes with water, allow to soak 20 minutes, drain well. Saute the soy protein cubes in the olive oil. Add the sliced mushrooms and saute them. Add evaporated milk, beef bouillon, garlic, pepper and nutmeg. The evaporated skim milk may be a little sweet; a teaspoon of lemon juice may be added if necessary. Some people prefer to add dill rather than nutmeg. Serve over eggless fettucini or eggless noodles.

Serves 4		161 calories per 4 oz. serving			
Fat	7.1 G	Cholesterol ...	4 mg	Fiber .... .3 G	Diabetic exchanges:
saturated .	1.1 G	Protein	7.0 G	Vitamin C .. 2 mg	1 lean meat, ½ fat
mono	5.1 G	Carbohydrate ..	11.4 G	Calcium . 249 mg	1 low fat milk
poly	.6 G			Sodium .... 353 mg	

*Indicates high sodium content

TOFU STROGANOFF

This tastes better than it looks, to paraphrase Mark Twain.

½ pound tofu, cut into ¾ inch cubes
2 tablespoons olive oil
8-10 large mushrooms, sliced
1 clove garlic, minced
2 tablespoons flour
2-3 teaspoons chicken flavored
   bouillon granules*

½ teaspoon dry chervil
¼ teaspoon freshly ground pepper
¾ cup skim milk
1-2 tablespoons low fat yogurt (optional)

Drain the tofu well on paper towels. Heat oil in a skillet, saute tofu until starting to brown on all sides. Remove tofu from skillet and set aside. Add mushrooms to skillet and saute until soft, add garlic, stir and immediately remove mushrooms and garlic from skillet. Combine the bouillon granules, flour, chervil and pepper, stir in the skim milk gradually, stirring until well blended. Add milk mixture to pan and bring to a boil, stirring constantly. Add tofu, mushrooms and garlic and mix thoroughly; cook to sauce consistency. Add yogurt if you are using it, stir. Serve over noodles.

Analysis is for sauce only. Add 80 calories for ½ cup noodles.

Serves 4	142 calories per ½ cup serving		
Fat .... 9.8 G	Cholesterol ... 1 mg	Fiber .... 1.1 G	Diabetic exchanges:
saturated . 1.4 G	Protein .... 7.2 G	Vitamin C .. 1 mg	1 vegetable, 1 medium
mono .... 5.7 G	Carbohydrate .. 7.6 G	Calcium ... 127 mg	fat meat, 1 fat, (½ cup
poly ...... 2.2 G		Sodium .... 170 mg	noodles = 1 starch)

*Indicates high sodium content

BRAISED TEXTURED "BEEF TIPS"

This is a fooler—your guests will think they are eating beef.

20 beef flavored soy protein cubes
2 tablespoons olive oil
1 medium onion, chopped
12 mushrooms, sliced
⅛ green pepper, finely diced
⅓ carrot, sliced thin and diced
½ stalk celery, sliced thin
½ cup canned tomatoes*

1 beef bouillon cube*
1-2 teaspoons low salt beef bouillon
garlic powder
salt (taste first, may not be necessary)*
freshly ground pepper
1 package brown gravy mix*
water to cover

Cover the soy protein cubes with water and allow to soak 20 minutes. Drain well. Saute the cubes in the olive oil to improve the texture. Place all ingredients except brown gravy mix into a sauce pan and simmer 20 minutes. Stir gravy mix into ½ cup water and add to the saucepan, stirring thoroughly. Simmer 2 more minutes.

Serve over biscuits or mashed potatoes.

Serves 4	99 calories per 5 oz. serving				
Fat	7.3 G	Cholesterol ... 0 mg	Fiber	1.7 G	Diabetic exchanges:
saturated .	1.1 G	Protein .... 1.9 G	Vitamin C ..	17 mg	½ lean meat, 1 fat,
mono	5.1 G	Carbohydrate .. 6.8 G	Calcium ...	23 mg	2 vegetable
poly......	.7 G		Sodium	600 mg	

"BEEFLESS" BURGUNDY

This doesn't have to be cooked for hours since the soy protein cooks rapidly.

20 beef flavored soy protein cubes
1 large onion, chopped
½ teaspoon salt*
10 twists pepper
2 tablespoons olive oil
½ teaspoon marjoram, hand rubbed

1 teaspoon thyme
1 cup burgundy or other red wine
1 beef bouillon cube in 1 cup water*
½ pound mushrooms, sliced
1 package brown gravy mix*

Simmer soy protein cubes in beef broth for 10 minutes. Drain. Saute soy cubes and onions in olive oil. Add marjoram, thyme and pepper. Stir in mushrooms and wine. Simmer 5 minutes more. Add brown gravy mix which has been dissolved in small amount of water. Simmer 5-10 minutes more. Serve with eggless noodles, rice or mashed potatoes.

Serves 4	153 calories per 8 oz. serving				
Fat	7.6 G	Cholesterol ... 1 mg	Fiber	.9 G	Diabetic exchanges:
saturated .	1.2 G	Protein .... 2.3 G	Vitamin C ..	3 mg	½ lean meat, 2 fat,
mono	5.2 G	Carbohydrate .. 7.7 G	Calcium ...	43 mg	½ starch
poly......	.6 G		Sodium	780 mg	

*Indicates high sodium content

FETTUCCINI ALFREDO, MODIFIED

Although the Parmesan cheese is higher in fat than is desired, the flavor of the freshly grated cheese is necessary. Simmering the vegetables in the milk makes the flavor very similar to the original recipe in side by side taste testing.

1 lb. fettuccini, cooked in salted water
1 can evaporated skim milk
4 tablespoons Butter Buds®*
3 tablespoons olive oil
1 clove garlic

½ stalk celery
⅛ segment green pepper
½ medium onion
½ cup freshly grated parmesan cheese*

Simmer the garlic, celery, green pepper, and onion in the skim milk for approximately 10 minutes. Remove and discard the vegetables. Add the Butter Buds®, stir until completely dissolved. Add fettuccini and warm thoroughly. Slowly add ½ cup freshly grated parmesan cheese, stirring thoroughly with each addition. Add salt and pepper to taste.

(Compare with 376 calories for original recipe)

Serves 8	196 calories per 1 cup serving		
Fat......... 7.0 G	Cholesterol ... 6 mg	Fiber .... 1.0 G	Diabetic exchanges:
saturated . 1.7 G	Protein .... 8.1 G	Vitamin C .. 1 mg	¾ starch, ½ fat
mono .... 4.2 G	Carbohydrate .. 25.0 G	Calcium ... 199 mg	1 low fat milk
poly...... .6 G		Sodium .... 243 mg	

MUSHROOM TOMATO SPAGHETTI SAUCE

The use of slightly more onion than usual and the liberal use of low salt bouillon enhances the flavor of the sauce.

1 large onion, diced
1 can tomatoes, chopped*
10 medium sized fresh mushrooms, chopped
1 teaspoon oregano, hand rubbed

1 chicken bouillon cube*
1 teaspoon low salt chicken bouillon
1 tablespoon olive oil
freshly ground pepper to taste
spaghetti

Saute onions in the oil; when translucent, add mushrooms, cook the mushrooms until the liquid starts to disappear. Add the tomatoes, oregano and bouillons. Add freshly ground pepper to taste. Simmer at least 20 minutes. Serve over spaghetti.

Analysis is sauce only. For ½ cup cooked spaghetti, add 80 calories.

Serves 4	74 calories per ½ cup serving		
Fat......... 4.1 G	Cholesterol ... 0 mg	Fiber .... 2.3 G	Diabetic exchanges:
saturated . .6 G	Protein .... 2.3 G	Vitamin C .. 21 mg	1½ vegetable, ¾ fat,
mono .... 2.6 G	Carbohydrate .. 8.8 G	Calcium ... 47 mg	(½ cup spaghetti =
poly...... .6 G		Sodium .... 465 mg	1 starch)

*Indicates high sodium content

SPAGHETTI WITH RED CLAM SAUCE

This spaghetti sauce provides 7.8 milligrams of iron in each serving.

1 can minced clams, drained,
  reserve liquid*
1 tablespoon olive oil
1 clove garlic, minced
1½ tablespoons chopped parsley
½ teaspoon oregano

⅛ teaspoon basil
1 chicken bouillon cube*
1½ cups canned tomatoes*
½ cup tomato sauce*
spaghetti
freshly grated parmesan cheese*

Drain the liquid from the clams and reserve it. Heat the olive oil in a saucepan, add garlic, saute briefly, do not brown. Stir in remaining ingredients except clams. Cook uncovered for 30 minutes. Add clams, reheat and serve over spaghetti. Sprinkle with freshly grated parmesan cheese.

Analysis is for the sauce only. Add 80 calories for ½ cup spaghetti.

Serves 4	99 calories per ¾ cup serving		
Fat . . . . 4.4 G	Cholesterol . . . 17 mg	Fiber . . . . 1.5 G	Diabetic exchanges:
saturated . .6 G	Protein . . . . 7.9 G	Vitamin C . . 20 mg	1 lean meat, ½ starch,
mono . . . . 2.7 G	Carbohydrate . . 8.1 G	Calcium . . . 63 mg	(½ cup spaghetti =
poly . . . . . . .6 G		Sodium . . . . 684 mg	1 starch)

SPAGHETTI WITH ONION AND GARLIC

This one is seductive.

3 green onions, cut into 1 inch pieces
2 cloves garlic, sliced thinly
2 tablespoons freshly grated
  parmesan cheese*

black pepper to taste
2 tablespoons chopped parsley
2 tablespoons olive oil
spaghetti

Cook the spaghetti according to package directions. Meanwhile, heat the olive oil in a heavy skillet. Add the green onions and cook until softened, stir in garlic. Continue to cook until the garlic is soft, do not brown. Remove from heat. Drain the pasta well and put it into a mixing bowl. Add the oil and onion mixture and toss. Add cheese and toss again. Add salt and pepper to taste, add parsley and toss. Serve immediately.

Analysis is for sauce only. For spaghetti, add 80 calories per ½ cup.

Serves 3	102 calories per 2 tablespoons		
Fat . . . . 10.0 G	Cholesterol . . . 3 mg	Fiber . . . . .5 G	Diabetic exchanges:
saturated . 1.9 G	Protein . . . . 1.8 G	Vitamin C . . 8 mg	½ vegetable, 2 fat,
mono . . . . 6.9 G	Carbohydrate . . 1.6 G	Calcium . . . 60 mg	(½ cup spaghetti =
poly . . . . . . .8 G		Sodium . . . . 65 mg	1 starch)

*Indicates high sodium content

GREEK TOMATO SAUCE

The only purpose of the carrots is to add sweetness.

1 tablespoon olive oil
1 medium onion, chopped
2 cloves garlic, minced
¼ cup green pepper, chopped
2 cups tomato sauce*
2 cups water
2 beef bouillon cubes*
1 chicken bouillon cube*

⅔ carrot, sliced with vegetable peeler
2 teaspoons lemon juice
freshly ground pepper
1 teaspoon oregano
1 teaspoon mint
1½ teaspoons basil
¼ teaspoon thyme
spaghetti

Saute onion, garlic and green pepper in oil. Add remaining ingredients and cook to sauce consistency. Serve with freshly grated Parmesan or Romano cheese over pasta.

Analysis is for sauce. For ½ cup cooked pasta add 80 calories.

Serves 6	75 calories per ½ cup serving		
Fat .... 2.8 G	Cholesterol ... 0 mg	Fiber .... 2.7 G	Diabetic exchanges:
saturated . .5 G	Protein .... 2.4 G	Vitamin C .. 38 mg	½ fat, 2 vegetable,
mono .... 1.8 G	Carbohydrate .. 12.0 G	Calcium ... 37 mg	(½ cup spaghetti =
poly ...... .3 G		Sodium .... 548 mg	1 starch)

MOSTACCIOLI

This is very low fat-less than one gram. Homemade tomato sauce and low salt bouillon will dramatically lower the sodium content.

2 cups tomato sauce*
2 beef bouillon cubes*
2 teaspoons low salt bouillon
1 large onion, chopped fine
1 small carrot, chopped fine
⅛ green pepper, chopped fine

1 tablespoon oregano, hand rubbed
¼ teaspoon cinnamon
½ teaspoon nutmeg
12 mushrooms, sliced
freshly ground pepper
¼ teaspoon sugar, or to taste

Combine all ingredients, simmer 25 minutes. Serve over cooked mostaccioli pasta and top with freshly grated parmesan cheese.

Analysis is for sauce only, for ½ cup cooked pasta add 80 calories.

Serves 4	75 calories per ½ cup serving		
Fat .... .9 G	Cholesterol ... 0 mg	Fiber .... 3.5 G	Diabetic exchanges:
saturated . .3 G	Protein .... 3.1 G	Vitamin C .. 28 mg	3 vegetable
mono .... .2 G	Carbohydrate .. 16.0 G	Calcium ... 55 mg	(½ cup pasta =
poly ...... .2 G		Sodium .. 1258 mg	1 starch)

*Indicates high sodium content

109

LASAGNA

The secret to the flavor is plenty of tomatoes and plenty of herbs. You may even want to add more herbs.

½ pound lasagna noodles
½ onion, diced
½ stalk celery, diced
¼ cup diced carrots
1 clove garlic
1 16 ounce can tomatoes*
¾ cup tomato sauce*
¼ pound ground pork tenderloin or
   ground turkey

2 beef bouillon cubes*
⅓ cup white wine (optional)
⅛ teaspoon nutmeg
1 tablespoon oregano, hand rubbed
1 teaspoon basil, hand rubbed
salt and freshly ground pepper to taste*
2 tablespoons olive oil
⅓ cup skim milk
2 teaspoons flour

Saute the meat in olive oil just until it loses its pink color. Add onion, celery, carrot, saute until vegetables are tender, add garlic. Cook another minute. Add wine to deglaze bottom of pan, simmer until reduced to ½. Stir in tomatoes, including their juice, tomato sauce, nutmeg, oregano, basil, salt, pepper and bouillon cubes. Cover and simmer for 2 hours, stirring occasionally. Combine the skim milk and flour, stir into the sauce, cook until thick, about 10 minutes.

BECHAMEL SAUCE
2 tablespoons olive oil
¼ cup flour

2 cups skim milk
salt and pepper*

Heat olive oil, stir in flour and cook for 1 minute. Whisk in milk and bring to a boil, stirring constantly. Reduce heat, add salt and pepper. Simmer 20 minutes.

Freshly grate about ¾ cup parmesan cheese.

Cook the pasta until tender, drain and freshen in cold water. Pour a thin layer of meat sauce into the bottom of a 11 x 7 inch baking dish. Arrange a layer of pasta on top, cover with ⅓ of the meat sauce, ⅓ of the bechamel sauce, sprinkle with ⅓ of the parmesan; make 2 more layers.

Bake the lasagna in a 400 degree oven for about 20 minutes or until heated through.

Serves 8	246 calories per 8 oz. serving		
Fat .... 12.9 G	Cholesterol ... 33 mg	Fiber .... 2.0 G	Diabetic exchanges:
saturated . 4.0 G	Protein .... 12.0 G	Vitamin C .. 14 mg	1¼ fat, 2 vegetable
mono .... 7.0 G	Carbohydrate .. 20.0 G	Calcium ... 236 mg	1 lean meat, 1 starch
poly ...... 1.4 G		Sodium .... 685 mg	

*Indicates high sodium content

110

PASTITIO

Pastitio has been called the Greek lasagna, but this controlled fat tossed dish is more tasty and has fewer calories. Serve with a salad and you have a complete meal.

1 can tomatoes, chopped, with juice*
1 can tomato sauce*
4 ounces beef flavored
    ground turkey (see recipe)
1 tablespoon oregano, hand rubbed
1 teaspoon cinnamon
1 teaspoon nutmeg

freshly ground pepper
2 medium onions, minced
1 large clove garlic, minced
2 tablespoons olive oil
½ pound mostaccioli
½ cup freshly grated parmesan cheese*
salt to taste*

Saute the onions and ground turkey in the olive oil; at the last moment, add garlic. Add oregano, cinnamon, nutmeg and pepper. Saute long enough to mingle flavors. Add tomatoes with their juice and tomato sauce and simmer until liquid is reduced to thick consistency. Add salt to taste.

Meanwhile cook mostaccioli according to package directions. Drain. Combine the mostaccioli with the sauce, stirring well. When cool, stir in the grated cheese and toss. Warm the pastitio in the microwave so as to not melt the cheese. Serve.

Serves 4	316 calories per 12 oz. serving		
Fat .... 14.7 G	Cholesterol ... 32 mg	Fiber .... 4.3 G	Diabetic exchanges:
saturated . 4.4 G	Protein .... 17.0 G	Vitamin C .. 31 mg	3 vegetable, 2¼ fat,
mono .... 7.5 G	Carbohydrate .. 31.0 G	Calcium ... 235 mg	1 lean meat, 1 starch
poly ...... 1.9 G		Sodium .... 751 mg	

*Indicates high sodium content

111

QUICHE

If you have one, your favorite recipe can be substituted. A good source of calcium.

2 cups evaporated skim milk
2 egg whites, beaten to stiff peaks
1 small onion, diced
10 mushrooms, diced
4 fresh tomatoes, chopped
2 tablespoons olive oil

¾ cup Egg Beaters®
1-2 tablespoons lemon juice
 (to adjust sweetness)
½ cup freshly grated parmesan cheese*
6-7 black olives, sliced in rings*

Prepare 8 inch olive oil pie shell, bake at 375 degrees for 8-10 minutes. Cool.

Saute onions, mushrooms and tomatoes in oil until most of the liquid is gone. Beat Egg Beaters® and milk in a bowl. Set aside. Pour tomato, onion and mushroom mixture into prebaked pie shell, cover with cheese. Fold beaten egg whites into milk mixture and pour over vegetables in pie shell. Decorate top with black olive rings. Bake at 425 degrees for 10 minutes, then reduce heat to 350 degrees and bake for another 15-20 minutes or until lightly browned on surface. Cool and serve.

Analysis is for filling only. With pie crust add 129 calories per serving.

Serves 6	197 calories per 1/6 quiche		
Fat .... 9.0 G	Cholesterol ... 9 mg	Fiber .... 1.6 G	Diabetic exchanges:
saturated . 2.4 G	Protein .... 15.0 G	Vitamin C .. 17 mg	¼ vegetable, 1 fat,
mono .... 5.0 G	Carbohydrate .. 14.9 G	Calcium ... 370 mg	1 low fat milk, 1 lean
poly...... 1.1 G		Sodium .... 338 mg	meat

*Indicates high sodium content

112

PIZZA

We decided to get the toughest audience—beer drinkers—to test this.

DOUGH:

1½ cups flour
½ teaspoon salt*

2 teaspoons yeast
¾ cup water

Combine flour and salt in small bowl. Dissolve yeast in warm water. Mix ingredients to form a firm dough and knead until smooth. Put into a clean bowl and cover with a damp cloth. Let rise in a warm place. After dough has risen, flatten into a 12 inch pizza pan and bake for 5 minutes in 350 degree oven.

SAUCE:

2 cups tomato sauce*
2 teaspoons onion powder
1 teaspoon garlic powder
2 tablespoons oregano, hand rubbed

freshly ground pepper
3 ounces cooked beef flavored
    ground turkey (see recipe)

Combine all sauce ingredients, mix well. Since the turkey is precooked, the sauce does not need additional cooking. Spoon sauce over dough.

TOPPINGS:

Sauteed (in olive oil)
    ground turkey meat or ground pork
tenderloin
sliced mushrooms

green pepper slivers
sauce
oregano
salt and pepper

Top with cheese—equal parts grated farmers cheese and 1% cottage cheese mixed well in the food processor.
Bake about 20-30 minutes in 400 degree oven or until done.

Serves 6	180 calories per 1/6 pizza		
Fat .... 2.5 G	Cholesterol ... 12 mg	Fiber .... 2.6 G	Diabetic exchanges:
saturated . .8 G	Protein .... 8.7 G	Vitamin C .. 12 mg	1 starch, ½ lean meat,
mono .... .8 G	Carbohydrate .. 32.0 G	Calcium ... 50 mg	3 vegetable
poly ...... .7 G		Sodium .... 690 mg	

*Indicates high sodium content

DOLMADES
(Rice Stuffed Grape Leaves)

The original recipe cooks the rice with lamb. The combination of herbs we found in a Persian recipe, but the taste of Greece and the Middle East are intertwined due to the violence of their history. At any rate, this is the taste of my childhood without the meat.

2 tablespoons olive oil
½ cup finely chopped onions
1 teaspoon salt*
freshly ground black pepper to taste
¾ cup uncooked rice
1 tablespoon dried dill weed
¼ cup parsley, finely chopped

1 teaspoon dried mint, hand rubbed
½ teaspoon oregano, hand rubbed
juice of ½ lemon
1 cup water
1 jar grape leaves (about 40)
2 beef bouillon cubes*
2 teaspoons low salt beef bouillon

Parboil the rice by stirring the rice into 2 cups of boiling water and boiling it for 5 minutes. Drain in a sieve and set aside. Saute the onions in the oil until they are soft. Add bouillon, rice, parsley, dill, mint, lemon juice, oregano, salt, pepper and water. Cook until the water is evaporated. Set aside, off the heat.

Meanwhile bring 3 quarts of water to boil. Drop the grape leaves into the water, turn off the heat and let the leaves soak for one minute. Pour off the water and plunge the leaves into a pan of cold water. Gently separate the leaves and put them on a towel to drain.

Layer the bottom of a large heavy pan with 10 leaves. Lay a grape leaf dull side up and spoon about 1 teaspoon of stuffing into the center of the leaf, fold up the stem end, then fold over each side to enclose the stuffing. Starting at the stem end, roll the leaf firmly into a compact package. Lay the stuffed leaf, seam side down, in the pan. Roll remaining leaves, place in pan, add 1 cup water. Bring water to boil, reduce heat to simmering and simmer for about 50 minutes. Watch closely so they do not burn. Serve either warm or cold.

Makes 30		27 calories per leaf					
Fat	1.0 G	Cholesterol ...	0 mg	Fiber	.2 G	Diabetic exchanges:
saturated .	.2 G	Protein	.4 G	Vitamin C ..	1 mg	¼ starch,
mono	.7 G	Carbohydrate ..	4.0 G	Calcium ...	5 mg	¼ vegetable
poly	.1 G			Sodium	140 mg	

*Indicates high sodium content

114

RED BEANS AND RICE

We don't know if this is Cajun or Creole, but we know it tastes good!

1 cup dry red beans
3 cups water
½ cup chopped onion
½ cup chopped celery
¼ cup chopped green pepper
1 clove garlic, minced
1 teaspoon fresh thyme or ⅛ dried
1 small bay leaf

¼ teaspoon hot pepper sauce
2 teaspoons Worcestershire sauce
¼ cup catsup*
2 teaspoons ham or
   beef flavored bouillon*
freshly ground pepper to taste
2 cups cooked rice

Soak the beans overnight. Drain and rinse. Combine all ingredients except rice and cook until beans are tender. Serve the beans over rice.

Analysis is for beans only; for ⅓ cup cooked rice add 80 calories.

Serves 6	135 calories per ½ cup serving		
Fat .... .6 G	Cholesterol ... 0 mg	Fiber .... 8.1 G	Diabetic exchanges:
saturated . .1 G	Protein .... 8.4 G	Vitamin C .. 10 mg	2 vegetable, 1 starch,
mono .... .1 G	Carbohydrate .. 25.1 G	Calcium ... 39 mg	(⅓ cup cooked rice
poly ...... .3 G		Sodium .... 303 mg	= 1 starch)

FIVE FIBER CASSEROLE

This easy to make casserole always receives compliments.

2 cups chicken broth (see recipe)*
1 cup thinly sliced carrots
1 (8 ounce) can red beans with liquid*
½ cup quick cooking barley
¼ cup oat bran

¼ cup chopped onion
¼ cup snipped parsley
3 tablespoons bulgur
1 clove garlic, minced
¼ cup freshly grated parmesan cheese*

Preheat oven to 350 degrees. Combine all ingredients, except cheese, in a 1 quart casserole and bake, covered, for about 50 minutes or until barley and carrots are tender. Sprinkle the parmesan cheese over the casserole and bake 2-3 minutes more.

Serves 6	143 calories per 1 cup serving		
Fat .... 1.7 G	Cholesterol ... 3 mg	Fiber .... 6.7 G	Diabetic exchanges:
saturated . .8 G	Protein .... 6.6 G	Vitamin C .. 4 mg	1¾ starch
mono .... .4 G	Carbohydrate .. 27.5 G	Calcium ... 76 mg	
poly ...... .3 G		Sodium .... 478 mg	

*Indicates high sodium content

STUFFED ZUCCHINI

I never liked zucchini until our Peruvian friend cooked a recipe her Palestinian grandmother taught her.

4 small zucchini
¼ pound pork tenderloin,
   ground or cubed
½ teaspoon cumin
½ teaspoon curry powder

½ cup uncooked rice
1 small tomato, peeled and diced
1 clove garlic, minced
salt and pepper to taste

Scoop soft seedy center from zucchini (there is a tool!) or use an apple corer. Discard pulp. Set the zucchini aside. Combine the remaining ingredients and loosely stuff the zucchini. Place the stuffed zucchini in a large pan and simmer in the following sauce until zucchini are done, about 1 hour.

Sauce
8 oz. tomato sauce*
1 small onion, chopped
1 clove garlic, minced

1 beef bouillon cube*
salt and pepper to taste*
water to cover zucchini

Combine all ingredients and pour over zucchini. If sauce is not served over zucchini, the sodium intake is lowered.

Analysis is for stuffed zucchini only.

Serves 4		193 calories per 8 oz. serving			
Fat	4.6 G	Cholesterol ... 30 mg	Fiber .... 2.5 G		Diabetic exchanges:
saturated .	1.5 G	Protein .... 13.0 G	Vitamin C .. 20 mg		3 vegetable, ½ starch,
mono	1.9 G	Carbohydrate .. 25.0 G	Calcium ... 40 mg		½ fat, 1 lean meat
poly	.7 G		Sodium .... 29 mg		

Analysis for tomato sauce.

Serves 4		26 calories per 8 oz. serving			
Fat	.3 G	Cholesterol ... 0 mg	Fiber .... 1.1 G		Diabetic exchanges:
saturated .	.1 G	Protein .... 1.2 G	Vitamin C .. 8 mg		1 vegetable
mono	.1 G	Carbohydrate .. 5.6 G	Calcium ... 17 mg		
poly	.1 G		Sodium .... 603 mg		

*Indicates high sodium content

PAELLA

Our version of the well known Spanish dish. Vary the meat to your desire.

1 medium onion, chopped
1 small green pepper, chopped
2 cloves garlic
1 tablespoon olive oil
½ chicken breast, boned,
    skin removed and cut into cubes
½ pound shrimp, peeled and deveined
1 teaspoon oregano

½ teaspoon basil
1 chicken bouillon cube*
freshly ground pepper to taste
¼ cup frozen peas
pinch saffron threads
¾ cup uncooked rice
3 cups chicken broth (see recipe)*

Saute chicken cubes in olive oil until browned, remove from skillet. In same oil saute onion and green pepper until onion is soft. Return chicken to skillet, add garlic, 1 cup chicken broth, oregano, basil, bouillon cube and pepper. Cook until chicken is done, about 10 minutes. Stir in the rice, 1½ cups chicken broth and saffron and simmer for 15 minutes. Stir in shrimp, peas and an additional ½ cup chicken broth. Cook 5-8 minutes or until shrimp is done.

Serves 6	199 calories per 8 oz. serving		
Fat .... 4.1 G	Cholesterol ... 89 mg	Fiber .... 1.3 G	Diabetic exchanges:
saturated . .8 G	Protein .... 16.4 G	Vitamin C .. 14 mg	1 lean meat, 1 starch,
mono .... 2.2 G	Carbohydrate .. 22.9 G	Calcium ... 51 mg	2 vegetable
poly...... .8 G		Sodium .... 690 mg	

*Indicates high sodium content

BEEF FLAVORED EGGPLANT

This was adapted from a Persian recipe called "Bademjan" or lamb with eggplant, and was taught to us by our Iranian friend while on a fishing trip.

1 eggplant, sliced in ⅜ inch
   thick slices
1 cup beef stock (see recipe)*
1 teaspoon low salt beef bouillon
½ teaspoon turmeric
1 pkg. brown gravy mix*

1 onion, chopped
1 tablespoon tomato paste*
pepper to taste
1 tablespoon olive oil
2 cups cooked rice

Peel and slice the eggplant, salt liberally, place on absorbent paper to release the bitter juices, about 20 minutes. Wipe both sides with a paper towel. Broil the slices until they are nicely browned. (Watch carefully). Saute the onion in olive oil, add the eggplant, water, bouillon, tomato paste and pepper. Cook covered for about 45 minutes. Add the brown gravy mix which has been mixed with about ½ cup water. Cook about 10 minutes more. Serve over rice.

Analysis is for sauce, for ⅓ cup cooked rice, add 80 calories.

Serves 4	70 calories per ½ cup serving			
Fat......... 3.9 G	Cholesterol ... 0 mg	Fiber .... 2.4 G	Diabetic exchanges:
saturated . .7 G	Protein .... 1.7 G	Vitamin C .. 5 mg	¾ fat, 1½ vegetable
mono .... 2.7 G	Carbohydrate .. 8.2 G	Calcium ... 38 mg	(⅓ cup cooked rice
poly...... .4 G		Sodium .... 406 mg	= 1 starch)

*Indicates high sodium content

Vegetables

♥ Atherosclerosis increases with the advent of the male hormone testosterone in adolescents. Women are protected by the female hormone estrogen until the menopause, when their rate of vascular disease approaches that of men. This is the best reason for taking estrogen replacement, not osteoporosis.

♥ Don't rely on exercise alone to lower cholesterol or lose weight. Diet is more important. Exercise has other benefits.

♥ To ripen tomatoes, including hot house tomatoes, put them in a plastic bag with an apple for 2-3 days. The ethylene gas from the apple is a ripening agent.

♥ A cholesterol determination by itself may be misleading. Some authorities recommend against a single value. I am uncomfortable with a single value.

VEGETABLES

ORIENTAL STYLE GREEN BEANS

Fresh green beans prepared in a spicy manner.

½ pound fresh green beans
1 tablespoon olive oil
3 tablespoons water
1 teaspoon sugar

1 teaspoon soy sauce*
¼ teaspoon ground ginger
1 small clove garlic, minced

Stem fresh green beans, leave whole. Heat oil in skillet and saute beans for 1-2 minutes. Add water and sugar and cook another 2-3 minutes. Stir in soy sauce, garlic and ginger. Cook only until tender crisp.

Serves 3	66 calories per 3 oz. serving		
Fat......... 4.6 G	Cholesterol ... 0 mg	Fiber .... 1.7 G	Diabetic exchanges:
saturated . .6 G	Protein .... 1.6 G	Vitamin C .. 13 mg	1 vegetable, ¾ fat
mono .... 3.3 G	Carbohydrate .. 6.0 G	Calcium ... 31 mg	
poly...... .4 G		Sodium .... 119 mg	

BABY LIMA BEANS

Lima beans are high in fiber and calcium. A hint of curry.

8 ounces frozen baby lima beans
1 clove garlic, crushed
½ teaspoon curry powder
¼ teaspoon freshly ground pepper
dash cayenne pepper
2 tablespoons olive oil
2 heaping tablespoons freshly
   grated parmesan cheese*

1 tablespoon chopped fresh parsley
½ teaspoon dried basil leaves, crushed
3 chopped green onions
1 teaspoon lemon juice
salt to taste

Cook the lima beans as package directs. While they are cooking prepare the dressing by combining the remaining ingredients and blending them well. While the beans are still hot, pour the dressing over them. Serve the beans hot as a vegetable side dish.

Serves 4	170 calories per ½ cup serving		
Fat......... 7.8 G	Cholesterol ... 2 mg	Fiber .... 8.0 G	Diabetic exchanges:
saturated . 1.5 G	Protein .... 7.3 G	Vitamin C .. 11 mg	1¼ starch, 1¼ fat,
mono .... 5.2 G	Carbohydrate .. 18.7 G	Calcium ... 71 mg	¼ lean meat
poly...... .7 G		Sodium .... 74 mg	

*Indicates high sodium content

121

BAKED BEANS

Low fat and spicy.

2 cans pork and beans*
2 teaspoons substitute bacon bits*
1 medium onion, chopped
¾ cup catsup*

½ teaspoon brown sugar substitute
½ teaspoon garlic powder (optional)
freshly ground pepper to taste

Combine all ingredients thoroughly and pour into baking dish. Bake in 350 degree oven until center of mixture bubbles and edges darken.
Alternative: cook in the microwave oven for 20 minutes, stirring after 10 minutes.

Serves 4	284 calories per 1 cup serving		
Fat .... 2.6 G	Cholesterol ... 15 mg	Fiber .... 14.0 G	Diabetic exchanges:
saturated . .9 G	Protein .... 13.0 G	Vitamin C .. 16 mg	3½ starch,
mono .... 1.1 G	Carbohydrate .. 59.0 G	Calcium ... 143 mg	¼ vegetable
poly ...... .4 G		Sodium .. 1532 mg	

COOKED CABBAGE

If you always thought you couldn't stand cooked cabbage, try this one before you make a final decision.

1 head cabbage
1 tablespoon olive oil
1 teaspoon sugar
¼ teaspoon freshly ground pepper

1 chicken bouillon cube*
½ teaspoon caraway seeds
½ cup water

Slice the cabbage into six wedges and put it in a saucepan. Add remaining ingredients, except caraway, cover and cook over moderate heat for about 15 minutes. Baste the cabbage occasionally with the pan juices. Just before the cabbage is done, add the caraway seeds.

Serves 6	28 calories per wedge serving		
Fat .... 2.4 G	Cholesterol ... 0 mg	Fiber .... .3 G	Diabetic exchanges:
saturated . .3 G	Protein .... .3 G	Vitamin C .. 6 mg	¼ vegetable, ½ fat,
mono .... 1.7 G	Carbohydrate .. 1.6 G	Calcium ... 7 mg	almost free
poly ...... .2 G		Sodium .... 188 mg	

*Indicates high sodium content

HARVARD BEETS

Standard taste, lower calorie.

1 can (16 oz.) diced or sliced beets*	freshly ground pepper to taste
1 tablespoon cornstarch	1 teaspoon vinegar
dash each onion and garlic powder	1 package sweetener (not aspartame)

Drain juice from beets into small saucepan and set beets aside. Stir cornstarch into beet liquid and cook until thickened. Add remaining ingredients and beets and cook until beets are heated through.

Serves 4	43 calories per ½ cup serving		
Fat .... .1 G	Cholesterol ... 0 mg	Fiber .... 1.8 G	Diabetic exchanges:
saturated .. 0 G	Protein .... 1.0 G	Vitamin C .. 5 mg	1 vegetable, ¼ starch
mono ..... 0 G	Carbohydrate .. 10.0 G	Calcium ... 17 mg	
poly .... 0 G		Sodium .... 324 mg	

LENTILS WITH RICE

One of the many ways to prepare this economical, nutritious meat substitute.

1 cup lentils	2 teaspoons salt or to taste*
water to cover by 2 inches	1 tablespoon olive oil
½ teaspoon turmeric	½ teaspoon cumin seeds
10-15 mushrooms, sliced	1 teaspoon coriander seeds
1 medium green pepper, sliced	¼ teaspoon freshly ground pepper
1 medium onion, chopped	hot sauce to taste
1 tablespoon Worcestershire sauce*	2 cups hot cooked rice

Wash lentils, discard debris. Put lentils in saucepan and cover by 2 inches with water. Bring to boil, reduce heat and simmer for 1 hour or until done. Add turmeric, mushrooms, green pepper, onion, Worcestershire sauce, salt and hot sauce; simmer 20 minutes. Heat oil in a small skillet, add coriander, cumin and pepper. Heat 2 minutes, stirring constantly, add to lentils. Serve over cooked rice.

Rice is not in analysis; for ⅓ cup cooked rice add 80 calories.

Serves 6	139 calories per ½ cup serving lentils		
Fat .... 2.8 G	Cholesterol ... 0 mg	Fiber .... 4.5 G	Diabetic exchanges:
saturated . .4 G	Protein .... 9.5 G	Vitamin C .. 14 mg	¼ lean meat,
mono .... 1.8 G	Carbohydrate .. 20.5 G	Calcium ... 35 mg	1½ starch, (⅓ cup
poly ...... .4 G		Sodium .... 722 mg	cooked rice =
			1 starch)

*Indicates high sodium content

BRAISED LEEKS

This seldom-used vegetable makes an appetizing side dish.

3-4 large leeks
1 tablespoon olive oil

¾ cup water

SAUCE:

1 cup peeled, seeded, chopped tomato
1 tablespoon olive oil
1 clove garlic, minced
1 teaspoon lemon juice

1 chicken bouillon cube*
pepper to taste
2 tablespoons chopped parsley

Trim the leeks to 6 inch lengths, be careful not to separate the white root. Wash thoroughly to remove all sand. Preheat oven to 350 degrees. Place the leeks in a shallow baking dish in one layer. Mix 1 tablespoon olive oil with ¾ cup water and pour over the leeks. Bring the liquid to a boil over high heat then cover loosely and bake in the 350 degree oven for 30 minutes. Don't overcook.

Meanwhile prepare the sauce: Pour 1 tablespoon olive oil into a skillet over moderate heat, add garlic and stir constantly for a minute or two. Add the tomatoes, lemon juice, bouillon cube and pepper and cook briskly until the moisture is evaporated. Remove from heat, stir in the parsley.

When the leeks are done, thin the tomato sauce with 2 tablespoons of the braising liquid, discard any remaining liquid on the leeks. Spread the tomato sauce over the leeks and serve.

Serves 6	58 calories per 3 oz. serving		
Fat .... 4.8 G	Cholesterol ... 0 mg	Fiber .... .8 G	Diabetic exchanges:
saturated . .7 G	Protein .... .8 G	Vitamin C .. 11 mg	¼ vegetable, 1 fat
mono .... 3.4 G	Carbohydrate .. 3.5 G	Calcium ... 14 mg	
poly...... .5 G		Sodium .... 191 mg	

"FRENCH FRIED" POTATOES

These look and taste like French fries, but there is no fat.

Scrub long slender white potatoes well. Do not peel, cut them into quarters. Rub the cut surfaces together until the starch appears on the cut surface. Place on ungreased baking sheet and allow to set 15-20 minutes. Bake in 400 degree oven until puffed and brown—about 30-35 minutes. Serve immediately.

If desired, garlic-olive oil dressing and/or parmesan cheese may be sprinkled over.

One potato	93 calories per serving		
Fat .... .1 G	Cholesterol ... 0 mg	Fiber .... .6 G	Diabetic exchanges:
saturated .. 0 G	Protein .... 3.0 G	Vitamin C .. 20 mg	1 starch
mono ..... 0 G	Carbohydrate .. 21.0 G	Calcium ... 9 mg	
poly....... 0 G		Sodium .... 4 mg	

*Indicates high sodium content

OKRA

This much maligned vegetable has an excellent flavor that is more difficult to detect in soups and stews. The following gives a taste of okra I think you will like.

2 cups okra, sliced lengthwise   salt and pepper to taste
garlic powder   olive oil
flour

Sprinkle the cut okra with garlic powder. Put flour into a plastic bag and add the okra. Toss to coat with flour. Saute in olive oil until brown. Sprinkle with salt and pepper to taste.

Serves 4	94 calories per ½ cup serving		
Fat .... 5.3 G	Cholesterol ... 0 mg	Fiber .... 2.6 G	Diabetic exchanges:
saturated . .7 G	Protein .... 2.6 G	Vitamin C .. 19 mg	1½ vegetable, 1 fat,
mono .... 3.8 G	Carbohydrate .. 10.9 G	Calcium ... 73 mg	⅛ starch
poly ...... .5 G		Sodium .... 6 mg	

COOKED RICE

Its easy. Twice the amount of water as raw rice, a little salt. Bring to boil, reduce heat and simmer, covered for 20 minutes. Don't peek.

Brown rice - about 2⅓ cups of water to each cup of raw rice, cook covered for 30 minutes.

Analysis for white rice

Serves 1	76 calories per ⅓ cup serving		
Fat .... .1 G	Cholesterol ... 0 mg	Fiber .... .3 G	Diabetic exchanges:
saturated .. 0 G	Protein .... 1.4 G	Vitamin C .. 0 mg	⅓ cup = 1 starch
mono ..... 0 G	Carbohydrate .. 16.9 G	Calcium ... 7 mg	
poly .... 0 G		Sodium .... 0 mg	

Analysis for brown rice

Serves 1	79 calories per ⅓ cup serving		
Fat .... .4 G	Cholesterol ... 0 mg	Fiber .... 1.1 G	Diabetic exchanges:
saturated . .1 G	Protein .... 1.7 G	Vitamin C .. 0 mg	⅓ cup = 1 starch
mono .... .1 G	Carbohydrate .. 16.9 G	Calcium ... 8 mg	
poly ...... .1 G		Sodium .... 0 mg	

POTATOES WITH GARLIC AND ROSEMARY

This is for garlic lovers.

1 tablespoon olive oil
1 large potato
2 cloves garlic, thinly sliced

½ teaspoon dried rosemary
salt and pepper to taste

Pour a teaspoon of oil into a 2 cup oven proof casserole. Slice the potato (either peeled or unpeeled) into ⅛ inch slices and place a layer of potato slices in the casserole. Top with slices of garlic, salt and pepper, and sprinkle of rosemary. Pour on a little more oil. Repeat layers until potato slices are used. Bake in 325 degree oven for 45 minutes. When potatoes are tender, remove from oven and serve.

Serves 2		152 calories per ½ cup serving			
Fat	6.9 G	Cholesterol ...	0 mg	Fiber .... 1.6 G	Diabetic exchanges:
saturated .	.9 G	Protein	1.9 G	Vitamin C .. 9 mg	1¼ starch, 1¼ fat
mono	5.0 G	Carbohydrate ..	21.3 G	Calcium ... 15 mg	
poly......	.6 G			Sodium .... 6 mg	

SPICY LENTILS

Lentils are an excellent source of fiber, protein and iron but be sure to include a grain with the meal for complete protein.

1 cup dried lentils
2 tablespoons olive oil
⅓ cup diced onion
2 cloves garlic, finely chopped
1½ teaspoons paprika

½ teaspoon dried thyme
¼ cup diced pimento
½ teaspoon freshly ground pepper
4 cups water
2 beef bouillon cubes*

Wash the lentils well, picking out any debris. Heat the oil in a medium saucepan, add the onion and cook until softened, about 3 minutes. Add the garlic, paprika, thyme and pimento and stir for about 1 minute. Add lentils to the pan, stir to mix ingredients. Add 4 cups water and the boullion cubes. Bring to a boil, lower heat and simmer until the lentils are tender, about 20 minutes. Remove 1 cup of the lentils and puree them in the blender, return to the pan. Add the freshly ground pepper, taste for seasoning.

Serves 6		162 calories per ½ cup serving			
Fat	5.1 G	Cholesterol ...	0 mg	Fiber .... 4.5 G	Diabetic exchanges:
saturated .	.8 G	Protein	9.7 G	Vitamin C .. 12 mg	1¼ starch, ¼ fat,
mono	3.5 G	Carbohydrate ..	20.8 G	Calcium ... 30 mg	1 lean meat
poly......	.6 G			Sodium .... 348 mg	

*Indicates high sodium content

CAULIFLOWER WITH LEMON SAUCE

Instead of the usual cheese sauce, try this version.

½ head cauliflower,
  broken into flowerettes
1 tablespoon olive oil
1 clove garlic, minced

1 tablespoon flour
1 chicken bouillon cube*
⅔ cup skim milk
2 tablespoons lemon juice

Steam cauliflower until just tender, about 6 minutes, don't overcook. Heat oil in saucepan, add garlic and sauté briefly. Stir in flour and cook about 1 minute. Add skim milk and bouillon cube and cook until thickened. Stir in lemon juice. Pour sauce over cauliflower and serve.

Serves 4	70 calories per ½ cup serving			
Fat......... 3.8 G	Cholesterol ... 1 mg	Fiber .... 1.4 G	Diabetic exchanges:
saturated . .6 G	Protein .... 2.9 G	Vitamin C .. 40 mg	1½ vegetable, ¾ fat
mono .... 2.6 G	Carbohydrate .. 7.1 G	Calcium ... 69 mg	
poly...... .4 G		Sodium .... 307 mg	

GREEK POTATOES

Can you believe it? No garlic!

2 whole unpeeled white baking potatoes
1 tablespoon olive oil
1 teaspoon lemon Juice

½ teaspoon oregano
⅛ teaspoon pepper
salt to taste (may be omitted)

Scrub potatoes well; cut into sixths and arrange in baking dish in a single layer with the cut side up. Combine the olive oil, lemon juice, oregano and pepper. Brush the potatoes with the oil mixture and bake in 350 degree oven, uncovered, for 40 minutes. Keep adding water for basting until toward the end of the baking period when the pan should be allowed to become dry. Potatoes should become slightly browned. Salt to taste, if desired.

Microwave method: Prepare as above. Cook, covered, in the microwave on high until potatoes are tender. Remove cover and place potatoes under oven broiler until browned. Salt to taste, if desired.

Serves 4	89 calories per ½ potato			
Fat......... 3.5 G	Cholesterol ... 0 mg	Fiber .... 1.1 G	Diabetic exchanges:
saturated . .5 G	Protein .... 1.2 G	Vitamin C .. 6 mg	¾ starch, ½ fat
mono .... 2.5 G	Carbohydrate .. 13.8 G	Calcium ... 8 mg	
poly...... .3 G		Sodium .... 4 mg	

*Indicates high sodium content

BAKED POTATO

Most baked potatoes are an abomination, especially those wrapped in foil. A potato is rubbed with olive oil and baked in a 400 degree oven for about 1 hour. The skin is crusty and the inside is mealy. Anything besides salt and pepper that you do to it is downhill. Eat skin and all!

Serves 1		93 calories per potato			
Fat	.1 G	Cholesterol ...	0 mg	Fiber .... 0.6 G	Diabetic exchanges:
saturated ..	0 G	Protein	3.0 G	Vitamin C .. 20 mg	1 starch
mono	0 G	Carbohydrate ..	21.0 G	Calcium ... 9 mg	
poly........	0 G			Sodium .... 4 mg	

SCALLOPED POTATOES

This version gives considerable savings in calories, fat and sodium when compared to a standard recipe using butter, whole milk and cheddar cheese.

3 cups thinly sliced,
  peeled, raw potatoes
¼ cup thinly sliced onion
1 tablespoon chopped parsley(optional)
2 tablespoons flour
⅛ teaspoon freshly ground pepper

1 chicken bouillon cube*
2 tablespoons olive oil
1 tablespoon chopped onion
1 cup skim milk
¼ cup freshly grated parmesan cheese*

Heat olive oil in saucepan, sauté 1 tablespoon chopped onion until transparent. Blend in flour, add milk and chicken bouillon cube. Add pepper. Cook for 10 minutes, stirring frequently. Spray a 1 quart casserole dish with pan spray, add a layer of potatoes, a layer of onions, spoon over some sauce; continue making layers until all potatoes are used. Top with sauce and sprinkle with the parmesan cheese. Cover the casserole and bake in 350 degree oven for 1 hour, remove cover and bake another 30 minutes. Garnish with chopped parsley and serve.

(compare to 228 calories, 9.5 g saturated fat, 515 mg sodium)

Serves 6		162 calories per ½ cup serving			
Fat	5.9 G	Cholesterol ...	3 mg	Fiber .... 1.6 G	Diabetic exchanges:
saturated .	1.4 G	Protein	4.9 G	Vitamin C .. 8 mg	1 starch, 1 fat,
mono	3.7 G	Carbohydrate ..	23.0 G	Calcium ... 109 mg	⅓ low fat milk
poly......	.5 G			Sodium .... 275 mg	

*Indicates high sodium content

CURRIED POTATOES

The secret to this dish is the preparation of the spices. Another example of the range of curry in cooking.

1 inch cinnamon stick	1 teaspoon mustard seeds
½ teaspoon cardamon seeds	3 whole cloves
1 teaspoon cumin seeds	1 teaspoon peppercorns
1 teaspoon coriander seeds	

Put the spices in a heavy skillet over low heat and toast them for 5 minutes. Coarsely grind the spices in a blender. These will keep in a spice jar for about a year. Indian cooks don't have a standard curry powder as you find in the store, but make a curry from a variety of spices for each dish. You can readily see that there can be a lot of different curries, each subtly flavored differently.

3 potatoes, thickly sliced
1 tablespoon olive oil

Heat 1 tablespoon olive oil in skillet. Add 1 teaspoon spice mixture and sauté briefly, add sliced potatoes which have been briefly precooked in either water or the microwave. Sauté until the potatoes are tender. Add salt and pepper to taste. Serve with sliced raw onions.

Serves 4	126 calories per ½ cup serving		
Fat .... 3.8 G	Cholesterol ... 0 mg	Fiber .... 2.0 G	Diabetic exchanges:
saturated . .5 G	Protein .... 2.0 G	Vitamin C .. 14 mg	1¼ starch, ½ fat
mono .... 2.6 G	Carbohydrate .. 22.0 G	Calcium ... 24 mg	
poly ...... .4 G		Sodium .... 7 mg	

SCALLOPED CORN WITH CRAB

Ah, New Orleans!

2 tablespoons chopped scallions	1 cup cream style corn*
2 tablespoons chopped celery	1 tablespoon catsup*
1 tablespoon olive oil	1 6 oz. can crab meat
1 cup cornbread crumbs	1 teaspoon Creole seasoning*
¼ cup skim milk	

Sauté scallions and celery in olive oil until vegetables are soft. Stir in remaining ingredients. Pour into 9 inch baking dish and bake at 350 degrees for 30-35 minutes. Serve as a side dish with fish.

Serves 6	140 calories per 3 oz. serving		
Fat .... 3.5 G	Cholesterol ... 16 mg	Fiber .... 1.4 G	Diabetic exchanges:
saturated . .6 G	Protein .... 6.8 G	Vitamin C .. 4 mg	1 vegetable, 1 starch,
mono .... 2.0 G	Carbohydrate .. 21.0 G	Calcium ... 54 mg	½ fat
poly ...... .5 G		Sodium .... 337 mg	

*Indicates high sodium content

MASHED POTATOES

The taste is not altered by the lack of fat.

3 potatoes, peeled and quartered
⅓ cup skim milk

1 tablespoon Butter Buds®
salt and pepper to taste

Cook potatoes in the usual fashion, drain off water, (don't forget to save the water for your homemade bread). Add skim milk, Butter Buds®, salt and pepper. Mash until fluffy.

Variation:
Add 2 teaspoons lemon juice and 1 clove garlic pressed through garlic press to the mashed potatoes. We thank the Greeks for this variation.

Serves 5	80 calories per ½ cup serving		
Fat .... .1 G	Cholesterol ... 0 mg	Fiber .... 1.2 G	Diabetic exchanges:
saturated .. 0 G	Protein .... 1.9 G	Vitamin C .. 6 mg	1 starch
mono ..... 0 G	Carbohydrate .. 17.3 G	Calcium ... 24 mg	
poly .... 0 G		Sodium .... 51 mg	

HIMMEL UND ERDE
(Heaven and Earth)

The Germans, bless them, will have to forgive me, I took the saturated fat out.

1 large potato, diced (unpeeled)
1 large apple, diced (unpeeled)
1 16 oz. can sauerkraut*
1 beef bouillon cube*

¼ teaspoon pepper
1 teaspoon caraway seeds
1 small clove garlic, minced
4 weiner sausages (see recipe)

Combine potato, sauerkraut, bouillon cube, pepper, caraway and garlic; cook together until the potatoes are tender. Add the apple and cook until apple is done. Add sausages and cook until the sausages are heated through.
The weiner sausages are precooked; the apple becomes mushy if overdone while the potatoes cook slowly in the salty sauerkraut liquid.

Analysis is without the sausage.

Serves 4	120 calories per 8 oz. serving		
Fat .... .7 G	Cholesterol ... 0 mg	Fiber .... 4.7 G	Diabetic exchanges:
saturated . .2 G	Protein .... 2.9 G	Vitamin C .. 29 mg	1 starch, 1 vegetable,
mono .... .1 G	Carbohydrate .. 27.7 G	Calcium ... 50 mg	¼ fruit
poly ...... .2 G		Sodium .. 1039 mg	

For the sausage add 166 calories, ¼ starch, 1½ lean meat, 1½ fat.

*Indicates high sodium content

DILLED POTATOES

An old Polish recipe served to us first in San Francisco by the wife of an orthopedic surgeon friend, modified, and frequently on our table.

Boil 3 medium potatoes, peeled and quartered, until done. Drain them (save the water for the homemade bread), and add:

1 tablespoon Butter Buds®
salt and pepper to taste

1 tablespoon chopped fresh dill or
½ teaspoon dried dill weed

Cover and let flavors mingle.

Serves 4		94 calories per ½ cup serving					
Fat	.1 G	Cholesterol ...	0 mg	Fiber	1.5 G	Diabetic exchanges:	
saturated ..	0 G	Protein	1.8 G	Vitamin C ..	8 mg	1⅛ starch	
mono	0 G	Carbohydrate .. 21.8 G		Calcium ...	9 mg		
poly	0 G			Sodium	55 mg		

SAUTEED TOMATO SLICES

This is a way to serve tomatoes before they start tasting good—green tomatoes. This also works well for hot house tomatoes.

½ cup all-purpose flour
½ cup dry bread crumbs
¼ cup freshly grated parmesan cheese*
¾ teaspoon dried thyme, crumbled

salt and pepper to taste*
2 hot house or green tomatoes
1 egg white beaten
2 tablespoons olive oil

Put the flour on a sheet of waxed paper. On another sheet of waxed paper, put the bread crumbs, cheese, thyme, salt and pepper and combine well. Lightly beat the egg white. Slice the tomatoes into ⅓ inch slices. Dip one tomato slice at a time into the flour, then into the egg white, then into the bread crumb mixture. Heat the olive oil in a heavy skillet over moderately high heat. Sauté the tomato slices for 1½ to 2 minutes on each side or until they are golden. Transfer to a heated platter.

Serves 4		205 calories per 4 oz. serving					
Fat	9.2 G	Cholesterol ...	5 mg	Fiber	1.9 G	Diabetic exchanges:	
saturated .	2.1 G	Protein	6.8 G	Vitamin C ..	11 mg	2 vegetable, 1¾ fat,	
mono	5.7 G	Carbohydrate .. 24.1 G		Calcium ...	98 mg	1 starch	
poly	.9 G			Sodium .... 204 mg			

*Indicates high sodium content

HASH

Hash, properly made, has a brown crust and is a delight to the senses. Without the crust, it should be avoided.

1 potato, peeled and finely diced
1 small onion, finely diced
1 beef bouillon cube*

1 teaspoon olive oil
freshly ground pepper

Put the potato and onion in a non-stick skillet and add water to cover. Cook until the water is evaporated. Add water to cover again and cook until the potatoes are soft. Add the oil, bouillon cube and pepper. Continue to cook until the potatoes can be separated into portions. Continue cooking until a brown crust is formed. Turn hash over and brown to a crust on the other side.

Serves 2	146 calories per 5 oz. serving		
Fat......... 2.7 G	Cholesterol ... 0 mg	Fiber .... 2.2 G	Diabetic exchanges:
saturated . .5 G	Protein .... 2.9 G	Vitamin C .. 11 mg	1½ starch, ½ fat
mono .... 1.8 G	Carbohydrate .. 28.4 G	Calcium ... 15 mg	
poly...... .3 G		Sodium .... 517 mg	

POTATOES WITH CAPERS AND DILL

You have to be careful with these—they are habit-forming.

1 pound potatoes,
  cut into ½ inch cubes
3 tablespoons olive oil
1 tablespoon lemon juice
1 tablespoon minced fresh dill or
  ½ teaspoon dried dill weed

1 tablespoon capers, minced
1 teaspoon salt*
¾ teaspoon sugar
⅛ teaspoon freshly ground pepper

In a large skillet, heat 1 tablespoon olive oil and cook the potato cubes, covered, until brown and fork tender, about 15-20 minutes. Turn the potatoes frequently to keep them from sticking. Meanwhile, combine the remaining 2 tablespoons of olive oil and remaining ingredients in a large bowl. When the potatoes are done, add them to the bowl and toss to coat well. Serve immediately.

Serves 6	129 calories per ½ cup serving		
Fat......... 6.8 G	Cholesterol ... 0 mg	Fiber .... 1.2 G	Diabetic exchanges:
saturated . .9 G	Protein .... 1.4 G	Vitamin C .. 11 mg	1 starch, 1 fat
mono .... 5.0 G	Carbohydrate .. 16.0 G	Calcium ... 8 mg	
poly...... .6 G		Sodium .... 359 mg	

*Indicates high sodium content

POTATO PANCAKES

This is not a breakfast item. This is an excellent side dish, low in calories and sodium.

¾ cup grated raw potatoes
2 tablespoons chopped onions
2 egg whites
¼ cup whole wheat flour

¾ teaspoon baking powder
¼ teaspoon onion powder
¼ teaspoon garlic powder
olive oil

Mix potatoes and onion together. Beat egg whites until soft peaks form and fold them into the potato mixture. Add remaining ingredients (except oil) and blend well. Heat griddle and lightly coat with oil (or spray with pan spray). Spoon batter to make ½ inch thick pancakes. Brown on each side and serve hot.

Makes 6	57 calories per cake		
Fat .... 1.6 G	Cholesterol ... 0 mg	Fiber .... 1.0 G	Diabetic exchanges:
saturated . .2 G	Protein .... 2.2 G	Vitamin C .. 2 mg	⅔ starch
mono .... 1.1 G	Carbohydrate .. 8.7 G	Calcium ... 14 mg	
poly ...... .2 G		Sodium .... 59 mg	

TUSCAN RICE AND BEANS

This dish provides complete protein with lots of fiber.

1 cup dried white beans
2 tablespoons olive oil
1 medium onion, chopped
2 cloves garlic, minced
¼ cup chopped parsley

½ teaspoon dried basil
1 stalk celery, minced
16 ounce can tomatoes*
salt and freshly ground pepper to taste
1 cup rice

Soak the beans overnight, drain and rinse. Put beans in a pot, cover with water and cook until just tender, about 1½ hours. Meanwhile, heat the oil in a sauté pan, add the onion, garlic, parsley, basil, celery and cook until the vegetables are soft. Add tomatoes. Season with salt and pepper and simmer for 10 minutes. Add vegetable mixture to the beans, simmer. Meanwhile, cook the rice. Add cooked rice to the bean mixture, mix well. Serve hot.

Serves 6	220 calories per 1 cup serving		
Fat .... 5.2 G	Cholesterol ... 0 mg	Fiber .... 2.4 G	Diabetic exchanges:
saturated . .8 G	Protein .... 9.3 G	Vitamin C .. 16 mg	2 starch, 1 lean meat
mono .... 3.4 G	Carbohydrate .. 35.6 G	Calcium ... 87 mg	
poly ...... .7 G		Sodium .... 142 mg	

*Indicates high sodium content

WILD RICE

If you have wondered how to prepare wild rice, here is one way, without meat added.

½ cup chopped celery
2 tablespoons chopped green pepper
2 tablespoons chopped scallion
1 tablespoon chopped parsley
1 cup sliced mushrooms
1 tablespoon chopped pimento
2 tablespoons olive oil

2 cups beef broth (see recipe)*
½ cup wild rice
¼ cup brown rice
½ cup skim milk
1 tablespoon flour
½ teaspoon salt or to taste*
freshly ground pepper to taste

Heat olive oil in sauté pan; add celery, green pepper, scallion, parsley, mushrooms and pimento; sauté until vegetables are softened. Stir in wild rice and brown rice, cook until rice is lightly browned. Stir flour into milk and add to pan. Stir in beef broth. Add salt and pepper to taste. Pour into a 1 quart casserole which has been sprayed with pan spray. Bake in 350 degree oven for about 30-45 minutes, until rice is done and liquid is absorbed.

Serves 8	104 calories per ½ cup serving		
Fat .... 3.8 G	Cholesterol ... 0 mg	Fiber .... 1.7 G	Diabetic exchanges:
saturated . .6 G	Protein .... 3.4 G	Vitamin C .. 6 mg	½ starch, ¾ fat,
mono .... 2.6 G	Carbohydrate .. 14.3 G	Calcium ... 33 mg	1 vegetable
poly ...... .4 G		Sodium .... 345 mg	

GREEK VEGETABLE STEW

A different way to prepare vegetables for your table.

1 medium onion, sliced
1½ tablespoons olive oil
½ pound green beans
2 carrots, sliced
2 medium potatoes, cut in
  lengthwise strips

2 stalks celery, cut in 1 inch pieces
½ teaspoon basil, hand rubbed
1 teaspoon oregano, hand rubbed
2 cloves garlic, minced
salt and pepper to taste
1 cup peeled, seeded, chopped tomatoes

Heat the oil, sauté the onion until soft. Add the remaining ingredients and turn into an oven casserole. Cover and bake in 325 degree oven for 1 hour or until vegetables are tender.

Serves 6	108 calories per ¾ cup serving		
Fat .... 3.7 G	Cholesterol ... 0 mg	Fiber .... 3.2 G	Diabetic exchanges:
saturated . .5 G	Protein .... 2.4 G	Vitamin C .. 20 mg	½ starch, ¾ fat,
mono .... 2.5 G	Carbohydrate .. 17.9 G	Calcium ... 51 mg	1½ vegetable
poly ...... .4 G		Sodium .... 90 mg	

*Indicates high sodium content

BAKED ACORN SQUASH

High fiber.

1 Acorn squash
1 tablespoon olive oil
2 teaspoons Butter Buds®
½ teaspoon brown sugar substitute

salt to taste
cinnamon to taste
nutmeg to taste

Halve acorn squash, clean out seeds. Invert squash half on plate and microwave for 5 minutes. Turn squash upright and cook additional 3 mintues or until tender. Remove from microwave and sprinkle center with brown sugar substitute and Butter Buds®. Add a little olive oil, if desired. Sprinkle with cinnamon and nutmeg.

This may be baked in the conventional oven-put olive oil, sugar substitute, Butter Buds®, cinnamon and nutmeg in squash halves and bake for about 1 hour at 375 degrees.

Serves 2	130 calories per 4 oz. serving		
Fat .... 7.1 G	Cholesterol ... 0 mg	Fiber .... 3.0 G	Diabetic exchanges:
saturated . 1.1 G	Protein .... 1.2 G	Vitamin C .. 11 mg	1 starch, 1½ fat
mono .... 5.0 G	Carbohydrate .. 17.7 G	Calcium ... 53 mg	
poly ...... .6 G		Sodium .... 71 mg	

BREADED TOMATOES

This should be tart and sweet; a good counterpart to many meals.

1 can (16 oz.) tomatoes in juice*
¼ cup finely chopped onion
1 tablespoon flour

salt and freshly ground pepper to taste
2 slices bread
1 package sugar substitute

Drain tomato juice from tomatoes, set tomatoes aside. In saucepan, cook the onions in the juice until they are soft. Combine the flour with a little cold water to make a thin paste, stir into the juice and cook until slightly thickened. Add the tomatoes, salt and pepper to taste and torn bread slices. Continue to cook until tomatoes are well heated and bread is well saturated with juice. Remove from heat, stir in sugar substitute (or sugar, if desired).

Serves 4	76 calories per ½ cup serving		
Fat .... .5 G	Cholesterol ... 0 mg	Fiber .... 1.7 G	Diabetic exchanges:
saturated .. 0 G	Protein .... 2.8 G	Vitamin C .. 19 mg	1½ vegetable,
mono ..... 0 G	Carbohydrate .. 15.8 G	Calcium ... 37 mg	½ starch
poly ...... .2 G		Sodium .... 283 mg	

*Indicates high sodium content

VEGETABLE MELANGE

The vegetables should remain tender-crisp and be shiny with oil.

1 carrot, peeled,
   sliced into ½ inch slices
1 cup broccoli flowerettes
1 cup cauliflower flowerettes
½ green pepper, seeded,
   cut into strips
½ red pepper, seeded, cut into strips

1 large onion, cut into eighths
½ cup mushrooms, sliced
1 tomato, cut into eighths
2 tablespoons olive oil
garlic powder
salt and pepper to taste

Separately blanch carrot slices, broccoli and cauliflower flowerettes for 3 minutes in boiling water, remove from water and plunge the vegetables immediately into iced water until cool. Drain on towels.

Heat olive oil in skillet, add onion and quickly sauté it just until limp. Add carrot slices, broccoli, cauliflower and peppers. Sprinkle vegetables with garlic powder and saute, stirring constantly, for 3-5 minutes, so that all vegetables become coated with oil and are heated through. Add mushrooms and tomato and cook another 2-3 minutes. Season to taste with salt and pepper.

Serves 6	74 calories per ½ cup serving			
Fat .... 4.8 G	Cholesterol ... 0 mg	Fiber .... 2.4 G	Diabetic exchanges:
saturated . .6 G	Protein .... 1.8 G	Vitamin C .. 73 mg	1½ vegetable, ¾ fat
mono .... 3.3 G	Carbohydrate .. 7.4 G	Calcium ... 25 mg	
poly...... .5 G		Sodium .... 14 mg	

WHITE SAUCE

Use this for your scalloped potatoes, creamed peas, creamed macaroni dishes, etc.

2 tablespoons olive oil
1 tablespoon chopped onion
2 tablespoons flour

1 cup skim milk
1 chicken bouillon cube*

Heat olive oil in small saucepan, sauté onion until transparent. Stir in flour and cook briefly. Add milk, stirring constantly, to prevent lumps. Add bouillon cube and cook for 20 minutes.

Makes 1 cup	100 calories per ¼ cup serving			
Fat .... 7.1 G	Cholesterol ... 1 mg	Fiber .... .1 G	Diabetic exchanges:
saturated . 1.0 G	Protein .... 2.8 G	Vitamin C .. 0 mg	½ starch, 1¼ fat
mono .... 5.1 G	Carbohydrate .. 6.4 G	Calcium ... 80 mg	
poly...... .6 G		Sodium ....310 mg	

*Indicates high sodium content

FRIED RICE CAKES

An excellent way to use left over rice. This is high in protein and calcium.

2 cups cold cooked rice
½ cup Egg Beaters®
2 tablespoons bacon substitute pieces*
⅓ cup finely chopped green pepper
¼ cup freshly grated parmesan cheese*

2 tablespoons finely chopped onion
⅛ teaspoon salt*
⅛ teaspoon freshly ground pepper
2 tablespoons olive oil for frying

In a large bowl, combine all ingredients except the oil. Cover and chill for at least 1 hour or overnight. Heat the olive oil in a large non-stick skillet. Place ½ cup rice mixture in the hot oil, forming patties. Cook for about 5 minutes on each side or until patties are set and golden. Garnish with parsley if desired.

Serves 4	194 calories per ½ cup serving			
Fat .... 6.0 G	Cholesterol ... 4 mg	Fiber .... .6 G	Diabetic exchanges:
saturated . 1.7 G	Protein .... 8.0 G	Vitamin C .. 10 mg	1½ starch, ½ lean
mono .... 3.2 G	Carbohydrate .. 26.0 G	Calcium ... 99 mg	meat, 1 fat
poly ...... .9 G		Sodium .... 214 mg	

*Indicates high sodium content

Notes

Cakes,
Cookies
& Desserts

♥ The oils in egg yolks are similar to the oils in bacon fat.

♥ Diabetics seldom die of sugar problems: strokes, heart attacks and gangrene are caused by their arteries.

♥ In my opinion, the second most dangerous disease is non–insulin dependent diabetes mellitus, ranking right behind cancer.

♥ When a recipe is cooked, use saccharin instead of aspartame. New cookable sweeteners are on the way.

♥ Sugar–containing snacks are being tested for routine inclusion in diabetic diets.

CAKES, COOKIES & DESSERTS

PEACH-PINEAPPLE UPSIDE DOWN CAKE

This is the lightest of this kind of cake I have ever tasted.

Topping

½ teaspoon brown sugar substitute
1 tablespoon brown sugar
1 tablespoon Butter Buds®*

2 tablespoons olive oil
Sliced canned peaches, well drained
Sliced canned pineapple, well drained

Spray an 8 inch cake pan with pan spray. Mix sugar, sweetener, Butter Buds® and olive oil and press the mixture into the bottom of the cake pan. Arrange the well drained fruit over the mixture and set aside.

Cake

¾ cup cake flour
¾ teaspoon baking powder
¼ teaspoon salt*
2 egg whites
¼ cup Egg Beaters®

⅓ cup skim milk
2 tablespoons olive oil
1 teaspoon vanilla extract
¼ cup Sprinkle Sweet®
1 tablespoon sugar

Combine all dry ingredients except sugar in large bowl. In another bowl, beat egg whites until soft peaks form, add the tablespoon of sugar and beat to stiff peaks. Combine all liquid ingredients, beat together then fold in the stiffly beaten egg whites. Fold in the flour mixture ¼ cup at a time. Mix just until incorporated. Pour onto prepared topping and bake in a preheated 350 degree oven for 25 minutes or until tests done. (Test for doneness with toothpick.) Invert onto serving dish and allow to cool for 3-5 minutes, remove pan. Serve warm or cold.

Serves 8	164 calories per ⅛ slice cake		
Fat......... 7.7 G	Cholesterol ... 0 mg	Fiber .... .8 G	Diabetic exchanges:
saturated . 1.1 G	Protein .... 3.0 G	Vitamin C .. 4 mg	¼ starch, 1 fruit,
mono .... 5.2 G	Carbohydrate .. 21.2 G	Calcium ... 46 mg	½ lean meat, 1 fat
poly...... 1.1 G		Sodium .... 155 mg	

*Indicates high sodium content

CHOCOLATE CAKE

Chocolate lovers! Cover it with frosting! Ice water improves the texture.

6 tablespoons cocoa
½ cup olive oil
1½ cups Sprinkle Sweet®
2 tablespoons sugar
4 egg whites

2 teaspoons vanilla
2 cups cake flour
1½ teaspoons baking powder
1 tablespoon Butter Buds®*
1 cup ice water

Preheat oven to 350 degrees. Oil and lightly flour two 8 inch round cake pans. Combine oil, sweetener and sugar and beat. Add egg whites and vanilla and beat well. Combine flour, cocoa, baking powder, and Butter Buds® and add to liquid mixture; blend well. Add 1 cup ice water and beat until smooth. Pour into prepared pans and bake for 25-30 minutes or until done. Cool in pans for 5 minutes before turning out onto cooling rack.

Serves 12	180 calories per 1/12 cake		
Fat .... 9.7 G	Cholesterol ... 0 mg	Fiber .... 1.3 G	Diabetic exchanges:
saturated . 1.5 G	Protein .... 2.9 G	Vitamin C .. 0 mg	1¼ starch, 2 fat
mono .... 6.8 G	Carbohydrate .. 21.3 G	Calcium ... 9 mg	
poly ...... .9 G		Sodium .... 143 mg	

CHOCOLATE BUTTERMILK CAKE

Chocolate lovers! Rich and good.

1⅔ cups cake flour
1 cup Sprinkle Sweet®
2 tablespoons sugar
½ cup cocoa powder
1 teaspoon baking powder

½ teaspoon baking soda
½ teaspoon salt*
1 cup 1% buttermilk
½ cup olive oil
2 teaspoons vanilla

Preheat oven to 350 degrees. Oil and flour two 8 inch round cake pans. Mix flour, sweetener, sugar, cocoa powder, baking soda, baking powder and salt in a bowl. Add buttermilk, oil and vanilla and beat until smooth. Pour into prepared pans. Bake 20-25 minutes. Cool 4 minutes in pans and then remove from pans and finish cooling on a rack. Cool completely then frost. (see recipe)

Serves 12	160 calories per slice		
Fat .... 10.0 G	Cholesterol ... 1 mg	Fiber .... 1.5 G	Diabetic exchanges:
saturated . 1.7 G	Protein .... 2.4 G	Vitamin C .. 0 mg	2 fat, 1 starch
mono .... 6.9 G	Carbohydrate .. 16.7 G	Calcium ... 32 mg	
poly ...... .9 G		Sodium .... 180 mg	

*Indicates high sodium content

COTTAGE PUDDING CAKE

Basic white cake—or strawberry short cake?

1½ cups flour
2 teaspoons baking powder
1 tablespoon Butter Buds®*
½ cup Sprinkle Sweet®

1 tablespoon sugar
½ cup olive oil
½ cup skim milk
2 egg whites

Oil and lightly flour 8 inch square pan. Preheat oven to 350 degrees. Mix flour, baking powder, Butter Buds®, sweetener and sugar in a bowl. Mix oil, skim milk and egg whites together; add to dry ingredients, mix well. Pour into prepared pan and bake for about 25 minutes or until done. Cool in pan for 5 minutes before turning out onto cooling rack.

Serves 16	115 calories per 2 inch square		
Fat .... 6.9 G	Cholesterol ... 0 mg	Fiber .... .3 G	Diabetic exchanges:
saturated . .9 G	Protein .... 1.9 G	Vitamin C .. 0 mg	¾ starch, 1 fat
mono .... 5.0 G	Carbohydrate .. 11.4 G	Calcium ... 35 mg	
poly...... .6 G		Sodium .... 61 mg	

ORANGE CARROT CAKE

This recipe is adapted from one put out by the local home extension office.

1 cup all-purpose flour
1 teaspoon baking powder
1 teaspoon ground allspice
½ teaspoon cinnamon
¼ teaspoon baking soda
⅛ teaspoon salt*

½ cup Egg Beaters® or 3 egg whites
½ cup sugar
⅓ cup olive oil
⅓ cup orange juice
1 cup grated carrots

Combine flour, baking powder, allspice, cinnamon, soda and salt in a bowl; set aside.

Combine Egg Beaters®, sugar, oil and juice in a large bowl, beat well. Add flour mixture and carrots, stirring until well blended. Pour into an 8 inch square pan which has been sprayed with pan spray. Bake at 350 degrees for about 30 minutes or until done. Cool cake in pan; dust lightly with powdered sugar if desired or frost with orange frosting. (see recipe) Cut into squares.

Serves 16	105 calories per 2 inch square		
Fat .... 4.8 G	Cholesterol ... 0 mg	Fiber .... .1 G	Diabetic exchanges:
saturated . .7 G	Protein .... 1.9 G	Vitamin C .. 3 mg	¾ starch, 1 fat
mono .... 3.4 G	Carbohydrate .. 13.7 G	Calcium ... 13 mg	
poly...... .5 G		Sodium .... 66 mg	

CAKE FROSTING

My wife said it could not be done!

¼ cup low fat cream cheese
6 tablespoons Sprinkle Sweet®
½ cup 1% cottage cheese*

3 tablespoons cocoa powder
½ teaspoon vanilla
Skim milk to consistency

Combine the cottage cheese and skim milk in the blender and process to a thick liquid. Add cream cheese and blend well. Add cocoa powder, vanilla and Sprinkle Sweet®. Add milk or more cream cheese to correct consistency. Chill before applying to cake as it will thicken as it gets cold. Cake must be refrigerated when this frosting is used.

Note: always add cocoa, vanilla and sweetener before adjusting consistency. To make vanilla frosting, use 1 teaspoon vanilla and eliminate cocoa. Vary the flavor of the frosting by using different flavored extracts.

Frosts 1-8 inch layer	21 calories per 1/12 cake		
Fat .... .7 G	Cholesterol ... 1 mg	Fiber .... .4 G	Diabetic exchanges:
saturated . .4 G	Protein .... 2.0 G	Vitamin C .. 0 mg	¼ fat, ⅛ starch (free)
mono .... .2 G	Carbohydrate .. 2.0 G	Calcium ... 16 mg	
poly .... 0 G		Sodium .... 49 mg	

LEMON ICING

This is old German cooking, modified.

¼ cup Egg Beaters®
1 cup sugar or Sprinkle Sweet®
¼ cup lemon juice
2½ tablespoons flour

grated peel of 2 lemons
  (or 2 drops lemon oil)
1 tablespoon olive oil
1 tablespoon Butter Buds®*

Beat the Egg Beaters®, stir in sweetener. Add lemon juice, lemon peel, Butter Buds® and olive oil. Stir the mixture until it comes to a boil, be careful it doesn't burn. Chill before using.

Makes 1½ cups	85 calories per 1 oz. serving		
Fat .... 1.6 G	Cholesterol ... 0 mg	Fiber .... 0 G	Diabetic exchanges:
saturated . .2 G	Protein .... .7 G	Vitamin C .. 3 mg	1 fruit, ¼ fat
mono .... .9 G	Carbohydrate .. 17.7 G	Calcium ... 5 mg	
poly ...... .4 G		Sodium .... 25 mg	

*Indicates high sodium content

CHEESECAKE

There are two ways to make this—for diabetics and non diabetics. Counting the olive oil, there is not over 16 grams of saturated fat in the whole cake. There is as much saturated fat in one piece of standard cheesecake as there is in this whole cake.

Crust
1 cup fine graham cracker crumbs   ¼ teaspoon cinnamon
4 tablespoons olive oil   ¼ teaspoon nutmeg

Mix graham cracker crumbs, cinnamon and nutmeg in the blender. Pour into a bowl and add 4 tablespoons olive oil and mix well. Spray a 9 inch springform pan with pan spray and line pan bottom and about 1½ inches up the sides with the crumb mixture. Put in the refrigerator until ready to fill.

Filling
24 ounces 1% cottage cheese*   1 teaspoon vanilla
1½ cups Sprinkle Sweet® (or sugar)   4 egg whites, beaten
6 tablespoons Egg Beaters®   2 tablespoons sugar
3 tablespoons flour

Combine cottage cheese, sweetener, flour, Egg Beaters® and vanilla in food processor bowl and process until very smooth. Beat egg whites until stiff, adding 2 tablespoons sugar. Fold whites into cottage cheese mixture. Pour into prepared crust. Put into preheated 400 degree oven and immediately lower temperature to 250 degrees (otherwise top will crack if temperature is too high) and bake until done, about 1 hour. Check for doneness by gently shaking; when done the center should feel firm but quiver upon shaking. Let cool completely before removing pan sides.

Serves 12	163 calories per 1/12 slice cake			
Fat .... 6.4 G	Cholesterol ... 3 mg	Fiber .... .3 G	Diabetic exchanges:
saturated . 1.3 G	Protein .... 10.0 G	Vitamin C .. 0 mg	⅔ fat, ¾ starch,
mono .... 4.0 G	Carbohydrate .. 16.0 G	Calcium ... 45 mg	1 lean meat
poly ...... .8 G		Sodium .... 328 mg	

*Indicates high sodium content

OLIVE OIL PASTRY

This is the basic pastry recipe for this book.

2 cups all purpose flour
1 teaspoon salt*
⅓ cup olive oil

4 tablespoons ice water
¼ teaspoon baking powder
1 heaping teaspoon potato starch

Combine dry ingredients in a bowl. Stir in olive oil and with a fork mash and stir until mixture resembles small crumbs. Add ice water and stir until mixture forms into a ball.

This is enough pastry for a double crust 9 inch pie.

Makes 1-9 inch pie	194 calories per ⅛ recipe		
Fat .... 9.2 G	Cholesterol ... 0 mg	Fiber .... .8 G	Diabetic exchanges:
saturated . 1.2 G	Protein .... 3.2 G	Vitamin C .. 0 mg	1½ starch, 2 fat
mono .... 6.6 G	Carbohydrate .. 24.0 G	Calcium ... 10 mg	
poly ...... .8 G		Sodium .... 270 mg	

BANANA CREAM PIE

Another forbidden taste made possible for your diet.

1 prebaked 9 inch olive oil
   pie crust (see recipe)
½ cup Sprinkle Sweet®
1 tablespoon sugar
¼ cup cornstarch

2 cups evaporated skim milk
½ cup Egg Beaters®
1 teaspoon vanilla
1 tablespoon Butter Buds®*
1 banana, sliced

Prepare and bake pie shell, cool. Place sliced bananas in shell. Combine the sweetener, sugar and cornstarch in medium saucepan. Gradually stir in the milk, mixing until smooth. Bring to boiling over medium heat, remove from heat. Stir half of mixture into Egg Beaters®, mix well, pour back into saucepan. Bring back to boiling, stirring. Remove from heat. Stir in Butter Buds® and vanilla. Pour immediately into prepared pie shell. Cool. May be sprinkled with nutmeg. May be topped with false whipped cream (see recipe).

Analysis includes pie crust.

Serves 8	203 calories per ⅛ pie slice		
Fat .... 5.3 G	Cholesterol ... 3 mg	Fiber .... .7 G	Diabetic exchanges:
saturated . .8 G	Protein .... 8.4 G	Vitamin C .. 2 mg	1 low fat milk, 1 fruit
mono .... 3.5 G	Carbohydrate .. 30.0 G	Calcium ... 199 mg	
poly ...... .7 G		Sodium .... 264 mg	

*Indicates high sodium content

CUSTARD PIE

And you thought you would never taste this again on your diet!

2 cups evaporated skim milk
¾ cup Egg Beaters₍ᴿ₎
2 egg whites
¾ cup Sprinkle Sweet₍ᴿ₎

1 teaspoon vanilla
nutmeg
9 inch unbaked olive oil pie shell
(see recipe)

Combine the skim milk, Egg Beaters₍ᴿ₎, sweetener and vanilla, mix well. Fold in the stiffly beaten egg whites. Pour into a 9 inch unbaked olive oil pie shell. Sprinkle with nutmeg. Bake at 425 degrees for 10 minutes, reduce heat to 350 degrees and bake for an additional 15-20 minutes or until set.

Analysis includes the crust.

Serves 8	172 calories per ⅛ pie slice		
Fat .... 5.6 G	Cholesterol ... 3 mg	Fiber .... .4 G	Diabetic exchanges:
saturated . .9 G	Protein .... 10.0 G	Vitamin C .. 1 mg	1 low fat milk, ½ starch
mono .... 3.6 G	Carbohydrate .. 19.7 G	Calcium ... 204 mg	
poly ...... .8 G		Sodium .... 262 mg	

PUMPKIN PIE

Even topped with false whipped cream (see recipe), it's still ⅓ the fat.

1 9 inch unbaked olive oil
   pie crust (see recipe)
1 can (16 oz) pumpkin
½ cup Egg Beaters₍ᴿ₎ or 2 egg whites
¼ cup sugar
½ cup Sprinkle Sweet₍ᴿ₎

½ teaspoon salt*
1 teaspoon cinnamon
½ teaspoon ginger
¼ teaspoon cloves
1 can (12 oz) evaporated skim milk

Combine all ingredients and beat well. Pour into a 9 inch unbaked pie shell. Bake in 425 degree oven for 15 minutes. Reduce heat to 350 degrees and bake for 45 minutes longer or until knife inserted near center comes out clean. Cool.

Note: Non diabetics may want to use ¾ cup sugar in place of the sugar and sweetener.

Analysis includes pie crust.

Serves 8	188 calories per ⅛ pie slice		
Fat .... 5.4 G	Cholesterol ... 2 mg	Fiber .... 1.5 G	Diabetic exchanges:
saturated . .8 G	Protein .... 7.3 G	Vitamin C .. 0 mg	1 low fat milk, 1 fruit,
mono .... 3.5 G	Carbohydrate .. 28.0 G	Calcium ... 156 mg	
poly ...... .7 G		Sodium .... 348 mg	

*Indicates high sodium content

DUTCH APPLE PIE

If you must have pie, try one with only one crust.

9 inch unbaked olive oil pie shell (see recipe)

Topping:
½ cup flour
2 tablespoons brown sugar
1 teaspoon brown sugar substitute

2 tablespoons olive oil
1 teaspoon Butter Buds®*

Filling:
6 cups apple slices
1 tablespoon lemon juice
1 tablespoon flour
¼ cup sugar

½ cup Sprinkle Sweet®
2 teaspoons Butter Buds®*
1 teaspoon cinnamon

Prepare the pie shell and refrigerate until ready to use. Combine the topping ingredients, rubbing them with your hand until it resembles coarse cornmeal. Set aside. Toss apple slices with lemon juice. Combine the remaining filling ingredients and toss with the apples. Turn the filling into the pie shell, spreading evenly. Cover with the topping; bake in a preheated 400 degree oven, covered with foil for 30 minutes. Remove the foil and continue to bake an additional 10-15 minutes or until the apples are tender.

Analysis includes the crust.

Serves 8	246 calories per ⅛ pie serving		
Fat......... 8.3 G	Cholesterol ... 0 mg	Fiber .... 2.5 G	Diabetic exchanges:
saturated . 1.1 G	Protein .... 2.7 G	Vitamin C .. 4 mg	1½ fruit, 1½ fat,
mono .... 5.8 G	Carbohydrate .. 40.6 G	Calcium ... 16 mg	1 starch
poly...... .8 G		Sodium .... 138 mg	

*Indicates high sodium content

GRASSHOPPER PIE

Uncooked egg whites usually are used in recipes of this type, but this version removes any problems associated with uncooked eggs.

Crust:

1¼ cups graham cracker crumbs
  (about 24)
4 tablespoons olive oil

2 tablespoons cocoa powder
2 packages sweetener
  (Do not use aspartame)

Mix all ingredients and press into a 9 inch pie pan, making a slightly raised edge. Bake in 375 degree oven for 8 minutes. Cool.

Filling:

1 package unflavored gelatin
¾ cup water
¼-½ teaspoon instant coffee granules
1½ cups 1% cottage cheese*
2 tablespoons sugar

4 packages sweetener
3 tablespoons creme de menthe
½ package gelatin
½ cup water

Sprinkle 1 package gelatin over ¾ cup water. Sprinkle ½ package gelatin over ¼ cup water. Let set 5 minutes. Gently warm the gelatin mixtures separately until the gelatin dissolves. Set aside. In the food processor put the cottage cheese, coffee, sugar, sweetener and creme de menthe. Process until smooth. Add the gelatin in the ¾ cup water and process until thoroughly mixed. To the gelatin in ¼ cup water, add ¼ cup water and set the bowl in a bowl of ice water. Beat with the electric mixer until stiff peaks form. (If the gelatin starts to gel too quickly, remove it from the ice water and continue to beat.) Fold the whipped gelatin into the cheese mixture. A whisk may be needed to break up the fluffs. Pour into the prepared pie crust and chill until firm.

Serves 8	214 calories per ⅛ pie slice		
Fat .... 9.4 G	Cholesterol ... 2 mg	Fiber .... 1.1 G	Diabetic exchanges:
saturated . 1.9 G	Protein .... 8.0 G	Vitamin C .. 0 mg	1½ starch, 1½ fat
mono .... 6.0 G	Carbohydrate .. 22.0 G	Calcium ... 37 mg	¼ low fat meat
poly ...... 1.1 G		Sodium .... 290 mg	

*Indicates high sodium content

CHARLIE'S SHEPHERD PIE

With all the cooking and taste testing, Charlie had to get in on the action. This is his creation.

2 cups canned sliced peaches,
    drained well
1 cup all purpose flour
1 tablespoon sugar
1 teaspoon baking powder

dash salt
¼ cup Egg Beaters®
½ cup skim milk
⅛ teaspoon cinnamon
⅛ teaspoon nutmeg

Preheat the oven to 375 degrees. Place the well drained peach slices in a 9 inch square baking pan. Combine the dry ingredients in a bowl. Combine the Egg Beaters® and milk and pour into the dry ingredients. Stir just until combined and pour evenly over the fruit. Bake in the preheated oven for 20 minutes or until lightly browned on top. Cut into 3 inch squares.

Serves 9		92 calories per serving				
Fat	.4 G	Cholesterol	0 mg	Fiber	1.0 G	Diabetic exchanges:
saturated	.1 G	Protein	3.1 G	Vitamin C	2 mg	1 starch, ¼ fruit
mono	.1 G	Carbohydrate	19.2 G	Calcium	33 mg	
poly	.2 G			Sodium	59 mg	

GREEN TOMATO MINCEMEAT

"End of the garden" green tomatoes can be used all year long for pie or oat bran cookies.

2 cups chopped green tomatoes
    (about 1¼ pounds)
1 cup seedless raisins
½ cup light brown sugar
2 tablespoons cider vinegar
½ cup apple juice concentrate
juice of 1 orange (about 4 tablespoons)

Grated zest of 1 orange
¼ teaspoon salt*
½ teaspoon ground cinnamon
½ teaspoon ground cloves
¼ teaspoon ground nutmeg
¼ teaspoon ground allspice

In a non-aluminum 2 quart saucepan, combine the tomatoes, raisins, brown sugar, vinegar, cider, orange juice, zest and salt; simmer about 40 minutes, until tomatoes are tender and juices are reduced by approximately one half. Add cinnamon, cloves, nutmeg, and allspice. Stir until heated through, 5 to 6 additional minutes.

Each serving will be reduced by 40 calories if the ½ cup brown sugar is replaced with 1 tablespoon sugar and 2 teaspoons brown sugar substitute.

Makes 2 cups		149 calories per ½ cup serving				
Fat	.3 G	Cholesterol	0 mg	Fiber	1.9 G	Diabetic exchanges:
saturated	.1 G	Protein	1.2 G	Vitamin C	13 mg	2 fruit, 1 vegetable
mono	0 G	Carbohydrate	38.1 G	Calcium	32 mg	
poly	.1 G			Sodium	84 mg	

*Indicates high sodium content

FALSE WHIPPED CREAM

Pretty close to the real thing, so I sneaked in some olive oil.

2 cups skim milk	2 teaspoons olive oil
2 tablespoons sugar	1 teaspoon vanilla
1 tablespoon cornstarch	

Heat 1 cup skim milk with sugar and vanilla, stirring constantly until it boils. Remove from heat. Stir the cornstarch into 1 cup cold skim milk and add it to the cooked skim milk. Add the olive oil, return the mixture to heat and cook, stirring constantly, for 3 to 4 minutes. Cool and chill in the refrigerator overnight. Just before serving, whip the mixture to stiff peaks. Serve immediately.

Makes 2 cups		20 calories per 1 ounce serving					
Fat	.5 G	Cholesterol	0 mg	Fiber	0 G	Diabetic exchanges:	
saturated	.1 G	Protein	.9 G	Vitamin C	0 mg	1 oz. is free	
mono	.4 G	Carbohydrate	3.0 G	Calcium	32 mg		
poly	0 G			Sodium	13 mg		

WHIPPED CREAM SUBSTITUTE

Use this as a topping for pie, gelatin desserts, etc.

1 cup 1% cottage cheese*	½ teaspoon vanilla
¼ cup Sprinkle Sweet® or sugar	skim milk

Blend all ingredients in the food processor or blender. Add skim milk to adjust consistency.

Makes 1 cup		45 calories per ¼ cup serving					
Fat	.6 G	Cholesterol	2 mg	Fiber	.1 G	Diabetic exchanges:	
saturated	.4 G	Protein	7.3 G	Vitamin C	0 mg	¾ lean meat	
mono	.1 G	Carbohydrate	2.3 G	Calcium	51 mg		
poly	0 G			Sodium	233 mg		

*Indicates high sodium content

BAKED APPLES OR BAKED APPLE SLICES

Use this to prepare both whole apples or apple slices. Olive oil and Butter Buds® give a very hearty taste to the apples. Add sweetener after cooking to avoid a bitter taste.

1 apple, cored (or sliced)	⅛ teaspoon cinnamon
½ teaspoon olive oil	⅛ teaspoon nutmeg
½ teaspoon Butter Buds®*	1 package sweetener

If the whole apple is used, core it and place it in a glass baking dish. Pour ½ teaspoon olive oil in each core; add nutmeg, cinnamon, Butter Buds®, salt and water to cover the bottom of the dish. Cook on high power in the microwave oven for 2-4 minutes, depending on doneness. The liquid bubbles up through the apple. Serve immediately or cool.

(For neatness sake and when only one apple is cooked, place the apple in a Pyrex measuring cup for cooking.)

Serves 1		89 calories				
Fat	2.7 G	Cholesterol ...	0 mg	Fiber	2.7 G	Diabetic exchanges:
saturated .	.4 G	Protein	.2 G	Vitamin C ..	6 mg	1 fruit, ½ fat
mono	1.7 G	Carbohydrate ..	17.4 G	Calcium ...	11 mg	
poly......	.3 G			Sodium	34 mg	

COOKED APPLES WITH MERINGUE

This dessert will impress your guests without adding undue fat and calories.

3 cups peeled sliced apples	3 egg whites
½ cup apple juice	3 tablespoons sugar
1 tablespoon lemon juice	½ teaspoon finely shredded lemon zest
3 inches stick cinnamon	

Combine the apples, apple juice, lemon juice and cinnamon stick together and cook to boiling. Reduce heat and simmer, stirring occasionally, until the apples are tender. Remove from heat and let set for 20 minutes, then remove cinnamon stick. While the apples are setting, beat the egg whites to soft peaks, gradually beating in 1 tablespoon of the liquid from the apples, the lemon peel and the sugar. Beat the egg whites to stiff peaks. Put the apples into individual oven proof serving dishes, top with meringue and bake in 325 degree oven until the meringue is browned, about 10 minutes. Serve warm.

Serves 6		76 calories per ½ cup serving				
Fat.........	.2 G	Cholesterol ...	0 mg	Fiber	1.3 G	Diabetic exchanges:
saturated ..	0 G	Protein	1.8 G	Vitamin C ..	3 mg	1 fruit, ¼ lean meat
mono	0 G	Carbohydrate ..	17.4 G	Calcium ...	10 mg	
poly.......	0 G			Sodium	26 mg	

*Indicates high sodium content

GERMAN APPEL PFANNKUCHEN
(APPLE PANCAKE)

I have trouble rationing myself with this dish.

FRUIT MIXTURE

4 packages sweetener
   (or 1 teaspoon sugar)
   (don't use aspartame)
1 teaspoon cinnamon
1 tablespoon Butter Buds®*

2 large cooking apples, peeled,
   cored and cut into ¼ inch slices
⅓ cup raisins
¼ cup apple juice

BATTER

½ teaspoon baking powder
½ cup Egg Beaters®
½ cup skim milk
½ cup flour

1 tablespoon Sprinkle Sweet® (or sugar)
½ teaspoon salt*
1 tablespoon Butter Buds®*
2 tablespoons olive oil

In a small sauce pan combine apples, raisins, apple juice, sweetener, cinnamon and Butter Buds®. Cook, stirring, for 3-4 minutes until apples are tender. Remove from heat, drain.

In a bowl, combine Egg Beaters®, milk, flour, sweetener, salt, Butter Buds® and 1 tablespoon olive oil. Mix thoroughly until no lumps remain. In an 8 inch non stick skillet put 1 tablespoon olive oil to cover bottom of skillet. Pour in batter and then spoon the drained apple mixture into the center; do not mix together. Keep heat on low, cover and cook slowly for 20 minutes.

Serves 6	185 calories per 1/6 pancake		
Fat .... 5.6 G	Cholesterol ... 1 mg	Fiber .... 2.6 G	Diabetic exchanges:
saturated . .8 G	Protein .... 4.7 G	Vitamin C .. 5 mg	2 starch, ¼ fruit
mono .... 3.5 G	Carbohydrate .. 30.3 G	Calcium ... 58 mg	
poly ...... .9 G		Sodium .... 321 mg	

*Indicates high sodium content

153

CHERRIES WITH TAPIOCA

This dessert can be served as is or put into a prebaked olive oil pie shell and served as cherry pie.

2 tablespoons quick tapioca
1 cup cherries, fresh, canned or frozen (unsweetened)
1 cup water or liquid from cherries
3 packages sugar substitute
¼ teaspoon almond extract

Soften the tapioca in cold water for 5 minutes. Add the cherries and cook until the mixture is thickened. Allow to cool. Stir in the sugar substitute and almond extract. Serve chilled. May be topped with whipped cream substitute (see recipe).

Serves 4	75 calories per ½ cup serving		
Fat .... .1 G	Cholesterol ... 0 mg	Fiber .... .6 G	Diabetic exchanges:
saturated .. 0 G	Protein .... .7 G	Vitamin C .. 3 mg	½ fruit, ½ starch
mono ..... 0 G	Carbohydrate .. 18.6 G	Calcium ... 10 mg	
poly .... 0 G		Sodium .... 3 mg	

STRAWBERRY DESSERT

This tastes richer and more fattening than it is.

2 packages unflavored gelatin
½ cup cold water
1 cup skim milk, heated to boiling
2 tablespoons sugar
2 packages sweetener
1 teaspoon almond extract
2 cups unsweetened frozen strawberries, slightly thawed

Sprinkle the gelatin over the cold water in a blender container, let stand 3-4 minutes. Add the hot milk and blend at low speed until the gelatin is dissolved, about 2 minutes. Add remaining ingredients and process at high speed until the strawberries are pureed. Pour immediately into dessert dishes and chill until firm.

Serves 8	42 calories per ½ cup serving		
Fat .... .1 G	Cholesterol ... 0 mg	Fiber .... 1.2 G	Diabetic exchanges:
saturated .. 0 G	Protein .... 2.7 G	Vitamin C .. 16 mg	⅓ starch, ¼ fruit,
mono ..... 0 G	Carbohydrate .. 8.0 G	Calcium ... 44 mg	
poly .... 0 G		Sodium .... 18 mg	

*Indicates high sodium content

BESSIE'S PRUNE WHIP

My mother used to make this and I was always leery of it because of what it did to me.

½ cup Whipped Cream Substitute (see recipe)
1 package sugar-free lemon gelatin

½ cup chopped pecans
10 cooked, pitted prunes, chopped

Prepare gelatin according to package directions. While the gelatin is jelling, prepare the whipped cream substitute. Cut the gelatin into cubes and combine with the whipped cream substitute, pecans and prunes just until cubes are well coated. Serve.

Serves 6	100 calories per ½ cup serving		
Fat .... 7.0 G	Cholesterol ... 0 mg	Fiber .... 1.4 G	Diabetic exchanges:
saturated . .6 G	Protein .... 3.3 G	Vitamin C .. 1 mg	½ low fat milk, ½ fat
mono .... 4.2 G	Carbohydrate .. 7.6 G	Calcium ... 25 mg	
poly ...... 1.7 G		Sodium .... 78 mg	

SCANDINAVIAN FRUIT SOUP

A common taste in Europe which we hope to bring here.

1½ cups dried apricots
1 cup dried prunes
2 cups dried apples
2 whole cinnamon sticks
½ lemon
1 teaspoon ground cardamom

⅓ cup quick tapioca
¼ cup raisins
¼ cup currants
1 teaspoon salt*
apple juice (optional)

Dice the dried fruit and put them into a stainless steel pot and cover with 10 cups water. Let stand 30 minutes. Add cinnamon, lemon, cardamom and tapioca. Bring to a boil, stirring frequently scraping the bottom of the pot to prevent sticking. Simmer, stirring frequently, for 10 minutes, turn off heat. Add raisins, currants and salt. Let soup cool then chill. If a thinner soup is desired, add apple juice.

Serves 20	74 calories per ½ cup serving		
Fat .... .1 G	Cholesterol ... 0 mg	Fiber .... 2.6 G	Diabetic exchanges:
saturated .. 0 G	Protein .... .7 G	Vitamin C .. 2 mg	1¼ fruit
mono ..... 0 G	Carbohydrate .. 19.5 G	Calcium ... 13 mg	
poly .... 0 G		Sodium .... 116 mg	

*Indicates high sodium content

COTTAGE CHEESE DESSERT

This can be prepared so quickly that it can be made while the table is being cleared (if you forgot to prepare dessert).

1 cup 1% cottage cheese*	**skim milk**
¼ cup sweetener or sugar	**cinnamon**

Blend all ingredients except the cinnamon in the food processor or blender. Add skim milk to adjust consistency. Spoon the mixture into serving dishes, sprinkle with cinnamon. Top with well drained canned peaches, apricots or other stewed fruit. Fresh fruit in season may be used.

Analysis is for topping only.

Serves 4	45 calories per ¼ cup serving		
Fat .... .6 G	Cholesterol ... 2 mg	Fiber .... .1 G	Diabetic exchanges:
saturated . .4 G	Protein .... 7.3 G	Vitamin C .. 0 mg	¾ lean meat
mono .... .1 G	Carbohydrate .. 2.3 G	Calcium ... 51 mg	
poly .... 0 G		Sodium .... 233 mg	

MODIFIED BANANAS FOSTER

Your guests' enjoyment of this dessert will be enhanced if you prepare it at tableside in an electric teflon skillet and flambe it with 2 tablespoons heated brandy or other liqueur of your choice.

1 cup freshly squeezed orange juice	**1 tablespoon olive oil**
½ cup Sprinkle Sweet®	**2 tablespoons Butter Buds®***
1 teaspoon brown sugar substitute	**4 bananas, peeled and split**
½ teaspoon corn starch in	
** 1 tablespoon cold water**	

Combine all ingredients except bananas and cook over low heat, stirring constantly, until the mixture is thickened. Add split bananas and cook just until the edges of the bananas become soft. To serve, arrange sliced bananas around a scoop of olive oil vanilla ice cream (see recipe) in serving dish. Spoon sauce over top.

Serves 8	91 calories per serving		
Fat .... 2.0 G	Cholesterol ... 0 mg	Fiber .... 1.3 G	Diabetic exchanges:
saturated . .3 G	Protein .... .8 G	Vitamin C .. 21 mg	1 fruit, ½ fat
mono .... 1.3 G	Carbohydrate .. 19.0 G	Calcium ... 7 mg	
poly ...... .2 G		Sodium .... 29 mg	

*Indicates high sodium content

BREAD PUDDING

This tastes as good as if it were made with saturated fat.

2 cups French style bread cubes
2 cups skim milk
2 tablespoons Sprinkle Sweet®
1 tablespoon sugar

½ cup Egg Beaters®
1 tablespoon Butter Buds®*
1 teaspoon vanilla
nutmeg

Combine the skim milk, Sprinkle Sweet®, sugar, Egg Beaters®, Butter Buds® and vanilla. Pour over bread cubes, sprinkle with nutmeg. Pour into 1 quart baking dish which has been sprayed with pan spray. Place in a larger dish with 1 inch hot water in it. Bake at 350 degrees for 35 minutes or until done.

Serves 6	87 calories per ½ cup serving		
Fat .... 1.2 G	Cholesterol ... 2 mg	Fiber .... .2 G	Diabetic exchanges:
saturated . .4 G	Protein .... 6.1 G	Vitamin C .. 1 mg	½ milk, ½ starch
mono .... .4 G	Carbohydrate .. 12.6 G	Calcium ... 124 mg	
poly...... .4 G		Sodium .... 164 mg	

LEMON PUDDING WITH PINEAPPLE

Lemon oil transforms the vanilla pudding into lemon pudding.

1 cup pineapple chunks, drained
1 package instant
  sugar free vanilla pudding*

2 drops lemon oil
2 cups skim milk

Prepare the pudding according to package directions with skim milk. Add the lemon oil drops. Mix with drained pineapple chunks. Serve Immediately or it liquifies.

Serves 6	70 calories per ½ cup serving		
Fat .... .2 G	Cholesterol ... 1 mg	Fiber .... .4 G	Diabetic exchanges:
saturated . .1 G	Protein .... 3.0 G	Vitamin C .. 5 mg	1 starch
mono ..... 0 G	Carbohydrate .. 14.5 G	Calcium ... 106 mg	
poly....... 0 G		Sodium .... 256 mg	

*Indicates high sodium content

CHOCOLATE MOUSSE

Chocolate Lovers! You aren't going to believe how rich this tastes!

½ cup Egg Beaters®
1⅔ cup evaporated skim milk
4 packages sweetener
  (don't use aspartame)
1 package unflavored gelatin
3 tablespoons cocoa powder

2 tablespoons olive oil
1 tablespoon Butter Buds®*
2 tablespoons sugar
1 teaspoon vanilla
½ cup water

Combine Egg Beaters®, milk, sweetener, cocoa, oil, Butter Buds®, sugar and vanilla in the top of a double boiler. Cook, stirring constantly with a wire whisk, until hot throughout. Meanwhile, sprinkle the gelatin over ¼ cup cold water in a small bowl, let set 5 minutes. Heat gelatin mixture until gelatin is dissolved. When dissolved, set the pan of gelatin in a bowl of ice cubes. Add the remaining ¼ cup water and beat the gelatin until it is the consistency of stiffly beaten egg whites, putting the pan of gelatin in and out of the ice as necessary to keep it from jelling too quickly. Place chocolate mixture over the ice and beat with a whisk until cooled. Fold whipped gelatin into the cooled chocolate mixture using a whisk to thoroughly mix. Pour into serving dishes, chill and serve topped with false whipped cream (see recipe).

Serves 5		144 calories per ½ cup serving		
Fat .... 5.8 G	Cholesterol ... 3 mg	Fiber .... 1.0 G	Diabetic exchanges:
saturated . 1.1 G	Protein .... 9.2 G	Vitamin C .. 1 mg	1 low fat milk, 1 fat
mono .... 3.7 G	Carbohydrate 14.6	Calcium ... 220 mg	
poly ...... .7 G		Sodium .... 153 mg	

*Indicates high sodium content

CHOCOLATE SQUARES

Chocolate lovers, both diabetic and non diabetic—the taste you love—without the calories! The olive oil is optional, but it does add richness.

4 packages unflavored gelatin
2 tablespoons sugar
½ cup Sprinkle Sweet®
1 ½ cups cold water

½ cup cocoa
1 tablespoon olive oil
1 teaspoon vanilla

Pour cold water into saucepan, sprinkle gelatin over water and allow to stand 1 minute. Stir over low heat until gelatin is dissolved. Stir in remaining ingredients except vanilla and continue stirring over low heat until sugar is dissolved and mixture is smooth. Stir in vanilla. Pour into an 8 inch baking pan which has been sprayed with pan spray. Chill until firm.

Serves 36	13 calories per 1½ inch square		
Fat .... .6 G	Cholesterol ... 0 mg	Fiber .... .5 G	Diabetic exchanges:
saturated . .2 G	Protein .... .9 G	Vitamin C .. 0 mg	2 squares would be free
mono .... .4 G	Carbohydrate .. 1.3 G	Calcium ... 2 mg	
poly .... 0 G		Sodium .... 1 mg	

CREAM PUFFS

Use these puffs with either appetizer or dessert filling.

¼ cup olive oil
½ cup boiling water
½ teaspoon salt*

½ cup flour
½ cup Egg Beaters®

Preheat the oven to 375 degrees. In a medium saucepan, heat the water and oil to boiling. Add salt and flour all at once, and stir vigorously until the flour is absorbed and mixture leaves the sides of the pan. Remove from heat and add the Egg Beaters® ¼ cup at a time, beating vigorously after each addition. The mixture will become spongy and shiny and should form a ball, leaving the sides of the pan. Spray a cookie sheet with pan spray. Drop mounds of batter by teaspoonfuls about 1 inch apart. Make them as round as possible. Bake in 375 degree oven for 30 minutes. Take one from the oven for a test, if it doesn't fall, they are done. When cool, cut open on one side near the top and fill.

Makes 3½ dozen	19 calories per puff		
Fat .... 1.4 G	Cholesterol ... 0 mg	Fiber .... 0 G	Diabetic exchanges:
saturated . .2 G	Protein .... .5 G	Vitamin C .. 0 mg	One puff is free
mono .... 1.0 G	Carbohydrate .. 1.1 G	Calcium ... 2 mg	
poly ...... .2 G		Sodium .... 18 mg	

*Indicates high sodium content

FROZEN YOGURT POPS

This is just as good frozen without the popsicle sticks for kids of all ages.

1 cup plain lowfat yogurt
¼ cup instant lowfat dry milk
1 package sweetener

1 cup sliced fresh or drained canned
fruit such as strawberries, bananas,
peaches, pineapple

In a blender container or food processor put the yogurt, dry milk and sweetener. Blend until dry milk is dissolved. Add the fruit and blend until smooth. Pour into 4 (4 ounce) paper cups and freeze until partially set. Put a popsicle stick in the center of each cup and freeze until firm. To unmold, roll cup between palms of hands to soften slightly, pull out pop.

Analysis is for pops made with strawberries.

Serves 4	63 calories per ½ cup serving		
Fat .... 1.0 G	Cholesterol ... 4 mg	Fiber .... .9 G	Diabetic exchanges:
saturated . .6 G	Protein .... 4.7 G	Vitamin C .. 22 mg	½ low fat milk, ¼ fruit
mono .... .3 G	Carbohydrate .. 8.8 G	Calcium ... 161 mg	
poly ...... .1 G		Sodium ... 64 mg	

VANILLA OLIVE OIL ICE CREAM

Diabetics should use 1 tablespoon sugar + ¾ cup Sprinkle Sweet® instead of the sugar. This reduces the calories to 192 per ½ cup serving.

½ vanilla bean
1 cup sugar
3 cups evaporated skim milk

½ cup Egg Beaters®
2.5 ounces olive oil

Break vanilla bean into smaller pieces and put them into a blender container and process to a coarse powder. Add sugar and continue to blend. (volume will decrease) This is best done in the smaller closed container. Pour evaporated skim milk, vanilla sugar, Egg Beaters® and olive oil into a saucepan. Heat, stirring constantly, to 160 degrees. Allow to cool. Beat 5 minutes with an electric mixer. Place mixture in freezer up to 40 minutes or until thoroughly chilled. Remove from freezer, beat 3 minutes more. Freeze in ice cream freezer according to manufacturer's directions. Spoon into containers and put into refrigerator freezer.

Serves 8	274 calories per ½ cup serving		
Fat .... 10.7 G	Cholesterol ... 4 mg	Fiber .... 0 G	Diabetic exchanges:
saturated . 1.6 G	Protein .... 8.8 G	Vitamin C .. 1 mg	½ starch, 1 fruit, 1 fat,
mono .... 7.0 G	Carbohydrate .. 36.2 G	Calcium ... 288 mg	1 low fat milk
poly ...... 1.7 G		Sodium .... 140 mg	

CHOCOLATE OLIVE OIL ICE CREAM

Chocolate lovers! This is a misnomer since it contains no cream, but the name categorizes the dish. It is not low in calories, but otherwise it is good for you. The secret in making ice cream is the amount of fat and trapped air.

6 tablespoons cocoa powder
1 cup sugar
½ cup Egg Beaters ®

1 teaspoon vanilla
2.5 ounces olive oil
3 cups evaporated skim milk

Combine all ingredients in a saucepan; cook over low heat, stirring constantly to 160 degrees. Remove from heat and allow to cool. Beat with egg beater for 5 minutes. Put in freezer container 20-30 minutes to chill thoroughly without freezing. Beat another 3 minutes. Freeze in ice cream freezer following manufacturer's instructions. Put in containers to store in freezer until serving time.

Serves 10	219 calories per ½ cup serving		
Fat . . . . 8.3 G	Cholesterol . . . . . 3 mg	Fiber . . . . 1.0 G	Diabetic exchanges:
saturated . 1.5 G	Protein . . . . 7.8 G	Vitamin C . . 1 mg	1 starch, 1½ fat,
mono . . . . 5.6 G	Carbohydrate . . 30.2 G	Calcium . . . 233 mg	1 low fat milk
poly . . . . . . .8 G		Sodium . . . . 111 mg	

CHOCOLATE OLIVE OIL ICE CREAM
FOR DIABETICS

Diabetic chocolate lovers! Still not low in calories, but you get a beneficial oil.

6 tablespoons cocoa powder
1 cup Sprinkle Sweet ®
1 tablespoon sugar
½ cup Egg Beaters ®

1 teaspoon vanilla
2.5 ounces olive oil
3 cups evaporated skim milk

Combine all ingredients in a saucepan; cook over low heat, stirring constantly to 160 degrees. Remove from heat and allow to cool. Beat with egg beater for 5 minutes. Put in freezer container 20-30 minutes to chill thoroughly without freezing. Beat another 3 minutes. Freeze in ice cream freezer following manufacturer's instructions. Put in containers to store in freezer until serving time.

Serves 10	156 calories per ½ cup serving		
Fat . . . . 8.3 G	Cholesterol . . . 3 mg	Fiber . . . . 1.0 G	Diabetic exchanges:
saturated . 1.5 G	Protein . . . . 7.8 G	Vitamin C . . 1 mg	1½ fat,
mono . . . . 5.6 G	Carbohydrate . . 14.0 G	Calcium . . . 233 mg	1 low fat milk
poly . . . . . . .8 G		Sodium . . . . 116 mg	

STRAWBERRY OLIVE OIL ICE CREAM

Although technically this isn't ice cream, I am hard put to think of another name for it.

3 cups evaporated skim milk
½ cup Egg Beaters®
6 ounces unsweetened
frozen strawberries, thawed

2.5 ounces olive oil
1 cup sugar

Combine milk, Egg Beaters®, olive oil and sugar in saucepan; cook over medium heat, stirring constantly, to 160 degrees. Remove from heat and allow to cool. Put mixture into blender container, add strawberries, reserving some berries to add later. Blend the mixture until smooth. Pour into a bowl and beat with the electric mixer for 5 minutes. Pour mixture into ice cream freezer container adding reserved berries. Freeze according to manufactuer's directions. Spoon into containers and put into the refrigerator freezer to freeze until firm.

In the summer when fresh berries are available, put 1 cup berries in the blender to be pureed with the one cup of sugar. Add ½ cup sliced fresh strawberries to mixture when putting it in the ice cream freezer.

Serves 8	281 calories per ½ cup serving		
Fat .... 10.7 G	Cholesterol ... 4 mg	Fiber .... .6 G	Diabetic exchanges:
saturated . 1.6 G	Protein .... 8.9 G	Vitamin C .. 10 mg	½ starch, 1 fruit, 1 fat,
mono .... 7.0 G	Carbohydrate .. 38.2 G	Calcium ... 291 mg	1 low fat milk
poly ...... 1.7 G		Sodium .... 141 mg	

STRAWBERRY OLIVE OIL ICE CREAM FOR DIABETICS

The calories and taste are present, but not the sugar.

3 cups evaporated skim milk
½ cup Egg Beaters®
1½ cups Sprinkle Sweet®

about 20 medium to large strawberries
2.5 ounces olive oil

Heat the milk, Egg Beaters® and sweetener in saucepan; cook over medium heat, stirring constantly, to 160 degrees. Remove from heat and allow to cool. Put mixture into blender container, add strawberries, reserving some berries to add later. Blend the mixture until smooth. Pour into bowl and beat with electric mixer for 5 minutes. Pour mixture into ice cream freezer container, adding reserved strawberries. Freeze according to manufacturer's directions. Spoon into containers and put into the refrigerator freezer to freeze until firm.

Serves 8	201 calories per ½ cup serving		
Fat .... 10.8 G	Cholesterol ... 4 mg	Fiber .... .5 G	Diabetic exchanges:
saturated . 1.6 G	Protein .... 8.9 G	Vitamin C .. 12 mg	1 fat, 1½ low fat milk
mono .... 7.0 G	Carbohydrate .. 17.2 G	Calcium ... 290 mg	
poly ...... 1.7 G		Sodium .... 149 mg	

CHOCOLATE COOKIES

Chocolate lovers! Just for the taste.

6 tablespoons cocoa powder
½ cup olive oil
1 cup Sprinkle Sweet®
1 tablespoon sugar
2 egg whites

½ teaspoon vanilla
1 tablespoon Butter Buds®*
¾ cup skim milk
2 cups flour

Beat olive oil, sweetener and sugar. Add egg whites, vanilla, Butter Buds®, cocoa and milk. Gently stir in flour and mix well. Drop by teaspoonfuls on ungreased cookie sheet. Bake at 375 degrees for 8-10 minutes.

Makes 36 cookies	48 calories per cookie		
Fat .... 1.8 G	Cholesterol ... 0 mg	Fiber .... .5 G	Diabetic exchanges:
saturated . .3 G	Protein .... 1.2 G	Vitamin C .. 0 mg	½ starch, ⅓ fat
mono .... 1.2 G	Carbohydrate .. 7.2 G	Calcium ... 9 mg	
poly ...... .2 G		Sodium .... 13 mg	

OATMEAL COOKIES

Standard taste with beneficial fat.

1½ cups flour
½ teaspoon baking powder
1 teaspoon cinnamon
1 tablespoon Butter Buds®*
2 egg whites, lightly beaten

⅓ cup Sprinkle Sweet®
¼ cup olive oil
1½ cups skim milk
1¾ cups rolled oats
½ cup raisins

Combine dry ingredients. Stir in skim milk, olive oil and egg whites. Drop by teaspoonfuls on cookie sheet sprayed with pan spray. Bake at 350 degrees for 8-10 minutes or until lightly brown.

Makes 24 cookies	85 calories per cookie		
Fat .... 2.7 G	Cholesterol ... 0 mg	Fiber .... 1.1 G	Diabetic exchanges:
saturated . .4 G	Protein .... 2.6 G	Vitamin C .. 0 mg	¾ starch, ½ fat
mono .... 1.8 G	Carbohydrate .. 13.6 G	Calcium ... 27 mg	
poly ...... .4 G		Sodium .... 26 mg	

*Indicates high sodium content

OAT BRAN COOKIES

If you're tired of muffins—these are easier to make, also.

2 cups oat bran
½ cup whole wheat flour
½ cup all-purpose flour
1 tablespoon baking powder
¼ cup brown sugar
1 teaspoon cinnamon

1 teaspoon nutmeg
1½ cups skim milk
2 egg whites
2 tablespoons olive oil
⅓ cup chopped dried fruit
   (apricots, dates, raisins, etc.)

Combine dry ingredients in a medium bowl. Combine liquid ingredients and stir into the dry ingredients, mixing well. Stir in dried fruit. Drop by spoonfuls onto baking sheet which has been sprayed with pan spray. Bake for about 6 minutes in 400 degree oven.

Variations
Add 1 cup of any of the following and reduce the milk by ½ cup: applesauce, peach puree, persimmon pulp or mincemeat.

Makes 16 cookies	103 calories per cookie		
Fat .... 2.4 G	Cholesterol ... 0 mg	Fiber .... 2.8 G	Diabetic exchanges:
saturated . .4 G	Protein .... 4.3 G	Vitamin C .. 0 mg	1 starch, ½ fruit
mono .... 1.5 G	Carbohydrate .. 21.2 G	Calcium ... 54 mg	
poly...... .4 G		Sodium .... 84 mg	

CHOCOLATE OAT BRAN COOKIES

Chocolate lovers! It's us against them, even in the fight for our arteries.

2 cups oat bran
½ cup whole wheat flour
½ cup all-purpose flour
1 tablespoon baking powder
½ teaspoon brown sugar substitute
2 egg whites

1 teaspoon cinnamon
1½ cups skim milk
2 tablespoons olive oil
6 tablespoons cocoa powder
1 teaspoon vanilla

Mix all dry ingredients thoroughly. Lightly whip egg whites; combine all liquid ingredients and add to the dry ingredients. Mix well. Drop by tablespoonfuls onto cookie sheet which has been sprayed with pan spray. Bake in preheated 400 degree oven for about 6 minutes or until done.

Makes 16 cookies	85 calories per cookie		
Fat .... 2.7 G	Cholesterol ... 0 mg	Fiber .... 3.1 G	Diabetic exchanges:
saturated . .6 G	Protein .... 4.6 G	Vitamin C .. 0 mg	1 starch, ½ fat
mono .... 1.6 G	Carbohydrate .. 16.1 G	Calcium ... 76 mg	
poly...... .4 G		Sodium .... 76 mg	

LEMON PRUNE PECAN BRAN COOKIES

This is probably good for the arteries in your lower tract.

2 cups oat bran
½ cup whole wheat flour
½ cup all-purpose flour
½ cup chopped pecans
⅔ cup cooked chopped prunes
1 tablespoon baking powder
¼ teaspoon baking soda
4 tablespoons Butter Buds®*

⅓ cup bottled lemon juice
10 drops lemon oil or grated zest
   of ½ lemon (or orange)
1⅓ cup skim milk
2 egg whites
2 tablespoons olive oil
¼ cup Sprinkle Sweet®
1 tablespoon sugar

Combine all dry ingredients. Combine all liquid ingredients except lemon juice and add to dry ingredients. Mix thoroughly then stir in lemon juice and mix well. Spray cookie sheets with pan spray and drop dough by tablespoonfuls onto prepared sheets. Bake in 400 degree oven for 6-7 minutes.

Makes 25	68 calories per cookie		
Fat .... 2.1 G	Cholesterol ... 0 mg	Fiber .... 2.0 G	Diabetic exchanges:
saturated . .2 G	Protein .... 2.9 G	Vitamin C .. 2 mg	1 starch, ½ fat
mono .... 1.1 G	Carbohydrate .. 12.9 G	Calcium ... 47 mg	
poly ...... .6 G		Sodium .... 89 mg	

CHOCOLATE BROWNIES

Alert! Chocolate lovers! This is the only time brownies will be beneficial to you. The oat bran makes them crunchy so you don't need to use nuts.

6 tablespoons cocoa
1 cup Sprinkle Sweet®
2 tablespoons sugar
1 tablespoon Butter Buds®*
1½ cups flour

½ cup oat bran
½ cup olive oil
½ cup skim milk
½ teaspoon vanilla
2 egg whites

Preheat oven to 375 degrees. Oil an 8 inch baking pan. Mix all dry ingredients together. Combine oil, milk, vanilla and egg whites and beat well with a whisk; add dry ingredients and mix well. This will have a thick consistency. Pour into an oiled 8 inch baking pan and bake at 375 degrees for 10-12 minutes. Cool and cut into 2 inch squares. Frost if desired.

Serves 16	132 calories per 2 inch square		
Fat .... 7.4 G	Cholesterol ... 0 mg	Fiber .... 1.4 G	Diabetic exchanges:
saturated . 1.2 G	Protein .... 2.8 G	Vitamin C .. 0 mg	1 starch, 1 fat
mono .... 5.2 G	Carbohydrate .. 15.7 G	Calcium .. 16 mg	
poly ...... .7 G		Sodium .... 27 mg	

*Indicates high sodium content

INDEX

Main Dishes

Vegetables

Cakes, Cookies & Desserts

Order Form

Use the order forms below for obtaining
additional copies of this cookbook.

The Healthful Chef™
is a great gift for friends and family.

Fill in Order Form Below - Cut Out and Mail

Please send _____ copies of **The Healthful Chef**® at $12.95 each plus $1.25 for shipping and handling.

Send Check or Money Order to: The Healthful Chef®
P. O. Box 2085
Danville, IL 61834-2085

Number of Books_____ @ **$12.95 ea.** = _____

Illinois Residents add 81¢ sales tax per book   = _____

Plus Shipping/Handling @ **$1.25 ea.** = _____

Total Due $_____

Mail books to:

Name _____

Address_____ Apt. No._____

City, State_____ Zip _____

Allow 4 to 6 weeks for Delivery

Fill in Order Form Below - Cut Out and Mail

Please send _____ copies of **The Healthful Chef**® at $12.95 each plus $1.25 for shipping and handling.

Send Check or Money Order to: The Healthful Chef®
P. O. Box 2085
Danville, IL 61834-2085

Number of Books_____ @ **$12.95 ea.** = _____

Illinois Residents add 81¢ sales tax per book   = _____

Plus Shipping/Handling @ **$1.25 ea.** = _____

Total Due $_____

Mail books to:

Name _____

Address_____ Apt. No._____

City, State_____ Zip _____

Allow 4 to 6 weeks for Delivery